The Climate Girl Effect

COMMUNICATING GENDER

Series Editors:
Diana Bartelli Carlin, Saint Louis University
Nichola D. Gutgold, Pennsylvania State University
Theodore F. Sheckels, Randolph-Macon College

Communicating Gender features original research examining the role gender plays in communication. It encompasses a wide variety of approaches and methodologies to explore theoretically relevant topics pertaining to the interrelation of gender and communication both in the United States and worldwide. This series examines gender issues broadly, ranging from masculine hegemony and gender issues in political culture to media portrayals of women and men and the work/life balance.

Recent Titles in This Series

The Climate Girl Effect: Fridays, Flint, and Fire by Carolyn M. Cunningham and Heather M. Crandall
Plasticity in Motion: Sport, Gender, and Biopolitics, by Robert M. Foschia
Electing Madam Vice President: When Women Run Women Win, by Nichola D. Gutgold
Communicating Intimate Health, edited by Angela Cooke-Jackson and Valerie Rubinsky
Misogyny across Global Media, edited by Maria B. Marron
Reimagining Black Masculinities: Race, Gender, and Public Space edited by Mark C. Hopson and Mika'il Petin
Intersectionality: Understanding Women's Lives and Resistance, edited by Dawn L. Hutchinson and Lori Underwood
Misogyny and Media in the Age of Trump, edited by Maria B. Marron
The Rhetorical Arts of Women in Aviation, 1911–1970: Name It and Take It, by Sara Hillin
Food Blogs, Postfeminism, and the Construction of Expertise: Digital Domestics, by Alane Presswood
Developing Women Leaders in the Academy through Enhanced Communication Strategies, edited by Jayne Cubbage

The Climate Girl Effect

Fridays, Flint, and Fire

Carolyn M. Cunningham and
Heather M. Crandall

LEXINGTON BOOKS
Lanham • Boulder • New York • London

Published by Lexington Books
An imprint of The Rowman & Littlefield Publishing Group, Inc.
4501 Forbes Boulevard, Suite 200, Lanham, Maryland 20706
www.rowman.com

86-90 Paul Street, London EC2A 4NE

Copyright © 2022 by The Rowman & Littlefield Publishing Group, Inc.

All rights reserved. No part of this book may be reproduced in any form or by any electronic or mechanical means, including information storage and retrieval systems, without written permission from the publisher, except by a reviewer who may quote passages in a review.

British Library Cataloguing in Publication Information Available

Library of Congress Cataloging-in-Publication Data

ISBN 978-1-7936-3955-4 (cloth)
ISBN 978-1-7936-3956-1 (electronic)

Contents

Acknowledgments	vii
Chapter 1: Girls on Earth	1
Chapter 2: The Greta Effect	23
Chapter 3: The Flint Girl Effect	43
Chapter 4: Indigenous Climate Girl Effect	63
Chapter 5: Technofeminist Climate Girl Effect	81
Chapter 6: Grassroots Climate Girl Effect	97
Chapter 7: Lawyer Up Climate Girl Effect	119
Chapter 8: The Future of the Climate Girl Effect	137
References	149
Index	169
About the Authors	187

Acknowledgments

First, we want to thank the climate girls who are on the frontlines all over the world doing this difficult and inspiring work. Thank you to the climate activists who agreed to our interviews. They are Avery McRae, Sahara Valentine, Kehkashan Basu, and the communication team from Bye Bye Plastic Bags. We came away from each filled with gratitude, reeling from their insights, and filled with energy for the work ahead.

Immense gratitude to graduate assistant Zoe Zamora who asked the right questions to do the quality work. Graduate assistant Natasha Johnson researched global climate girl activists that added to our project. Brian Henning, who advances Gonzaga University's mission of care for the planet through the Cataldo Project and the Center for Climate, Society, and the Environment, provided an academic space and support for our project. Nicolette Amstutz at Lexington Books whose gentle monthly emails we counted on to make sure we were on deadline. Nichola Gutgold who advocates for scholarship on gender and communication. The anonymous reviewers who helped us see opportunities to clarify and strengthen our arguments. Thank you, Morgan Blue, for your genius indexing.

One sweet part of writing a book is being able to thank people for helping. We want to thank our immediate family: Daniel P. Nailen, Harvey Hartwell, Olive Merle Creed, Julie Johnson, Jim Crandall, and Robyn Winks! As well as Scarlett Madeline, Jack Curtis, and John Hinson. Your love, support, and well-being bring us peace and happiness all the time. Thank you to the Nailens. Thank you to our many friends who listen to us go on and on, who encourage us, and who distract us in wonderful ways. Kris Morehouse, as both our friend and colleague, we do not have enough time or space to thank you enough.

Thank you, Carmen Hoover and Kyle Pittman (Nez Perce/Yakama), for wading through drafts of our "Indigenous Climate Girl Effect" chapter and sending us scholarship recommendations and for helping us do what we said we were trying to do in that chapter. We want to thank colleagues who sent important articles our way (we are looking at you, Melissa and Casey). Thank you, John Caputo, Jonathan Rossing, Paul Soukup, S. J., and Lance Strate, as well as the party trolley ladies and the 80s casino concerts crew—all people who welcomed us to their teams. Thank you to WSCA, NWCA, and AJCU-CC. The people who make up these professional organizations are the best. Finally, we are always grateful for the creative, insightful conversations we have with current and former students.

This process of co-authoring was a blast. We continue to write, speak, teach, learn, and sip lobby wine with each other. We gain so much when we put our heads together to try to improve the world through our scholarship.

Chapter 1

Girls on Earth

As we write this book in Spokane, Washington, on the ancestral homelands of the Spokane Tribal People, we are experiencing a record shattering heat wave. We are advised to stay indoors because the air quality is unhealthy from wildfires burning in the area. Our region is experiencing its worst drought, further fueling the wildfire season. However, the impact of the climate crisis in our region barely compares to the devastation we are witnessing across the globe, ranging from deadly floods, hurricanes, forest fires, and heat waves. No wonder there is an increase of eco-anxiety among youth who feel that their future is at risk and feel powerless to do anything about it.

The story of the climate crisis is one of a battle between science, government and global capitalism. It is also a story of inequality, where developed countries with the highest carbon emissions are impacting countries with little say in the matter. In the Global North, the discourse is about sustainable capitalism and green energy. In the Global South, discourses are rooted in post-colonial environmentalism that honors Indigenous knowledges, survival, and a scathing critique of capitalism as sea rise threatens island countries and climate refugees flee to higher ground.

In the past decade, climate mitigation strategies and solutions have steadily grown. In December of 2015, the countries in the United Nations Framework Convention on Climate Change (UNFCCC) adopted the Paris Agreement, which was the first effort of its kind to, by agreement, hold each other legally accountable to reduce greenhouse gas emissions to pre-industrial levels. Three years later, a special report from this body articulated a deadline by which carbon emissions needed to be drastically reduced to keep global warming at 1.5°C above pre-industrial levels—2030. In August 2021, the IPCC (UNs Intergovernmental Report of Climate Change) report warned that their findings are a "code red" for humanity. Human-caused climate change has harmed ecosystems that are now irreversible. We are dangerously close to the tipping point of no full return. The large-scale social change necessary is stalled for many reasons due to conflicting interests between science, politics, and global capitalism.

The global health pandemic of 2020, caused by COVID-19, brought industrial processes to a grinding halt. It was and continues to be terrifying, but it also gave a hopeful glimpse of what a more sustainable world might look like. There were widespread reports of air and water pollution improvement, significant reductions in carbon emissions, and even dolphins swimming in Venice canals. Yet many argue that these reports only give us false hope.

It is in this context that we have come to admire girl leaders in the climate justice movement. We refer to these girls as "climate girls" because they have been given this title by mainstream media and, by extension, public discourse. However, we also see that while these girls participate in environmental justice in a variety of ways, from planting trees, beach cleanups, or pressuring politicians, the urgency of the climate crisis and girls' use of social media has united them under the umbrella of "climate" as the most pressing issue to act on. Perhaps the most famous climate girl is Greta Thunberg. Greta Thunberg, a Swedish girl who started the School Strike for Climate in 2018, is seen as the voice of her generation, taking world leaders to task for not doing enough to protect kids' future. She is not alone in her climate activism. Jamie Margolin, a queer Latinx feminist, heads This is Zero Hour, which organizes protests and participates in lobbying, directly connecting environmental justice with social justice. Indigenous girls, such as Autumn Peltier (Wiikwemkoong First Nation), are now taken more seriously when they advocate for protecting water and land rights. Climate girls seem to be everywhere: on the cover of magazines, speaking at international climate conferences, and leading efforts to get people in positions of power to recognize the gravity of the climate crisis.

Our admiration of these girls as leaders in the context of the climate crisis turned into a series of questions about the cultural, political, and social factors that allow girls to take such high prominence on the world's stage on issues of the climate crisis. They are gaining notoriety in part because of their savvy use of social media, as they respond to politicians and business leaders who dismiss their messages. As feminist media studies scholars, we wanted to learn more about how these climate girls use social media for social change, especially given their positionalities as girls. At the same time, mainstream media play an important role in mediating the climate crisis. When it comes to coverage of these activist girls, who gets to be recognized for doing this activist work? Whose voices are ignored and why?

We were also interested in understanding what rhetorical and technical strategies climate girls used to engage in the climate justice movement. Climate girls are learning from adult leaders in the climate justice movement, but they are remixing this discourse to push for the next level of action needed. In addition to their use of social media, climate girls are using technologies in innovative ways for their activism, designing videogames, apps, and water filters. What can we learn from their technological interventions in light of persistent gender inequality in STEM fields?

These girls begin their activism at a young age and grow into teens and young adults. As girls' studies scholars, we wanted to better understand the obstacles they face as they try to protect their future. What motivates these girls to circumvent them, especially given our concerns? These climate girls are the subject of misogynistic attacks and cyberbullying. They are critiqued for both their gender and their generation as they struggle to have their voices heard. Misinformation campaigns, trolling, and doxxing are all part of efforts to discredit them. Why are these attacks so prevalent and what do they say about girls' agency in a patriarchal society?

The answers to our questions lie at the confluence of mainstream media framing these girls as exceptional as well as the different rhetorical strategies that climate girls are using to get their messages across, through social media platforms, but also through the direct actions they lead. In this chapter, we introduce the core themes of our book including the dominant hegemonic narrative of climate girls, digital rhetorical strategies of climate girl activists, and girls as techno-savvy activists. In our analyses of climate girl activists, we show that as part of their actions and the ability to raise their voice that participatory culture affords (Jenkins et al., 2006), girl activists are invited to appear on international stages to help inform decision-making at the highest levels. We find the twists and turns of young girls who rise to prominence in their fight for a livable planet an important trajectory to trace for social movement scholars and environmental activists because this leads to several questions: Once on the international stage, are world leaders persuaded? What are the actual implications of this powerful platform? We argue the resulting social change packs more unintended influence than we realize.

Our goals as adult white women are to amplify climate girls' voices and to help form intergenerational alliances, partly because we need as many voices at the table to address the climate crisis, but also because environmental conditions will continue to worsen as these girls age and we want to help them build their capacities. Our aim, then, is to understand their strategies and tactics, how they are doing what they are doing, and what opportunities and challenges they face in that process. We recognize there are limitations and biases in our academic training and in our positionalities, and we acknowledge that as white thinkers and women raised in settler colonial ideologies, we often are outsiders. In light of our positionality, we have consciously drawn from scholarship in Black and Indigenous girls' studies, which help us to better understand and analyze girls' climate activism. To that end, our aim is to foreground climate girls' lived experiences in the cases in this book and hope their lived experiences become more central in public discussion.

WHO ARE CLIMATE GIRLS?

In our study of climate girl activists, we are focused primarily on teens who self-identify as girls. The girls in our cases range from 8–25 years old. We focus on these girls since those are the ones who are given the most media attention and who are spotlighted on the world stage in leadership roles for climate justice. Beyond the girls who are high-profile, we also draw attention to girls' technofeminist strategies for participating in the climate justice movement. While these girls are not singled out in media, we find that they offer unique insights into addressing the climate crisis.

The term "girl" can refer to one's gender identity or a person's subjective experience of their gender (Fixmer-Oraiz & Wood, 2019). Key to our analysis is a central understanding that gender identity is socially constructed and varies across cultures and over time. Additionally, gender also refers to one's subjectivity, especially how one's sense of self is situated within power relations. Feminist scholars have been critical of a binary notion of gender and, as Vanner (2019) writes, "with the recognition of trans and gender-nonconforming identities, the category of girl has expanded to encompass all who identify as such, regardless of the sex assigned to them at birth" (p. 120).

Additionally, we use the term "girls" in our case studies because that is how they are being referred to in popular culture and mainstream media. By labeling them "girls," they are seen as less threatening because of cultural constructs of girls as overreactive and angry.

While many of the girls in our cases do not invoke a gendered subject position (such as speaking as a girl or for girls), they operate within cultural contexts that rely on a gendered binary system. That said, Generation Z tends to embrace non-binary gender identifications, through actions such as pronoun use. They also embrace what we call "Gen Z radical" in which they challenge dominant discourses that are binary, not only in identity but also in relationship to the Earth. For example, they emphasize a reciprocal relationship between humans and the environment, which challenges capitalist neoliberal frameworks of exploiting the environment. Like ecofeminists who see an alliance between gender oppression and Earth's oppression, this generation of climate girl activists advocate for inclusivity, decolonialism, and degrowth.

One thing that unites the girls in our cases is that they are not able to participate in traditional politics, such as voting, because they are not considered adults. Thus, they use their youth subject position as a rhetorical strategy to implore adults to act. Speaking as youth, they make the case that they will inherit a world that they had no hand in creating, which leads to their involvement at high-profile climate conventions.

The girls in this book have grown up with the term "climate change" circulating in popular discourse and are witness to and victims of the severity of the global climate crisis. They have seen global efforts to address the climate crisis steadily increase (e.g., Paris Agreement, United Nations Framework Convention on Climate Change, IPCC reports), yet they are frustrated that more is not being done to address this crisis. Following the words of Greta Thunberg, they want adults to act as if their house is on fire.

The girls featured in our case studies have all come to the climate justice movement through a relationship to the natural world, whether through research in school, participation in an environmental club, or witnessing climate disasters such as hurricanes and wildfires. These climate girls did not set out to lead a movement, but to create needed change in ways that made sense for them. Social media and media coverage helped with the rhetorical strategies these climate girl activists created and tried. Swedish teen Greta's idea for her now-famous school strike came from the American youth who organized school strikes to protest gun violence as well as March for Our Lives (Stone, 2021). Other girls and youth climate activists took inspiration from Greta's act and organized what has been termed the "youth movement," known as Fridays for Future. Our goal, however, is to convey that there is not one environmental youth movement. Instead, we follow Wildemeersch et al.'s (2021) approach of studying youth activism as multi-faceted because it "emerges in different shapes and forms and at different places in the world: in study groups, in local policy actions, in forms of civil disobedience, in media events, [and] in the use of social media" (p. 3).

FROM GIRL POWER TO GLOBAL SAVIORS

Our research follows in the tradition of girls' studies. In her article, "Coalescing: The Development of Girls' Studies," Kearney (2009) documents the rise of girls' studies in the 1990s as a response to women's studies scholarship that narrowly focused on adult women without considering the context of girls' lives. Girls' studies was also a response to the marginalization of girls in youth studies research. As youth studies scholars point out, youth is a social construct that changes over time (Corsaro, 1997; Griffin, 1993; Lesko, 2012). Girlhood was seen as a developmental stage that girls were going through on their way to growing into adult women. However, girls' studies scholars drew attention to the unique perspectives that girls had, as well as the pressures they face given interlocking identities including socioeconomic status, race, ethnicity, sexuality, and ability. These scholars sought to amplify the voices of girls themselves. Girls' studies research encompasses a wide field, including the psychological development of girls especially in terms of self-esteem, body image, and aggression, girls' involvement in youth cultures, educational performance of girls, primarily in relation to STEM fields, and representations of girls in media, to name a few areas.

Kearney (2009) also identifies the sociocultural context that led to the field of girls' studies, particularly the attention that media and beauty and fashion industries paid to girls in the 1990s. The 1990s saw widespread "girl power" discourse that emerged from diverse origins, from the pop culture band the Spice Girls to Riot Grrl, the subcultural feminist punk music movement that also advocated for gender justice. At the time, girl empowerment seemed to infuse all aspects of popular culture sending the message that girls should be bold, fearless, and confident, even in the face of misogyny and racism. These mainstream media messages about girls' empowerment focused on their appearance, sexual commodification, and purchasing power (Harris, 2003). Scholars such as Anita Harris (2004) have critiqued the neoliberal underpinnings of girl power that celebrated individual achievement while masking structural inequalities. The empowerment discourse from the 1990s continues to follow (white) girls into adulthood, where they are encouraged as individuals to "lean in," as Sheryl Sandberg (2013) advocates, to their fears of success and climb the corporate ladder, even when structures do not support their participation.

As Driscoll (2002) argues, modern girlhood is enmeshed with anxieties about cultural norms and changes about what constitutes girlhood. Girls' studies are concerned with how femininity is commodified and how media create the concepts of girlhood. Girls' studies look historically at how social, cultural, and political influences impact these constructions. For example, Schrum (2004) highlights the emergence of teen girls in popular culture since World War I, with the rise of consumerism and the beauty industry. Teen girls continue to be the focus of media, especially as they are simultaneously celebrated for being influencers and critiqued for their foolishness. For example, in her *Vox* article, Grady (2021) asks if the teen girl is the most powerful force in pop culture. Grady comments on a range of influential teenage girls that have emerged in the public imagination, ranging from VSCO girls to pop stars like Olivia Rodrigo. Additionally, she comments on the new image of activist teens that have enjoyed media celebrity status in recent years:

> There is a bizarre, fetishistic quality to the attention adults pay these teen girl activists. We tend to focus on their youth, their femininity, and their bravery, taking pleasure from the disconnect between the seriousness of the work these girls are trying to accomplish and their social status as unserious, unrespected

teenage girls. And while we enjoy this juxtaposition, we tend to ignore the substance of their messages: We laud them for their bravery in demanding change, and then we refuse to make the changes they seek. Moreover, we tend to ignore the fact that teenage girls are, after all, still children, and therefore people to whom adults owe a responsibility. (Grady, 2021, para. 32)

Indeed, as Bent (2020) writes, there is so much scrutiny on girl activists that "while girl activists labor under the pressures associated with spectacular girl power, viewers learn to be complicit and entertained by and through girls' mediated suffering, which has the cumulative effect of warning others away from public feminist resistance" (p. 809). There are bound to be examples of mediated suffering of these teen girls' lives. For example, in 2021 Jamie Margolin, climate girl founder of Zero Hour, accused another high-profile girl activist of sexual assault (Cohen, 2021).

Within the field of girls' studies, there have been significant interventions to offer critiques of a lack of attention to intersectionality within this scholarship. For example, de Finney (2015) took girls' studies to task for the lack of scholarship about Indigenous girls and argued for the importance of reconceptualizing Indigenous girlhood in light of the way it is shaped under a Western neocolonial state. These scholars call for research that looks at how Indigenous girls themselves unpack stereotypes of what it means to be an Indigenous young woman growing up in a settler state. "The particularities of Indigenous girlhood in settler states are intersected by a tremendous diversity of perspectives, social locations, backgrounds and histories" (de Finney, 2015, p. 170). Our study of Indigenous girl climate activists contributes to this scholarship by highlighting their activist strategies and recognizing the threats they face, based on their race, class, age, gender, and geographic location.

Black girlhood studies scholars have also contributed to the field by showing the particular and important ways in which Black girls experience oppression. "Black girls have varied lived experiences, however, there is also a shared experience based on their intersecting identities" (Greene, 2021, p. 38) and in digital contexts, Black girls find themselves in "spaces steeped in anti-Blackness toward Black girls" (Greene, 2021, p. 38). These scholars show how Black girls in the United States continue to be marginalized, especially in schools. They are often perceived as less innocent and more adult than their white peers, which leads to them receiving more discipline (Epstein et al., 2017). To contribute to knowledge of the specific experience of Black girls in America, Muhammad and McArthur (2015) interviewed Black girls aged 12–17 about how they respond and want to be represented given a full-spectrum media-saturated environment that portrays them in narrow gendered and racialized ways. They "found that the ways the girls desired to be represented (as evident by their self-descriptions) were in opposition to the ways they felt society and media viewed them" (Muhammad & McArthur, 2015, p. 138). These scholars also examine Black girls' cultural production and engagement with popular culture (Owens et al., 2017). This body of research has illuminated the ways in which Black girls resist oppressive system through cultural production (Kelly, 2018; McArthur, 2016). Additionally, Field et al. (2016) describe how outside of the U.S., Black girlhood research projects are growing in the Americas, Africa, and the Caribbean.

More recently, scholars have introduced the concept of transnational girlhood to better understand the experiences of girls in a world in which borders are shifting and migration is common. Different than globalization (which refers to activities that take place in a global space), transnationalism refers to activities that are linked to multiple nation states, since many political, economic, and social activities occur across national boundaries. These scholars take a transnational feminist lens to examine the impacts of global capitalism on women, especially Indigenous and "racialized neo-colonial communities" (Vanner, 2019, p. 115). Vanner (2019) draws on other scholars who argue that girlhood emerged as a Western construct that has been imposed on non-Western girls. This Western-centric framework led to the creation of binaries that non-Western countries were oppressive and backward, whereas Western countries were progressive. Thus, Vanner's framework of transnational girlhood includes

> cross-border connections that build on the localized lived experiences of girls and speak to the linkages between global and local power structures; intersectional analyses . . . that prioritizes perspectives of girls from the Global South, girls of color, and other girls who have traditionally not been given equal opportunities to speak on an international stage; recognition of girls' potential agency as local, national, and global activists despite constraints imposed by global structures of patriarchy and (neo) colonialism; and a counter-hegemonic agenda that challenges oppressive global systems to create more equitable societies for all girls. (p. 126)

GIRLS AND ACTIVISM

The past ten years have seen a rise in girl activist research (Taft, 2020). As Driscoll (2008) writes, girl-led activism is not new, but each generation reinvigorates activist struggles with fresh perspectives. Girl activism challenges traditional notions of gender, age, and power, especially since girls are excluded from traditional politics because of their age. When they participate in activism, they are often dismissed. However, we see girl activists rising as celebrities of different social movements and they are received with some degree of success.

As Taft (2020) writes, girls have been involved in activism, especially related to labor and education, since at least the 19th century, yet since the 2000s, girl activists, such as Malala, have emerged as "global saviors" who are "defined by their hopefulness, harmlessness, and heroism" (p. 3). These girls are seen as what Projansky (2014) calls "spectacular" because media discourses promote stories of lone girls fighting what they see as an unjust system. Bent (2020) calls this girl power activism because it "gives the impression that sociocultural and political change happens as soon as one exceptional girl puts her mind to it" (p. 800).

As Taft (2020) writes, "changes in the political, social, and cultural landscape have made girl activists both more legible and more desirable for media attention and public consumption" (p. 2). Feminism has become more popular, through celebrities such as Beyoncè claiming the term. High-profile social movements, such as Black Lives Matter and #MeToo, have inspired girls to speak out against racial injustice, sexual violence, and school shootings. These social movements have a presence both online and offline, spreading their reach and allowing for multiple ways for people to engage in activism. This form of activism has inspired the climate girls in this book, especially since many of these movements are led by girls and women. Black Lives Matter took hold in 2013 in response to the acquittal of George Zimmerman in the murder of Trayvon Martin, a 17-year-old African American boy. Alicia Garza shared her love for her community on Facebook and Patrisse Khan-Cullors added the hashtag, which opened digital spaces for sharing information and organizing disparate conversations about police violence and racial justice. According to Jackson et al. (2020), "the Black Lives Matter movement not only relies on new technological infrastructures and potentials, it was birthed in the public consciousness by them" (p. 123). This online and offline activism led to the circulation of other hashtags to draw attention to racial justice, such as #SayHerName, which draws attention to the way violence against Black women and girls who are victims of state-sanctioned violence is eclipsed and erased in public discourse. The #MeToo movement empowered women and girls to share stories of sexual violence and also led to a number of other hashtags, including #YesAllWomen, which showed the impact of widespread misogyny (Mendes et al., 2019).

It is in this context that several girl activists have risen to prominence, taking on celebrity status as they speak out about injustice and their hope for a better world. Girl activists are seen as having the power to solve important global problems, like religious and political extremism, poverty, violence against women and girls, and now climate change. Media coverage shows girls being anxious about their future and activism becomes a source of hope, not only for them but it allows publics to feel optimistic about a better future. Taft (2020) argues that girl power activists are now positioned as "global saviors." Yet, despite their rise to prominence, several scholars, including Hesford (2013) and Taft (2020), argue that in the process, girls' radical views are diluted because they are seen as harmless based on their gender and age. Media contain girls' radical activism, making it more of a spectacle than a potential revolution. Additionally, focusing on girl saviors as single-handedly solving the world's problems draws attention away from the need for collective action (Ryalls & Mazzarella, 2021).

Bent (2020) argues that girl power activism is palatable for the public, yet puts pressures on girls, ensuring their girlhood is contained. As Bent writes, "one of the dangers associated with the exceptional girl trope is that it turns girl activists into public celebrities marked for continuous surveillance and scrutiny" (p. 800). In the process, "girl activists must therefore learn how to negotiate the terms of their public visibility without crossing the boundaries of normative girlhood and becoming too big for their so-called britches" (p. 800). This is why they simultaneously become saviors and objects of disgust and vitriol. They are always on stage, whether they like it or not. And many are waiting for them to fail.

Despite the tendency for media to frame girls as exceptional, Bent (2020) sees how girl activists are resisting these frames. In her analysis of Emma González, Bent argues that we should see her as a public intellectual. González sticks to the message that gun violence is connected to larger systems of oppression that continue to plague the U.S. The school-to-prison pipeline, unequal access to education based on geolocation, and gendered differences in the way girls and boys experience school, are just some of factors that contribute to school shootings. Her rhetorical strategies, including "We call B.S." (to shame adults who say they are doing everything they can) and her 6-minute silence at the March for Our Lives rally to symbolize the time it took for the mass shooting in Parkland to occur, demonstrate how she is able to keep attention on the problems at hand and draw them away from her as an exceptional girl.

Girls' Digital Activism

These girls are being labeled climate activists, yet climate justice is not their only concern. These girls identify with alternative forms of collective action and horizontal leadership, which eschews charismatic leaders at the center. These climate girls become eco-activist celebrities and in turn are made spokespeople for a movement. Many of the ways that girls enact their activism is through their participation in digital and social media. In recent years, digital media have allowed youth new avenues to participate in social movements. As Jenkins et al. (2016) write, "young people have refreshed and renewed the public's symbolic power as they fight for social justice; they often push back against inherited forms and search for new mechanisms for asserting their voice" (p. 2). Some might identify this contemporary form of activism as a fourth wave of feminism, in which women and girls use social media to draw attention to racism and misogyny, while also being explicitly intersectional (Munro, 2013; Zimmerman, 2017). Social media platforms, such as Instagram and Twitter, allow girls to learn about injustices and participate in social change through sharing, commenting, or remixing media messages.

There are several dynamics and affordances of social media that lend themselves to activism. Social media create what boyd (2010) terms "networked publics" in which publics are "restructured by networked technologies" (p. 39). Networked sites, such as Facebook, allow people to gather for a number of social, cultural, and civic purposes, but they allow for connections that span across people's networks. These sites reorganize the flow of information and how people interact with each other and explain the dynamics of how information can spread. They also make visible offline relationships and networks.

Social media also can encourage connective action, in which people share personalized content through social media networks (Bennett & Segerberg, 2012). Bennett and Segerberg (2012) argue that key to this kind of activism is how communication becomes an organizational process for social movements, which is different than the resource mobilization of traditional collective actions. Connective action allows for engagement with political issues and can mobilize audiences through issue framing and agenda-setting, allowing for more and diverse voices to enter the conversation and become involved.

The affordances of digital technologies have altered the way that people participate in social movements. In her study of social movements' use of digital technologies, Tufecki (2017) writes, "these technologies were not merely basic tools; their new capabilities allowed protesters to reimagine and alter the practice of protests and movement building on the path that they had already been traveling but could finally realize" (Tufecki, 2017, p. xxv). Through her research, she saw how digital technologies help create a networked public sphere: "it's a recognition that the whole public sphere, as well as the whole way movements operate, has been reconfigured by digital technologies" (p. 6). Climate girls are utilizing the power of digital technologies to enact a form of citizenship in which they call on those in power to act. They organize large-scale protests, such as Fridays for Future, and circulate digital content, such as photos, or connect to one another using hashtags.

Throughout the case studies in this book, we have documented how climate girls are using digital media to participate in activism in different ways.

Green (2020) argues that young people's use of digital media may be leading to a new understanding of citizenship where young people are able to make equal claims about their rights and their future in the same ways as those who are in power. Green writes that youth are using digital media to advocate for positive rights (e.g., a right to a healthy planet) as opposed to negative rights (e.g., protection from harm). As Green writes,

> never has it been as easy as it is now for young people to mobilise themselves and each other in support of what they claim as their citizenship rights without the help of adult mediators and facilitators. Because digital devices allow young people to connect sources of knowledge, paths for active engagement and the presentation of opinions and demands, they can perform citizenship, singly and collectively, in ways that were not previously possible. (p. 15)

In the end, Green argues that children's performance of citizenship rights through the use of digital media is having an impact. Social media provides a space for girls to participate in public conversations about political issues.

Another trend in the use of social media for social change is location-based activism. Location-based activism refers to the way activists digitally extend place, and thereby the social construction of that place, for both the people in that place as well as for those digitally connected to that place (Moors, 2019). In Chapter 3, we discuss the water crisis in Flint, Michigan. Location-based activism was important because citizens of Flint could use social media's connective affordances to disrupt the dominant negative narrative emerging from media coverage of Flint and simultaneously invite witnessing (Moors, 2019). Location-based activism via social media can be important in climate activism because too often Western audiences do not see the depth and breadth of the devastation that is occurring around the globe.

Despite the positive use of social media for social change, we share Rosenfeld's (2020) position that "we must question the role technology structures and affordances play in the liberation and suppression of identity and communication" (p. ix). For example, hashtag activism is the process of using hashtags (#) to create conversations or discursive communities around different populations (Crandall & Cunningham, 2016). It has been a popular form of activism among feminists (Horeck, 2014; Jackson, 2016; Rentschler, 2017; Williams, 2015). Yet, Mendes, Ringrose, and Keller (2019) question the impact of these campaigns since participating in hashtag activism can be both triggering and comforting, especially when sharing stories of sexual assault. Girls and women are more often victims of cyberharassment and cyberstalking than men (Phillips, 2015). As several scholars have documented, misogyny is rampant in online spaces (Citron, 2014; Jane, 2017; Shaw, 2014; Vickery & Everbach, 2018). Shaw (2014) found that Twitter is a negative space for women (Shaw, 2014). Banet-Weiser and Miltner (2016) identify "networked misogyny," which is not just about the technological affordances of social media that allow for misogyny to thrive online, but it is also the logic of misogyny itself which has become naturalized in Western culture (i.e., that girls and women are not welcome in the public sphere). Throughout this book, we document some of the ways in which climate girls have experienced networked misogyny through trolling and death threats as they participate in this public form of activism. Climate denialism is associated with masculinity and conversely, environmental activism is associated with femininity (Anshelm & Hultman, 2014; Brough & Wilkie, 2017; Gelin, 2019). Climate girls, like Jamie Margolin, recount how online attacks can reveal personal information, leaving a digital footprint that is now part of their identities (Hirji, 2019). Additionally, they have been the subject of misinformation and disinformation campaigns (Dave et al., 2020).

Girls' Techno-ecofeminist Activism

Given the many ways that girl climate activists are using digital media to mobilize for action, this book examines and extends knowledge of girls' technofeminist activism. First coined by Judy Wajcman in 2004, technofeminism is both a theoretical framework as well as a praxis that addresses gender inequality in the design and uses of technology. As Wajcman (2004) writes, "technology is both a source and consequence of gender relations" (p. 107). Thus, there is a mutual shaping of gender and technology that occurs on a number of different levels. Gender impacts technological design, both in terms of the gender identities of those who are in charge of innovation but also in how assumptions about gender are embedded in technological design.

Technofeminism emerged as a field in response to science and technology studies (STS) (MacKenzie & Wajcman, 1999). Moving away from a technological determinist view of technology, in which social change was thought to be caused by technology, STS took a constructivist view, examining the multiple factors that influence technological design and usage. A key argument in STS is that artifacts have politics that are embedded in their design (Winner, 1980). Technofeminism, then, as a response to a blind area in STS is conceptualized as the "mutually shaping relationship between gender and technology in which gender is both a source and consequence of gender relations" (Wajcman, 2004, p. 107). Wajcman argues that understanding women's relationship with technology is two-fold. It requires looking at the source of design as well as the use of technologies in women's everyday lives. To look at the source of design is to see the ways ideologies of gender are embedded (whether intentionally or unintentionally) in technological design. The design of technologies is largely shaped by men, which can limit a consideration of women's needs or interests. As Wajcman (2006) writes, "different groups of people involved with a technology can have different understandings of that technology, and consumers or users can radically alter the meanings and deployment of technologies" (p.16). Wajcman (2004) writes, "technology must be understood as part of the social fabric that holds society together; it is never merely technical or social. Rather, technology is always a socio-material product—a seamless web or network combining artefacts, people, organizations, cultural meanings, and knowledge" (p. 106). One main concern of technofeminists is female exclusion from design and management of technologies, and thus technofeminists advocate for diversity in the sources of innovation.

In our study of climate girls' activism, we noticed a technofeminist approach to specifically addressing environmental justice, which we label as "techno-ecofeminism." Few scholars have applied a technofeminist lens to examine the environmental movement, yet Sikka (2018) offers some insight into this shift. As Sikka (2018) writes, "technologies are formed as part of sociotechnical systems or sets of ensembles and thus should be understood not on only artifacts, but also as containing and encompassing social relationships and practices, frameworks of knowledge, and networks of actions" (p. 113). In relation to women in climate science and geoengineering, Sikka (2018) posits a technofeminist analysis looks at questions that are and are not asked, the methods used, and conclusions reached. Thus far, dominant approaches to climate science have emphasized efficiency, technical feasibility, and economic outcomes, connections between science and government policy, and what role corporate entities play in funding research. Instead, Sikka encourages a technofeminist and materialist ecofeminist methodology that is critical of the patriarchal values of Western science. She uses the example of the Green Revolution in India. In an effort to increase food production, Western corporations used a chemical intensive process that led to water erosion and agricultural monocultures. This process replaced traditional knowledge about sustainable food production practices that were primarily held by Indian women. Where Sikka (2018) calls for critique of green technologies, we see how techno-ecofeminism can be a strategy for creating technological solutions that are attuned to addressing environmental problems. Wajcman's (2006) own writing mentioned the way postcolonial technoscience draws attention to the bias of Western thinking in the field, global dynamics, and their gendered implications. Mining materials for technology, in her example, feeds military conflicts and has ecological consequences for women globally.

Ecofeminism, first coined by French feminist Françoise d'Eaubonne in 1974, recognizes that Western thinking encourages a separation between nature and culture that results in part to environmental degradation (Merchant, 2005). Ecofeminism challenges capitalism as inherently patriarchal, resulting in exploitation of women and the environment. Ecofeminists question hegemonic structures of power and promote innovative localized solutions to climate change as well as Indigenous knowledge. The way we conceptualize techno-ecofeminism, then, is about challenging the assumptions of accepted systems, structures, and networks which are rooted in patriarchy and capitalism. Techno-ecofeminism turns the attention to how technologies impact the environment, specifically for women. These same dynamics exist in discourses about gender and climate change. Women and girls are disproportionately affected by global climate change because of poverty, gender inequality, work and family responsibilities, reliance on natural resources for work, and limited financial and social resources. At the same time, they are seen as important agents of change in their communities. Skills are important for community-building, social interdependence, and cultural change. Women's political activism has been strongly associated with environment. Reports such as *Roots for the Future: The Landscape and Way Forward on Gender and Climate Change* (Aguilar et al., 2015) and *Girls' Education in Climate Strategies* (Kwauck et al., 2019) advocate for the importance of educating girls so that they can help create climate plans for their communities.

We recognize this important lens and used it to look at practices of techno-ecofeminism in girls' activism. They are not only using digital technologies to organize protests, promote young people to join their efforts, critique politicians, and sue governments through navigating legal systems, they are also bringing attention to the ways in which technological systems have caused harm to the planet. They critique global capitalist practices that extract natural resources as if they are limitless. And, they call attention to the gendered assumptions embedded in technological systems. The climate girls in this book are designing technologies in innovative ways to address their local environmental problems. For example, in Chapter 6, we look at how climate girls are starting nonprofits to engage young people and their communities in activism. Sisters who started Bye Bye Plastic Bags in Bali have trained local women how to make plastic bag alternatives and sell them to support themselves. Sisters who started Kids Against Plastic created an app that allows kids to log and track their plastic cleanups. In chapter 5, we explore the ways that girls are designing apps and video games to raise awareness about climate change. In chapter 4, we listen to Indigenous girls who support Indigenous ways of knowing to protect life on Earth against governmental and corporate greed.

WHAT IS THE CLIMATE GIRL EFFECT?

In 2012, the United Nations High Commissioner Navi Pillay dubbed the term the "Malala Effect" to criticize the selective attention of international news media on Malala's story (Pillay, 2012). Malala Yousafzai, an outspoken advocate for girls' education in Pakistan, was shot in the head in retaliation for her activism. Pillay criticized media for highlighting Malala as exceptional, ignoring and erasing the many stories of injustice that occur every day in the region. Malala herself tried to resist this framing of her as exceptional, yet as Hesford (2014) argues, the notion of exceptionalism plays into Western ideological frameworks. The Malala effect, "points to a rhetorical process whereby configurations of exceptionality are bound by composite images of repressed Muslim women and girls and normative story-lines that turn on simple oppositions, such as freedom and constraint" (Hesford, 2014, p. 142). In the process, Malala's message of human rights of children, and especially girls, does not register to audiences who want to believe that Muslim girls need to be saved by the more developed West. The Malala effect "is rooted in the logic of exceptionality that underwrites liberal internationalism and its differential distribution of vulnerability and valued lives" (p. 158).

Several international development programs have focused on how girl empowerment will save girls in the Global South (Koffman & Gill, 2013; Koffman et al., 2015; Switzer et al., 2016). For example, the Nike Foundation's campaign "The Girl Effect," is focused on girl empowerment, yet as Hesford (2014) argues, this discourse frames girls in the Global South as victims in need of a public voice and privileges "neoliberal narratives of girl empowerment" (p. 158), which are dominant in the U.S.

In her critique of the United Nations Foundation's Girl Up project, in which girls from the United States are encouraged to use girl power discourse to rescue girls in crisis in the Global South, Vanner (2019) is critical of how this activism uses consumerism and fundraising as a way to invest in these girls' futures. In the process, "the program encourages girls in the Global North to speak against barriers of harmful practices in the Global South, without identifying gender-based discrimination in their own lives" (p. 125).

We draw on the work of these scholars to bring together these dynamics that we are naming the "climate girl effect." We started by following the girls' rhetorical and technical strategies. Through this exploration, we started to see trends in how climate girls were participating in social change. All of these trends, then, made up the larger climate girl effect we found. We define the effect as both individual and collective. From an individual standpoint, we explore how individual girls relate to the broader climate justice movement. As mentioned previously, there isn't a singular movement that is leading climate justice. More accurately, there are multiple efforts that become linked through digital networks. While the overall project is to preserve a livable planet through practicing climate justice as a global norm, we note that there are so many efforts happening, which allows girls to participate in ways that are most meaningful to them. We see several dimensions of these effects.

USE OF THEIR PLATFORMS TO BRING ATTENTION TO THE ISSUES

While many girls in this book are framed as "exceptional" in the same ways that girl activists such as Malala and González are, they resist this framing in several ways. They insist that they don't want to be doing this work. That they want to be normal teenagers who go to school and listen to pop music. Instead, propelled by the lack of attention paid to the climate crisis and the reality of the ticking clock (e.g., https://climateclock.world), they are compelled to act. In the process, though, they use their platforms and agency to influence public discussions, mobilize like-minded people, and keep the climate emergency ever-present.

INTERSECTIONAL AND COALITIONAL LEADERSHIP

Bent (2020) illustrates how González "grounds her activism in the complexities of identity politics, signaling the coming together of her gender, race/ethnicity, sexuality, socioeconomic status, and age as fundamental to her political subjectivity" (p. 808). March for Our Lives activists made complicated arguments about gun violence that were rooted in identity privilege, geographic locations, and marginalization. They did not argue for simple solutions to injustice but gave complicated accounts. This is also true of climate girls. They are not focused on girl power and self-empowerment discourse. They identify with alternative forms of collective action, horizontal leadership, and not having a charismatic leader at the center of it all. They use the spotlight for collective resistance. Climate girl activists are following in the footsteps of other social movements like Black Lives Matter that favor "leaderful movements" and horizontal leadership, moving beyond identity politics that were a hallmark of earlier social movements (Cohen & Jackson, 2016).

INFLUENCERS

These climate girls become eco-activist celebrities through media coverage, sharing on social media networks, and their involvement in public events. These girls step up to be, or are made spokespeople of, a movement even as this is not their goal. However, they also find that they can use their status as known public figures to change things on multiple levels even as they are inevitably entangled in profit-driven systems. The relationship between environmental activism and consumerism has a long history. Pezzullo (2011) for example, examined the value of buycotts and boycotts as environmental activist strategies. She found that these actions do work in that they have been shown to mobilize collective action toward specific businesses or business practices. A different form of commodity comes up in Milstein et al.'s (2020) study of the radical, direct action cetacean protection organization, Sea Shepherd. Sea Shepherd successfully used celebrities to attract media attention that then draws attention to and support for their work. Citing Brockington (2009), Milstein et al. (2020) say, "the alliance of celebrity with environment is 'mutually supportive publicity' and combines conservation with capitalism nicely, which 'commodifies and commercializes environmental protection'" (p. 9). Riordan (2001) noted that commodification increases awareness, however, "when something becomes commodified, it is first co-opted, and co-optation tends to neutralize the radical potential of messages" (p. 295). In *Commodity Activism,* Marita Sturken (2012) writes, "activism is not what it used to be. Resistance was never what it was understood to be. And capitalism is always reinventing itself" (p. x).

METHODOLOGY: CASE STUDY METHOD

This book takes a case study approach to understanding the complexity of climate girl activism. In each chapter, we highlight the unique contributions that these climate girls make, ranging from launching national protests, starting nonprofits, and suing governments. For our methods, we used critical discourse analysis (CDA) (Fairclough, 1995). CDA looks at discursive practices that make up text production, distribution, and consumption. It delves into the ideologies that were present in the creation and circulation of stories. As Harvey (2021) writes, "discourse analysis examines language beyond individual sentences to investigate the meaning it makes within larger texts, considering its role in producing and reproducing social, cultural, and political ideologies" (p. 43). First, we looked at mainstream media coverage of high-profile climate girls. We draw on Entman's (1993) concept of framing, or how mainstream media select which aspect of these girls' actions to highlight. As Entman (1993) writes, "frames are constructed from and embodied in the key words, metaphors, concepts, symbols, and visual images emphasized in the news narrative" (p. 7). Thus, we looked at the choices of language used as well as what images accompanied the stories. Through the lens of framing, we saw that mainstream media highlight these girls as spectacular and thus rarely focused on the substance of their messages.

We also looked at the new media environment to understand alternative narratives and different arguments and assumptions the climate girl activists created for social change. Many of the girls in our cases participate in creating their own media, such as books, blogs, as well as their social media posts. These forms of participatory new media make room for different gender identities and intersectional activism. They also allow girls to create counter-frames to the dominant frames present in mainstream media. We looked at the girls' social media accounts to draw on what themes and concepts they were highlighting in their posts. Like Tufecki (2017), we wanted to get a sense of the feel of the movement.

When possible, we were able to interview some of these girls. We reached out to many of the girls through social media, but it was only fruitful in some cases and we were grateful for what their voices added. As mentioned, they are protecting themselves from predators, so it makes sense that they would be cautious. Moreover, they're crafting their own messages that are easily accessible and retrievable.

ORGANIZATION OF THE BOOK

Climate girl activism takes different forms, as we show in this book. Each chapter is focused on a different dimension of the climate girl effect. We also used O'Brien et al.'s (2018) dissent frameworks which include dutiful, disruptive, and dangerous. Each of these are represented in the book. Dutiful dissent refers to the ways in which youth participate in established institutions and decision-making, such as in sustainable development or working with nonprofits. Disruptive dissent challenges those in power, through petitions and boycotts. This form of protest is intended to change the system, rather than working within the system. Finally, dangerous dissent is about creating alternative systems and new ways of doing things, such as degrowth and anti-consumerist movements.

In Chapter 2: The Greta Effect, we look at the complicated polarizing public discourse about Greta Thunberg that made her and her climate activism so celebrated and so reviled. We examine the qualities of Greta and what she represents that made her iconic. We discuss Greta in light of feminism and what it means for a girl to be perceived as angry. We also look at the ways Greta uses social media and the role of participatory culture in making Greta's climate justice activism an iconic protagonist performance. The Greta Effect we find is along the lines of Taft's (2020) concept of girls as global saviors. Greta's climate activism is a gripping drama, where she takes on world leaders and big business publicly. She is an intersectional feminist iconic protagonist in that her activism and her actions do not fit hegemonic girl norms. She continues to advance the scientific arguments and continues to keep them on the public agenda, despite media framing her as spectacular and harmless.

In Chapter 3: The Flint Girl Effect, we focus on Flint, Michigan's ongoing water crisis and the history of environmental justice activism required of its residents. We specifically follow the rise of Amariyanna Copeny, ("Little Miss Flint"), who first gained national attention when she wrote a letter to then President Barack Obama, which led to his declaration of the state of emergency resulting from lead poisoning in the water supply in Flint. Soon thereafter, images of her holding hand-drawn messages about the ongoing situation with Flint's water circulated on social media (Twitter, Instagram, her webpage) and popular media featured her. We use Black feminist activist scholarship to examine these different messages and modes of messages. She is now 14, a global youth activist, and has spent a significant amount of time being a climate activist. This chapter ends in a discussion of Mari's techno-feminist activism and the potential of commodity activism. The Flint Girl Effect shows a different kind of climate girl activism that successfully merges public criticism about environmental racism, while also creating an activist brand premised on commodity activism and materiality. The Flint Girl Effect is sustained through her philanthropy, technological innovation, and her participation in image culture.

Chapter 4: Indigenous Climate Girl Effect, begins with an overview of arguments that frequently surface in climate justice discourse about Indigenous peoples. We then examine spectacular Indigenous climate activists fighting different fights with extractive industries and complicit governments in some of these frontline communities. We apply White Earth Ojibwe scholar Gerald Vizenor's (1999) concept of "survivance"—wherein narratives incorporate themes of survival and resistance that include Native presence to these girls' stories (as cited in Kelly & Black, 2018, p. 3). We understand Indigenous activism in the context of a femicide crisis in Indigenous communities in North America known as #MMIW. Using case studies of Indigenous girl activism during the Standing Rock protests and First Nation water activist Autumn Peltier, we trace some of qualities of the Indigenous Climate Girl Effect, which is about intersectional activist identities present in their efforts to recognize the large-scale shift that must occur in the way people relate to and care for the climate and frontline communities.

In Chapter 5: Technofeminist Climate Girl Effect we apply a technofeminist framework to examine environmental solutions girls come up with when they build apps and design video games. We start with the organizations that use computer programming to increase girls in STEM fields, namely Girls Who Code, Google Play's Change the Game, and Technovation. In our analysis, we examine not only what concerns girls have about the environment, but also the variety of tools they use to inspire social change. By looking at the underlying messages in these projects, as well as the aesthetics used to get their point across, we highlight how girls' technofeminist activism can be another avenue for environmental social change. Additionally, this work broadens the scope of technofeminist research to include the work of girls. The Technofeminist Climate Girl Effect offers hope. It shows how girls can use coding to address pressing environmental concerns. Both video games and apps offer strategies that include behavioral change, awareness of one's own consumption, empathy building, and simulation, which will be crucial to making long-term impacts to weather the climate crisis.

Climate girl activists are creating nonprofit organizations to participate in the environmental movement. In Chapter 6: Grassroots Climate Girl Effect, we analyze the efforts of girl-founded nonprofit organizations, including Kids Against Plastic, Zero Hour, Bye Bye Plastic Bags, the Sunrise Movement, and the Green Hope Foundation. We also examine how these organizations structure themselves, how they encourage youth to get involved, how they use digital media to inform their members and their publics about their actions, and how they keep momentum. The Grassroots Climate Girl Effect is about that the ways they structure their non-profits are encouraging a different kind of consumption that promotes sustainability. Climate girls can make an impact by raising money through philanthropy and investing that money back into their communities. By launching these organizations, girls are creating institutional interventions and avenues for increasing youth participation in the climate justice movement. Institutionalizing these efforts brings legitimacy and longevity to their activism.

Some girls are enacting their activism through the legal system, challenging corporations and governments who are not taking proactive steps to protect their futures. Cases have been filed in Canada, India, Pakistan, and the United States. In Chapter 7: Lawyer Up Climate Girl Effect, we look at girls as spokespersons for these legal battles, the nature of the cases, the form of arguments gathering momentum, and their techno-feminist activism. We highlight Lawyer Up climate girls in cases such as Kelsey Juliana who was fifteen when she co-filed a lawsuit with the nonprofit Our Children's Trust against the Oregon State Governor. We explore media coverage of these lawsuits and the theme that these girls are more than their activism. The Lawyer Up Climate Girl Effect is how storytelling becomes central to broadening public understanding of the climate crisis. We see that girls' involvement in these cases evoke both agency (because they are exercising their rights) as well as legacy (their stories are getting written into the legal documents).

The final chapter, Chapter 8: The Future of the Climate Girl Effect, offers syntheses of how our collection extends the field of girls' studies, digital rhetorical strategies of climate girl activists, and girls as techno-ecofeminist activists. We also highlight what can be learned from each case and how to be helpful for those seeking productive entry points. While this book has examined a first generation of high-profile climate girl activists, we hope it expands the research at these intersections and we hope it inspires collective action through a better understanding of what these climate activists are working for and against.

Chapter 2

The Greta Effect

Well-known climate girl activist Greta Thunberg believes "No one is too small to make a difference," which is also the title of her 2019 book that was recognized as a #1 *New York Times Bestseller*. She brought life to this mantra when, inspired by the March for Our Lives activists in America, she took it upon herself to go on strike in 2018 (Pickard, 2021). Rather than attend school, Greta handed out printed flyers to politicians coming to work in the Swedish Parliament. Her message, translated from Swedish, read,

> We kids most often don't do what you tell us to do. We do as you do. And since you grown-ups don't give a shit about my future, I won't either. My name is Greta and I'm in ninth grade. And I refuse school for the climate until the Swedish general election. (Pickard, 2021, para. 14)

Her initial strike lasted for three weeks. She was demanding that the Swedish government reduce carbon emissions as part of the Paris Agreement. Every day, she would sit outside the Parliament building with her sign that read *Skolstrejk för Klimatet* (School Strike for the Climate). A photo of her sitting alone with her handwritten sign quickly went viral, inspiring the youth movement Fridays For Future (FFF), where school-aged kids from all over the globe skip classes on Fridays to demand that political leaders take action to address climate change. By July 2021, there have been school strikes recorded in 213 countries with 14 million people reported striking (Fridays For Future, 2022). FFF demands that governments act to keep the global temperature rise below 1.5 degrees Celsius, work toward climate justice, and act according to science, not politics.

Greta has emerged as an icon of the climate justice movement and is seen as the voice of her generation (Murphy, 2021; Ryalls & Mazzarella, 2021). On the topic of the climate crisis, her picture is everywhere: on the cover of *Rolling Stone,* in memes on social media, in international news articles about the climate crisis. She was followed on social media as she traversed the

Atlantic Ocean in a solar-powered boat to attend the United Nations Climate Action Summit in New York City in 2019. And she is often pictured protesting with children across the globe in school strikes, which are now considered the largest environmental protests in human history (Murphy, 2021).

In this chapter, we examine the qualities of Greta, now 18 years old, that have made her so iconic, contributing to what some dub the "Greta Effect." Her iconic performance is significant because she has come to represent the innocence of youth who are demanding that those in power act, and act urgently, to protect their future. She harnesses the power of social media to challenge the system, especially when (mostly) adult white men bully and threaten her. Her iconic performance inspires others to act. Here, we sift through scholarship about Greta as iconic, how she is positioned and perceived, the legacy and social media dynamics of her climate activism, her position as an iconic protagonist and the challenges famous girl activists face as they try to hold together a social movement by refusing to splinter.

GRETA'S CLIMATE ACTIVISM

The story of how Greta became a climate justice activist is now well-known, documented in her book *No one is too small to make a difference,* in the documentary *I am Greta,* and repeated in mainstream media articles. Similar to other kids who were tuning into the reports about the damage done to the atmosphere and the scientific agreement that there is little time left to make significant changes before there becomes a point of no return, Greta became withdrawn, depressed, and anxious. She stopped eating and talking. At twelve years of age, she was diagnosed with Asperger's syndrome, which helped to explain why she had a hard time fitting in with other kids at her school. Yet, she wanted to do something to make a difference. And this is where the school strikes began.

As the school strikes continue to gain traction, Greta is often invited to speak on the world's stage about climate change. Her message is aimed at world leaders and policymakers in government. Yet, she expresses her rising frustration at world leaders who invite her to speak as a celebrity of the movement, but do not act in the face of her calls to action. Many climate justice activists understand her argument, the fight, the frustration, and the urgency of her activism. Her message especially resonates with youth who are inspired to act and follow her lead.

While Greta's message is inspiring, it is also polarizing. Many wonder what is wrong with this little white girl, calling her names, joking about her seriousness, and insisting she must be mentally unstable. She is often depicted in photos in which her face appears neutral, unhappy, or angry. Other common images of her that circulate through social media are of her on stages giving speeches, being interviewed, or protesting together with other youth. The way she appears in public is a topic of general interest as evidenced by both academic analysis and mainstream media coverage. Although she often uses science to back up her claims and has been invited to speak at high profile events such as the UN Climate Summit, "many prominent voices and powerful media institutions have tried to diminish her status" (Murphy, 2021, p. 194). One way this happens is when men in positions of power undermine her by calling her mentally unstable and overly emotional. Framing girls and women as overly emotional and hysterical have long been tactics in women's oppression. Kay and Banet-Weiser (2019) label this as "affective injustice" because women's display of anger is seen as hysterical and overly emotional, whereas men's anger is seen as an appropriate response (p. 605).

When girls and women do not conform to hegemonic gender roles (e.g., smile, defer) they are seen as angry, breaking the norms of femininity and expectations of being nice. Women protesting injustice are seen as angry or what Ahmed (2017) calls "killjoys," and this anger becomes a reason not to listen to women's messages. Critiquing women as angry has especially been a tool for undermining women in politics. Margaret Thatcher was seen as an Iron Maiden (Fixmer-Oraiz & Wood, 2019). In her memoir, Hillary Clinton (2017) writes about the pressure to not display any emotion that may be perceived as angry. President Trump famously called Clinton a "nasty woman," referring to her disagreement with his policies. He repeated the term to refer to Nancy Pelosi and Kamala Harris. In a feminist turn of events, women have embraced this term as a slogan to counter and resist Trump's misogyny.

However, Kay (2019) convincingly argues that anger is becoming an acceptable form of protest and expression, not only in public discourse but also in popular culture. She identifies the #MeToo campaign as contributing to this newly accepted form of rage. Through social media, women expressed their anger about pervasive violence against women. As Kay (2019) writes, "this new registering of rage is occurring not only in the sphere of politics and protest as they are normatively understood; women's anger is increasingly legible within popular and commercial cultural forms" (p. 591). Yet, she also questions whether this popularity of anger is simply a tool for capitalist media's profit. Indeed, many Black feminists have argued that it is important to see how race influences the reception of women's expression of anger. For example, Ahmed (2009) writes about how institutional efforts to increase diversity has led to Black women needing to be seen as happy and gracious, lest they are identified as angry and against diversity. As she writes, "diversity becomes a technology of happiness" (p. 46). In the case of Greta, media focus on her anger, rather than her message. Greta herself has noticed news media's attempts to direct attention away from the climate crisis and reminds journalists that she is not what is important.

Media outlets often ask why is Greta so angry? She says that she, and kids like her, are angry for good reasons because adults are refusing to do the right thing (Rincon, 2019). Yet anger becomes the dominant frame in defining her in media. In her speeches to international leaders, her anger and frustration come through. For example, oft-quoted through clenched teeth she proclaimed "You have stolen my dreams and my childhood. How dare you?" (UN Climate Conference, 2019). In the same speech, she warns that if political leaders do not act urgently to curb the devastating effects of climate change, "we will never forgive you." In a speech to the EU Parliament in 2018, she says "I want you to panic. I want you to act as if your house is on fire."

Nobody Puts Greta in a Corner

While she expresses her anger toward world leaders, it is clear that she does not get to be her own version of angry. In interviews, she clarifies that she is not angry. In the documentary *I am Greta,* she states, "there is this false image that I'm an angry, depressed teenager. But why would I be depressed when I am trying to do my best to change things?" When asked in an interview in the *New York Times Magazine* about being angry, she replies,

> I've never felt that angry. When I say: "How dare you? You have stolen my dreams and my childhood"—that doesn't mean anything. It's a speech. When I wrote it, I thought, OK, this is a once-in-a-lifetime opportunity to speak in the United Nations General Assembly, and I need to make the most out of it. So that's what I did, and I let emotions take control, so to speak. But I'm actually never angry. I can't remember the last time I was angry. (Marchese, 2020, para. 22)

What she does discuss is strategy. Greta says "it's all about communicating the crisis mode" (Marchese, 2020). Here is how she describes her communication strategy:

> The mainstream communication strategy for the last decades has been positivity and spreading inspiration to motivate people to act. Like: "Things are bad, but we can change. Just switch your light bulb." You always had to be positive, even though it was false hope. We still need to communicate the positive things, but above that we need to communicate reality. In order to be able to change things we need to understand where we are at. We can't spread false hope. That's practically not a very wise thing to do. Also, it's morally wrong that people are

building on false hope. So I've tried to communicate the climate crisis as it is. (Marchese, 2020, para. 8)

In addition, when asked why people are so moved by her style of communication, Greta says, "I don't think I have any specific wisdom. I don't have much life experience. One thing that I do have is the childlike and naïve way of seeing things. We tend to overthink things. Sometimes the simple answer is, it is not sustainable to live like this" (Marchese, 2020, para. 27). She especially does not want to be the center of attention because she is dealing with Asperger's. As Greta says in an interview for the *Atlantic,* "when I'm around too many people, I just shut off my brain, in a way to not get too tired because I can't take everything in" (Meyer, 2019). Kay and Banet-Weiser (2019) identify this display of emotion as "respair means fresh hope; a recovery from despair" (p. 607). As they write,

> it is not only that one might follow after the other, but also that they often simultaneously co-exist, are entangled and mutually dependent. The presence of despair does not equate to the absence of hope: and indeed, perhaps the presence of the former is a precondition for the meaningful existence of the latter. It is precisely the bland, empty optimism and the denial of anger and pain that render neoliberal and popular feminisms so devoid of any meaningful political power. It is only by embracing anger and despair—and recognizing them as legitimate aspects of our politics—that we can hope for genuine, transformative change. (p. 607)

Despite her repeating that she is not angry, the anger people perceive is the largest attack on her. When she was named *TIME* Magazine's person of the year in 2019, then President Donald Trump tweeted:

> So ridiculous. Greta must work on her Anger Management problem, then go to a good old fashioned movie with a friend! Chill Greta, Chill! (Trump, 2019)

Piers Morgan, on *Good Morning Britain* agreed that Thunberg was articulate, but "she's very young, and she seems very overemotional." In the *Daily Mail,* he called her "a vulnerable drama queen who should go back to school" (Morgan, 2019).

She has also been attacked for having Asperger's, most often that she is mentally ill rather than having a disability. For example, Maxime Bernier, a Canadian politician, tweeted that Greta "is clearly mentally unstable" (Bernier, 2019a). He also tweeted, "I'm also concerned about all the children that @GretaThunberg has irresponsibly encouraged to skip school, or who have become more anxious, distressed, and in some cases suicidal because they believe they have no future" (Bernier, 2019b). Bernier blames Greta for causing hysteria, despite how her message is based in sound reasoning, resonating with youth activists and inspiring them to act.

Fox News commentator Michael Knowles attacked Greta, stating, "the climate hysteria movement is not about science. If it were about science, it would be led by scientists, rather than by politicians and a mentally ill Swedish child who is being exploited by her parents and by the international left." His comments sparked an apology by the network (Koerner, 2019). Fox News host Laura Ingraham juxtaposed Greta's UN speech with a clip from the 1984 horror film *Children of the Corn* and joked "I can't wait for Stephen King's sequel *Children of the Climate*."

Many politicians and pundits have justified their attacks on the teen climate activist because she has become a public figure. Bernier (2019c), for example, tweeted "she has become an influential figure in a movement that is a threat to our prosperity and civilisation. If she wants to play that role, she should be denounced and attacked" Arron Banks (2019), former UK Independence party funder, tweeted about "freak yachting accidents do happen in August" (@Arron_ banks, August 14, 2019) when Greta was sailing across the Atlantic Ocean. Dinesh D'Souza (2019) tweeted, "Children—notably Nordic white girls with braids and red cheeks—were often used in Nazi propaganda. An old Goebbels technique! Looks like today's progressive Left is still learning its game from an earlier Left in the 1930s."

Despite this incommensurate cyberbullying, Greta frames her Asperger's as a "super power." She tweets, "when haters go after your looks and differences, it means they have nowhere left to go. And then you know you're winning! I have Asperger's and that means I'm sometimes a bit different from the norm. And—given the right circumstances—being different is a superpower." #aspiepower (Thunberg, 2019). Positive media frames of people with ASD are rare and Ryalls and Mazzarella (2021) argue that this is part of why she is framed as exceptional.

While Taft (2020) names girling as the process of media rendering girl activists as harmless, in their analysis of Greta, Ryalls and Mazzarella (2021) found a more nuanced dynamic which they termed "Girling Fierceness (the paradoxical construction of her as a powerful, fearless, female child)" (p. 5). About this construction, Ryalls and Mazzarella (2021) surmise, "perhaps these adult male journalists find [Greta] bewildering because her manner of speaking and cultural influence do not align with normative white girlhood" (p. 9). In their analysis, they found that news media coverage often framed Greta as rational, a rare association for girls, because of her plea that we all follow the science, also a rare association given the uneven numbers of women in STEM (Ryalls & Mazzarella, 2021, p. 9). Thus, pundits are off base about her and her arguments and climate activists are paying attention.

GRETA the Iconic Protagonist

Greta became famous rather quickly as her photo with her protest sign outside of the Swedish parliament went viral, raising her up as an icon of the climate justice movement. As Olesen (2020) writes, she is the "moral and political embodiment of today's struggle against climate change" (p. 2). Olesen (2020) explains that political icons have high public visibility and embody a political cause or social movement for large groups of people. They become political icons because they create "coherence, visibility, and motivation" around a social cause (p. 3). In the process of becoming an icon, they inspire emotional and moral connections with audiences. Iconic protagonists are part of a drama in which they take on risks and sacrifices for the higher goal of social change. To become an icon, protagonists create a "communicative relationship between protagonist and audience" (p. 2). Greta's message makes sense to millions, as it circulates on social media and in mainstream media.

Oleson (2020) argues that Greta's emergence as protagonist icon is different from other political icons because of the swiftness in which it happened. Greta had limited financial and organizational resources when she started her Fridays for Future protests, yet she quickly gained support because of the social media ecology in which her performance occurred (Oleson, 2020). Also, as Oleson (2020) writes, two things distinguish the social media ecology from previous phases: iconic protagonists now have wide degrees of control over their own performance as they set the agenda through tweets, memes and posts, and audiences are no longer mere receptors of iconic performances, but actively become co-performers through commenting on social media posts or sharing messages with their networks. Social media allow for what Bennett and Segerberg (2012) identify as connective action because activists can draw on their networks to grow a political movement. Greta strategically uses social media to respond to her critics who accuse her of being manipulated by adults and world leaders who bully her. Through social media, she is able to challenge mainstream media frames. And, she has a direct communication channel with other youth audiences who are typically excluded from participating in political discourse, inspiring children all over the globe to participate in the Fridays for Future campaign. These iconic performances can happen on multiple social media platforms simultaneously. As a result, audiences can create a para-social relationship with protagonists, through comments on posts, retweets, and sharing things to go viral. Parasocial relationships refer to the psychological connection audiences feel to celebrities that they have never physically met but feel connected to through watching their mediated performances. This is particularly important in this case because youth are empowered and inspired to enter the political arena through their feelings of connection with Greta.

Olesen (2020) also argues that Greta is photogenic and visually plastic. She has a distinct look with her braided hair, staring directly into the camera, rarely smiling. She is often wearing a yellow raincoat to symbolize that she is braving the elements to protest. This image has been drawn on murals around the world, circulating on social media, and printed on mugs and T-shirts.

Greta often evokes what Keller (2021) identifies as a "failed futurity" (p. 685), or a bleak future, in her iconic performance as she tries to make the system listen and react. For example, she proclaims, "what is the point of learning facts in the school system, when the most important facts, given by the finest science of that same school system, clearly mean nothing to our politicians and our society?" She argues that school is useless if there is no future. She also argues that adults are using children to provide hope for the future, yet she responds saying that children should be in school not doing the work of adults. While she does see youth as making change, she recognizes that she can't do this without the help of adults in power. Greta's insistence on a failed future challenges the framing of girl activists as representing hope for the future. As Keller (2021) writes, "as a figure of mediated transnational girlhood, Thunberg becomes a source of anxiety and threat . . . because she refuses to do what we have come to expect of girl activists who cross borders on our screens—making 'us' feel good about a future, and in this case, one that relies on the global use of fossil fuels" (p. 685).

Part of her iconic performance is about how she calls out adults. For example, in her speech, she warns, "the show is over . . . this is communication tactics disguised as politics" (Thunberg, 2021). Her logic calls out the politics of climate change, as she continues to use evidence of how emissions are rising at higher levels, even though politicians say they are doing the best they can. On the other hand, however, Greta is framed as "spectacular" (Projansky, 2014). Taft (2020) argues that this is because of neoliberal ideals of empowerment and individualism. This works to take away from the need for collective action.

People are tuning into Greta's social media to see what she will do next. What is the nature of this drama? How is it unfolding? In the following sections, we look at these dynamics.

Greta vs. World Leaders

Inspired by the survivors of the Parkland, Florida shooting, Greta is known for "clapping back" at her critics on her social media (Murphy, 2021, p. 202). Greta "famously turns bullies' words back on them" (Ryalls & Mazzarella, 2021, p. 11) in how she subsumes their attacks in the service of her call to action or turns mockery back on them when the time is right. For example, after her speech at the United Nations Climate Summit in 2019, Trump mocked her anger by tweeting that Thunberg seemed like "a very happy young girl with a bright and wonderful future." After that, she changed her Twitter bio to read "a very happy young girl looking forward to a bright and wonderful future." She changed her profile to read "a kind but poorly informed teenager" after Russian President Vladimir Putin called her that. And, after Greta tweeted about the murder of Indigenous people who were defending the Amazon, Brazilian president Jair Bolsonaro called her a pirrahla, Portugese for brat. Greta then changed her Twitter profile to pirrahla. At a virtual climate change summit on Earth Day in 2021, Johnson commented "It's vital for all of us to show that it is not all about some expensive politically correct green act of 'bunny-hugging' or however you want to put it" as he critiqued climate activists for their naivety about how economics is a part of the solution (Roche, 2021). As Murphy (2021) shows, the fact that she "attracts derision, especially from powerful figures" has actually fueled her celebrity status (p. 196).

Murphy (2021) found that Greta, "demonstrates an advanced capacity to tactically redirect criticism back at her critics—ironically a skill that often makes her sound like the adult in these exchanges" (p. 203). For example, in response to Australian News Corp columnist Andrew Bolt calling her "deeply disturbed," she responded: "I am indeed 'deeply disturbed' about the fact that these hate and conspiracy campaigns are allowed to go on and on and on just because we children communicate and act on the science. Where are the adults?" (Meade, 2019). The drama between Greta and world leaders continues to unfold. In response to Trump's Twitter post which read "STOP THE COUNT!" referring to the ongoing efforts to count absentee ballots and late ballots, Greta tweeted that he needed to work on his Anger Management problem (Reuters, 2020). On President Trump's last day in office, she posted a photo of him boarding Marine One with the quote, "He seems like a very happy old man looking forward to a bright and wonderful future. So nice to see!" (Thunberg, 2021).

Remixed Greta

One way that audiences become co-performers in producing iconic protagonists is through remixing. Remixing is part of what Jenkins (2006) identifies as participatory culture. Digital media reduces barriers to access so that users can create their own media. Remixes, where users take popular images, text, and audio and create new meaning through juxtaposing in new and innovative ways, allow users to have political commentary, satire, or amplify a message that is already circulating. There are several popular memes of Greta, with words from her speeches juxtaposed on different images, such as a meme that has an image of Greta staring at the camera with the words "Save the planet or you will re-Greta it" (https://in.pinterest.com/pin/224757837641037440/). The overall message is that Greta will be watching you, a riff on her UN speech telling them that the whole planet is depending on the decisions adults are making at the Climate Summit. Her profile picture, with her knuckles crossed resting her head on her hands and looking at the camera. Another viral meme was a side-by-side picture, one of Thunberg at a podium, the other of President Trump with his arms crossed in defiance staring into the camera. The caption reads "One of these people is a child who knows nothing about science and shouldn't be given a platform. The other is Greta Thunberg" (Mulligan, 2020). This meme riffs on the critiques that Greta is a child and turns it on its head saying that it is actually Trump who is the child.

Other people have used references to Greta in creating videos. For example, Evan Williams and Mark Humphries filmed a comedy sketch called the "Greta Thunberg helpline: For adults angry at a child." In the sketch, people are phoning into a call center to express their anger toward Greta. One caller says, "Hi. I'm a middle-aged man with an embarrassing problem. I get irrationally angry at a Swedish girl that wants to save the planet" (ABC News Australia, 2019). We see a series of white men talking to women in a call center about how much Thunberg upsets them.

Mashups, where users take the sound or images in one video and juxtapose with a different meaning, are also a form of remix. One mashup that went viral was Death metal mashup that took Greta's UN speech and turned it into a death metal song by John Mollusk. Greta enjoyed this mashup and commented that she would pivot her activism toward Death metal.

Additionally, hashtag activism allows users to connect with other social movements and extend the audience (Crandall & Cunningham, 2016). Hashtag activism is the process of identifying a discursive community around a number of topics.

Jung et al. (2020) found through a sentiment analysis (where posts are classified as positive, negative, or neutral) of twitter posts that mentioned Thunberg. They also looked at the influential users who were sharing her tweets or tagging her. Politicians, professors, journalists, actors. They would retweet the content and add a news link, video clip, or image to extend the arguments. Barack Obama was the most followed user. Celebrities and global leaders were commenting on her or criticizing her as a way to promote their own standpoints. But they also found that many of the hashtags used in the United States were related to the Trump election (#MAGA-Make America Great Again; #Trump2020; #KAG-Keep America Great).

The Dark Web Underbelly

One thing that is not present in Oleson's(2020) analysis of iconic protagonists is the dark side of being on the stage. However, trolling, cyberbullying, and sexually explicit memes are all too common for girls who have a public presence on social media.

The rise of climate girl activists has also led to gendered attacks and misogyny (Gelin, 2019). Research by Anshelm and Hultman (2014) identified that climate denialism was closely connected to a loss of masculinity, threatening a way of life. This led to an anti-feminist backlash. In the process, they found that climate science and its related activism was feminized and a threat to masculinity. Pulé and Hultman (2019) called it "industrial breadwinner masculinity," referring to the feeling that men were losing their social role status as breadwinners and that extracting profit from natural resources was a part of what humans were meant to do. Thus, climate activism is a struggle over identity, especially because as Brough and Wilkie (2017) found climate activism is perceived as a feminine activity.

Dave et al. (2020) found several examples of online misinformation and conspiracy theories about Greta. They found five main tropes: attacks on her mental ability, her connection to antifa (a supposed faction of left-wing protestors that are often blamed for inciting violence), connection to George Soros (a philanthropist that is hated by the right), that she was a puppet (being used by people in positions of power to get their way), and that she was part of the climate industrial complex (a network of corporate interests that promote green energy and sustainability). What they found is that these stories were circulating across different social media platforms and also across different countries. The tactics were used to not only discredit Thunberg but promote skepticism in mainstream environmental organizations. As they write "undermining her credibility is a proxy attack on the credibility of these organizations and movements" (p. 3). Another dynamic they found was how images of Thunberg were first circulated on satire sites, but then were circulated and taken out of context, suggesting that they were true and authentic. They write, "the variety of ways in which critics have claimed Thunberg is not authentic, genuine, or sincere—because she is a hoax as is climate change itself. In the same way that critics claim Thunberg is not really what she purports to be, they say the idea she represents is equally false" (p. 19). They make broader claims about how these conspiracy theory stories target minorities and women, which poses a greater threat as members of these groups use social media to participate in society. In a content analysis of user comments on the most popular, professionally produced videos on YouTube about Greta, Park et. al. (2021) found a majority of comments uncivil. Moreover, the comments were not about her climate activism. Instead, they were about her personal characteristics. Similarly, Park et al., (2021) conclude that users appear to attack Greta "because they cannot effectively argue the science of climate change" and likely because they are also attacking climate science.

Keller (2021) highlights two instances of mediated misogyny directed toward Greta. During a trip to Alberta, Canada in October 2019, in downtown Edmonton, there was a mural which was a closeup of Thunberg with one of her braids over her shoulder and an angry face. The mural was supposed to refer to the UN "How dare you" speech. The mural was quickly defaced, with someone blacking out her eyes and the phrases "stop the lies" and "this is oil country" written across the face. The French phrase, "petite salope" (English translation is little slut) was also graffitied on the mural. Keller also refers to a sticker that depicts a rape symbol with two hands pulling braids from behind and the silhouette of a naked girl. "Greta" is on her lower back, suggesting the connection between the rape imagery and Greta. The sticker also had X-site Energy Services, the company logo of an Alberta-based oil company. When the photo of the sticker went viral, the company took responsibility for distributing the sticker. Again, showing her toughness in the face of bullying, Greta responds that acts like that "show we are winning" (Gramenz, 2020).

More recently, an attack that can be characterized as "fat shaming" occurred by Chinese media (Chen, 2021). An article published in *China Daily* questioned whether or not Greta was a vegan and circulated a picture of her as overweight. Chinese journalist Tang Ge wrote "although she claims to be vegetarian, judging from the results of her growth, her carbon emissions are actually quite low" (Chen, 2021). Greta is outspoken about China's carbon emissions. Greta clapped back to the accusations, reasserting that China is increasing its carbon emissions and that being fat shamed was "a pretty weird experience even by my standards. But it is definitely going on my resume" (Zoellner, 2021).

Greta as a Hub in the Climate Activist Network

Greta uses her network in the service of unity. Through her social media posts, she draws attention to marginalized communities that are experiencing the worst of climate change. She also travels to these locations and brings together other youth activists.

Our findings are that many of these young climate activists are working together to help each other and refuse to be divided even as culture tries to divide them and even as they have to point out their generational differences to get adults with agency and power to listen. As previously detailed, one unique feature of Greta's activism is the way she participates in the global network of other youth climate activists through social media. She both amplifies the work of others and refuses to be the "face" of the movement.

On January 28, 2020, Greta tweeted, "there are countless of school strikers and young climate activists around the world. Not just me. They all have names and stories waiting to be told" (Thunberg, 2020). On February 19th, 2021, Greta posted a close-up picture of a smiling young woman of color and a German Shepherd dog on her Instagram page. The caption said, "Freedom of speech and the right to peaceful protest and assembly are non-negotiable human rights. These must be a fundamental part of any democracy. #StandWithDishaRavi." The next day, the post had amassed over 4000 comments and 254,696 likes. At first glance, all it took was a nod to something about freedom of speech, and an image of a girl and a dog. The next day *The Hindu's* headline read "Greta Thunberg extends support to Disha Ravi." A large photo of unsmiling Greta in a crowd looking right into the camera was the dominant image that accompanied the story. According to the article in *The Hindu,* Disha is a twenty-two-year-old activist who was jailed for sedition. BBC News' headline read, "Disha Ravi: The jailed Indian activist linked to Greta Thunberg." The dominant image was a close-up of Ravi and her dog. The article explained that Ravi's "arrest is part of a larger pattern on journalist and protestor intimidation" using archaic laws, and that she was part of helping "farmers protest new agriculture reform laws." According to the section of NBC News' Climate in Crisis section, Ravi "has emerged as a symbol of the Indian government's crackdown on dissent as the country confronts a growing crisis after months of protest from furious farmers." Disha Ravi co-founded India's chapter of Thunberg's Fridays for Future Youth Climate Strike movement. This is one example of how Greta uses her social media to connect and support climate activists all over the world as well as how networked and interrelated the youth climate activist movement is. Greta's style of activism has attracted support from traditionally marginalized groups (Murphy, 2021).

Besides the networked aspect of Greta's climate activism, we found many interviews and stories wherein girl climate activists talk about Greta in positive terms. She was their motivation to act, or to get involved. African climate activist Vanessa Nakate said she was inspired by Greta. Vanessa joined #FridaysforFuture in 2019 and started The Rise Up Movement in Africa (Srikanth, 2020). Other youth climate activists said Greta's message was "the boost they needed to kick up their own work" (Sawchuck, 2019). In this interview with 16-year-olds: Isra Hirsi, who co-founded and co-directed Youth Climate Strike US and Communications Director, Maddy Fernands, both described how Greta's message resonated with them: "She has a very pointed message and a very consistent message of how our current leaders today will be looked down on as the villains" who didn't act in the face of evidence, Fernands said. "Her voice and her goal—it's just hard to ignore her" (Sawchuk, 2019). In Greta's Instagam post about an open letter they wrote to "EU-and global leaders, signed by thousands of activists, scientists, representatives of civil society and influencers," Jamie Margolin commented that she was "Honored to have signed this letter and to be part of this! I hope our leaders listen. We must all unite to #facetheclimateemergency [Earth emoji]!" We discuss Margolin in Chapter Six of this book.

We find that Greta has inspired others, and that they do praise her and that they do not report her out for credit or personal gain. Indeed, she (and the other girls in this book) take on these roles reluctantly (Frazer-Carroll, 2019; Murphy, 2021), which as Oleson (2020) argues positions them as iconic protagonists.

Greta and other climate girl activists are more interested in collaborating as a united front even as they recognize the different climate work each are doing in their local contexts. Studying young feminist organizers in the global South, Bashi (2018) noted that "[Young feminists] are showing their ability to organize intersectionally (that is, recognizing and respecting differences between them arising from race, class, caste, disability, and other aspects of identity), with often extremely limited resources and support from their own communities. Young feminists are proving brave, creative, and resilient" (Bashi, 2018, p. 442). Based in Western conceptualizations of activism, O'Brien et al. (2018) studied youth climate activists in "high-emissions societies" and came up with an analytical typology that is not mutually exclusive of different ways youth challenge through dissent: dutiful, disruptive, and dangerous. Dutiful being the most common form. "Dangerous dissent challenges existing paradigms or ways of understanding the relationship between climate change and social change." It is dangerous in that "it generates new and alternative systems, new ways of doing things, new types of economic relationships, and new ways of organizing society. The 'danger' also lies in the way that youth are claiming, taking back, or generating their own power and strengthening their personal and political agency, or simply questioning what to others appears to be inevitable, such as a fossil fuel–based economy hyperconsumption, and increasing social inequality" (n.p.). Like Martín (2021), who studied representation of eco-feminist leadership in popular culture, we also see a larger social vision afoot that is important for the scale of the change that is needed and that these girl climate activists understand. As Martín (2021) observed, "Cooperative networks, female leaders and inclusive revolutionary processes have proliferated in the movies at the same time as networked world citizens have occupied squares, participated in international strikes and engaged in online activism" (p. 92). The network dynamics of Greta's climate crisis activism certainly reflects this, too.

The impulse to divide these climate activist girls is understandable given the way conflict arouses the attention needed in attention economies and given the habit of reinforcing cultural stereotypes of girls' relationships as manipulative and mean. Adults, who have been conditioned to expect respect from young people, and girls especially, are losing that respect as adults do not protect and care for them, and are being called out as a generation. In her now-famous 2019 UN speech, "the sixteen-year-old Swedish student emphasized the generation gap between the senior diplomats and policymakers and the community of young climate activists she represented, including outspoken Black, [I]ndigenous, and people of color (BIPOC) teen activists" (Houdek & Phillips, 2020, p. 369). Greta learned a great deal from other youth who have chosen to hold adults accountable. Parkland shooting survivor, Emma González, for example, spoke at a 2018 rally for gun control said, "Maybe the adults have gotten used to saying, 'it is what it is,' but if us students have learned anything, it's that if you don't study, you will fail. And in this case if you actively do nothing, people continually end up dead, so it's time to start doing something" (CNN, 2018).

Global media coverage of Greta is problematic, and Greta is aware. According to Murphy (2021), after the Vanessa Nakate AP incident wherein the Ugandan environmental activist was the only Black girl cropped out of a photograph of the group at the World Economic Forum, Greta held a press conference with fellow African eco-activists to raise awareness about this problem of invisibility. Indeed, climate girls of color are erased in media coverage (Gandhi, 2020), which is another problem. Indian climate activist, Licypriya Kangujam, who is also the youngest at 8 years old, objected to media stories that referred to her as "Greta of India." She acknowledged that she and Greta are friends, and used social media to describe the problem "Greta of India" as a mechanism that erases her identity and eclipses her story (Gandhi, 2020). Kangujam (2020a) tweeted "Dear Media, Stop calling me 'Greta of India.' I am not doing my activism to looks like Greta Thunberg. Yes, she is one of our Inspiration & great influencer. We have common goal but I have my own identity, story. I began my movement since July 2018 even before Greta was started." Kangujam also posts a video of her holding a handwritten sign that reads, "Dear Mr. Mode & MPs, Pass the Climate Change Law! Act Now!" In a series of tweets, she explains how she raised her voice in a UN event in Mongolia on July 4, 2018, and started her movement called "Child Movement," which in Hindi is "Bachpan Andolan." The goal was to call for action on climate change. She states that she was not interested in publicity and media coverage and instead focused on the movement. She also dropped out of school at age seven to focus on her activism. "If you call me 'Greta of India,' you are not covering my story. You are deleting a story" (Kangujam, 2020b).

Scholarship on news media coverage of Greta's constructed persona as outsized and unhelpful in the fight for an inhabitable planet reinforces division. For example, Ryalls and Mazzarella (2021) studied how journalists created the persona of Greta as they made sense of her in 21 mostly corporate-owned, left leaning articles about her. By centering Greta's autism spectrum disorder (ASD) and her whiteness, Ryalls and Mazzarella (2021) argue, news media contribute to the narrative that Greta is exceptional and erases "young climate change activists who do not meet a white, Western, middle-class standard" (p. 3). Ryalls and Mazzarella (2021) argue that the way news media construct Greta as hero means, while there is often space in the story for Indigenous girl activists and long-time environmental girl activists of color, Greta is the face, the voice, the inspiration, and their hero, which these scholars see as problematic. Greta herself recognizes this problem and employs several strategies to reduce this tendency (Murphy, 2021). Greta reiterates the environmental justice activism discourse about Indigenous leadership on her Instagram post. "Indigenous peoples make up 5 percent of the world's population, but take care of 80 percent of the remaining healthy ecosystems. They are almost always on the front line of the climate-and ecological crisis, but they are also leading the resistance. We have to listen to the guardians of the land and value their traditional knowledge to get out of this global crisis. The exploitation of nature, land and people needs to stop." While Greta is globally known, her own acts do not reflect exclusion. Rather Greta seeks to "share the spotlight with others" (Murphy, 2021, p. 197). Some have argued that it is because Greta is white that she gets so much attention, while activists of color are ignored in media. However, it is not helpful to aim collective animosity at Greta, as Frazer-Carroll (2019) notes, as "it's impossible for one person to truly represent everyone" anyway. What would be helpful is to recognize the way media systems produce Greta (Frazer-Carroll, 2019). "There were many girl activists working on climate change before Greta, and many of those were girls of color, including the founders of *This is Zero Hour* and the *Sunrise Movement* . . . there are many other girl activists who are also doing the hard work of social movement organizing but whose identities and political visions are perhaps more challenging to contain or less desirable for public consumption" (Taft, 2020, p. 8).

INTERGENERATIONAL PARADOX

We recognize a tension these climate girl activists try to navigate between needing adults to get on board and implement change at the same time that they need to take adults to task and shake them from complacency and inaction, which can foment a defensive posture. This is a counterpublic growing exasperated with the lack of change. Greta and climate crisis activists around the world are arguing that adults with power listen and act in the interests of humanity, they (and we) need the intergenerational alliances to achieve the 2030 pre-industrial global temperature targets. This generation of young activists see the "need to come together in solidarity to work towards gender equality, inclusion, and social justice. This includes working intergenerationally" (Bashi, 2018, p. 451). The methods Raging Grannies used to organize in Seattle's ShellNo Action Coalition in pressing their aged bodies, gender, roles, and whiteness into useful service after listening to the needs of young, diverse climate activists, is a good example (Chazan & Baldwin, 2019). These scholars think "generationally polarizing discourses are far too simplistic, and their tendency to incite and reify the divisions they portray is potentially dangerous to the kind of intergenerational and intersectional movement-building needed to protect life on this planet" (Chazan & Baldwin, 2019, p. 258). We see these climate activist girls coach other activists to avoid intergenerational divisions. In the 2020 book, *All We Can Save: Truth, Courage, And Solutions for the Climate Crisis*, about division, Xiye Bastida (discussed in chapter 4 of this book) writes,

> to me and a lot of other young people, it feels like we're rooted in awareness while the adults around us live in obliviousness. This is where "Okay, Boomer" came from, a phrase designed to describe the intergenerational disconnect of the movement . . . we cannot let phrases like "Okay, Boomer" divide us. The fossil fuel industry wants us to be divided in order to slow down the push for climate justice. But we refuse to let attempts at division affect our purpose. (Johnson & Wilkinson, 2020, p. 5)

What Greta and other high-profile climate girl activists are fighting for in this dynamic of unity and division is a future to do things with. Time is not abstract for them or the planet, whereas the adults they are appealing to are locked into their classist, racist, sexist, and ageist habits of their conditioned conceptions of limitless time and resources. Climate girl activists call adults to account because time is running out. "Underlying Thunberg's emphasis on the clash between generations and the urgent need for action is a distinct rhetorical emphasis on the now of the present moment" (Houdek & Phillips, 2020, p. 369). Houdek and Phillips (2020) discuss "temporal rhetorics" as those ritualistic and repetitious discourses, practices, and performances that produce and sustain how a given people views themselves as existing within time" (p. 371). To make a case for the notion that the temporal turn "can open up productive and critical space within rhetorical studies and the study of gender and communication more broadly," Houdek and Phillips (2020) assert the need "to challenge and rethink fundamental white and Western cultural constructs like temporality is as urgent as ever. We hope that elevating the question of temporality and the prospects for alternative views of temporality can contribute . . . to all those who seek to build, imagine, and occupy different possible futures" (p. 372). Place is also in play. Greta's networked intersectional climate crisis activism moves when needed. Take, for example, the 151st Friday School Strike on Greta's Instagram. It includes an image of six girls and boys on Climate Strike together on a tree plantation in Northern Europe. They're holding two handwritten protest signs that say, "Skol Strejk för Klimatet" (School Strike for the Climate), "Fridays for Future" and one larger printed banner that reads, "STAND WITH THE GUARDIANS OF THE LAND. RESPECT SAMMI RIGHTS = SAVE LIFE." The text below this image explains how forest companies clear-cut forests, which is bad because we need forests for biodiversity and for their role as carbon sinks. Trees are then replaced with non-local invasive tree species. Greta then explains the negative impact on the Indigenous Sami reindeer herders' land and lives. "It is not just the forest and carbon sinks that are being eliminated, but also the history, future and traditions of the Sami people." Greta exposes the lie of the use of the terms "renewable" and "carbon neutral" in the context of limited time. She explains the harms of burning biomass the way tree plantations "exacerbate their effects, increasing the devastation and suffering of people and wildlife." And the post ends with the hashtags: "#schoolstrike4climate #climatestrike #fridaysforfuture #IndigenousRights #StopFakeRenewables."

Discussion of finite time and images of location are both important features of Greta's recent crisis communication strategy on her social media. The young climate activists try to be invitational and educational as they appeal to the urgency of needing change and calls for adults to help.

WHAT IS THE GRETA EFFECT?

As an icon for the Climate Justice Movement, Greta wants to be an anti-icon. She eschews the celebrity status that is bestowed upon her, claiming that it only draws attention away from people doing something about the climate crisis. Still, Greta has become the face of the youth movement. A girl who uses the agency available to her to ask for a world that makes sense to her. She stays on point, she challenges those in authority, and connects with other youth online and offline. She joins school strikes around the world. She accepts invitations to speak about the climate crisis. And she listens to others and amplifies where helpful as climate activists share their stories.

Part of her iconic status comes through her rhetorical style, which against expectations, combines anger and logic to convince people to act. She notably criticizes those in power and engages with them on social media. She is also a target of bullying and misogyny.

Journalists and scholars have described different kinds of Greta effects. First, Greta's activism inspires people to make small changes and to feel hopeful that they too can make a difference. A survey of U.S. adults found a link between familiarity with Thunberg and collective efficacy, or the idea that individuals can work together for a common goal (Sabherwal et al., 2021). Those who are familiar with Greta feel they can help mitigate climate change. They are more willing to take action themselves. The more familiar they were with Thunberg, the more likely they felt their actions were effective and meaningful. Her lonely initial stand inspired millions of people. "no one is too small to make a difference." She inspires people to take collective action. "Greta Effect" also refers to girls' who were inspired to strike (Nevett, 2019). An article in BBC News titled "The Greta effect? Meet the schoolgirl climate warriors" features several girls from around the globe who are striking. Haven Coleman from Denver, Colorado cites her decision to strike inspired by Greta. She is the co-director of US Youth Climate strike. She founded the organization with Isra Hirsi, daughter of Ilhan Omar (democratic Congresspersonfrom Minnesota) and Alexandria Villaseñor. Leah Namugerwa lives in Uganda and at age twelve felt helpless against drought and famine and was inspired to act after learning about Greta.

Murphy (2021) described a media dynamic called "the other Greta Effect," which occurs when Greta sets the agenda. Greta mentions, say global eco-activists, and media then cover the story. Another "Greta Effect" is in travel choices. Swedes and others who are part of the "no-fly movement" (Murphy, 2021, p. 198) minimized domestic flights because they were inspired by her. Another "Greta Effect" is the pressure corporations face to be more sustainable. For example, Röderer (2020) identified the impact of Thunberg on corporate tweets. Many corporations felt they needed to make a stand on sustainability and climate. The emergence of Greta as protagonist icon forced people to respond.

We offer a more critical view of the "Greta Effect" along the lines of Taft's (2020) concept of girls as global saviors. Because media tend to frame Greta as exceptional (Ryalls & Mazzarella, 2021) they reduce the power of her message. At the same time, Greta herself does not want to be seen as exceptional but that message doesn't come through. Instead, her social media posts and subsequent media coverage create an activist drama. It is no longer about the actual steps that governments need to take to reduce carbon emissions, instead it is about the struggle between Greta and world leaders. This drama includes the dynamics of her as an iconic protagonist. And further, we see her as an intersectional feminist iconic protagonist in that her activism and actions challenge hegemonic girl norms.

Taken together, we identify The Greta Effect as empowering new kinds of participatory culture related to environmental activism and standing up to power structures. Through her social media, Greta posts photos of her striking as part of the Fridays for Future movement. These posts inspire others to keep going and being persistent. We can learn from the way that Greta participates in the political drama of taking on world leaders and encouraging her followers to take action. Her use of humor and clapback response increases her following and the attention she attracts draws people into the movement.

Additionally, the Greta Effect refers to how climate girls can set the public agenda through their iconic performances. Mainstream media look to Greta for responses when she is attacked by those in power. They follow her to climate conferences and report on her speeches, which are focused and to the point. She uses her platforms to amplify the reality of a diverse climate justice movement.

The Greta Effect calls on adults to work intergenerationally and inclusively. We can further this work by doing our part to keep focus on climate science and adult action. We can help by pressuring platforms that host gender violence and networked misogyny to remove those posts and tendencies. We can also demand platforms remove misinformation and disinformation related to climate change.

Chapter 3

The Flint Girl Effect

This chapter explores Little Miss Flint who, at age 8, became an activist during the Flint water crisis. She has spent her tween years in the public spotlight branding herself as an activist on both social and traditional media. "My generation will fix this mess of a government. Watch us" captures part of her approach to social change as a climate girl activist (Mari Copeny, 2021). In this chapter, we explore the intersections of age, race, and gender; national notoriety, politics, and activism; and social media use and media coverage to better understand what is involved in growing up online as a Black girl activist and public figure who advocates for the children of Flint in a long fight for environmental justice.

Demographically, the citizens of Flint, Michigan are majority poor to working poor and Black and, in the spring of 2014, were poisoned by their city and state government. It began undemocratically with a decision made (secretly) at the state level to divert the water supply from Lake Huron and the Detroit River to an untreated source, the Flint River, to save money. The results of this decision showed up in Flint's bodies: an outbreak of Legionnaires' disease, reports of rashes and hair loss, and long-term developmental problems the youth will suffer from their possible exposure to lead in the water. For 18 months, Flint residents, who knew their water source had changed, and who had experienced health problems polluted water causes, and who were lied to by their government about the safety of their drinking water, fought for environmental justice. As Pauli (2020) writes, "the Flint water crisis is one of the most significant environmental contamination events in recent American history" (n.p.).

The intersectional systemic obstacle of environmental racism and classism was formidable, partly because it was invisible and dismissible to many. Environmental racism "refers to any environmental policy, practice, or directive that differentially affects or disadvantages (whether intended or unintended) individuals, groups, or communities based on race or color" (Bullard & Johnson, 2000, p. 559). Flint's water crisis is exemplary environmental racism. Although some justice was served in 2021 when Flint residents reached a settlement for damage caused and criminal charges were leveled toward former Michigan governor Rick Snyder, Flint residents continue to distrust their water.

During Flint's water crisis, eight-year-old Amariyanna Copeny won a beauty pageant and was crowned Little Miss Flint. This title gave her a platform to raise her own voice (Thomas, 2020). She wrote a letter about her town's poisoned water supply to then President Barack Obama. This sweet, traditional, American ritual of school children writing the president made a difference. Her letter led to Obama's visit to Flint and subsequent declaration of the lead poisoning in Flint's water supply a national emergency. Copeny's activism didn't end there. Images of her holding hand-drawn written messages about the ongoing situation with Flint's water circulated on social media. "Mari" is now fourteen. She continues to remind people that the crisis in Flint is not over. Her ongoing efforts include her use of social media platforms to accomplish the justice she wants for her community. Her activism has expanded to include actions such as an anti-Trump rally in front of the White House and a GoFundMe crowdfunding effort to raise money for bottled water for Flint residents.

In this chapter, we first provide an overview of the Flint water crisis, especially how mainstream media reported on the events and local efforts to challenge dominant framing. Next, we analyze Mari's activist strategies, which includes creating a brand through which she packages herself as a Black girl activist. In the end, we discuss the Flint Girl Effect, which shows how place-based activism can draw attention to environmental racism.

WHO IS LITTLE MISS FLINT?

Mari, a self-proclaimed activist, was born in 2007. According to her website, "her youthful honesty prevents political leaders from being able to ignore the consequences of neglectful leadership. She gives voice to the unheard hardships of Americans trapped by a collapsing toxic infrastructure" (Mari Copeny, 2021).

In 2016, Mari rose to national fame when she wrote a letter to President Obama. The text of the letter reads:

> Mr. President,
>
> Hello my name is Mari Copeny and I'm 8 years old, I live in Flint, Michigan and I'm more commonly known around town as "Little Miss Flint." I am one of the children that is effected by this water, and I've been doing my best to march

in protest and to speak out for all the kids that live here in Flint. This Thursday I will be riding a bus to Washington, D.C. to watch the congressional hearings of our Governor Rick Snyder. I know this is probably an odd request but I would love for a chance to meet you or your wife. My mom said chances are you will be too busy with more important things, but there is a lot of people coming on these buses and even just a meeting from you or your wife would really lift people's spirits. Thank you for all that do for our country. I look forward to being able to come to Washington and to be able to see Gov. Snyder in person and to be able to be in the city where you live. (Meyer, 2016, para. 4).

President Obama heeded the call and made a visit to Flint to witness firsthand the water crisis and hear from residents. In photos of Mari and President Obama, she is wearing her beauty pageant sash looking up at a very tall Obama. Her identity as a girl who summoned him to the rescue is reinforced in photos of him picking her up and hugging her.

INTERSECTIONAL GIRLHOOD STUDIES

Mari's lived experience as a Black girl living in Flint, Michigan allows her to be critical of systemic racism while developing her own voice about injustices. We see Mari's activism as aligning with research from Black girlhood studies that have highlighted the ways in which Black girls navigate dominant narratives about them (which is that they are deviant), while also advocating for social change. As Kaler-Jones, Griffin, and Lindo (2020) write, "Black girlhood, as a framework, highlights how Black girls add critical perspectives of human experience, produce and validate knowledge that disrupts dominant deficit-based narratives, and use experience as a strength" (p. 162). Additionally, they write that "when Black girls examine their lived experiences, they come up with radically unique ideas about those experiences" (p. 162). Mari can also be understood as embodying Black girlhood which, Brown (2009) found, "transcends age and instead is the representations, memories, and lived experiences of being and becoming a body marked as youthful, Black, and female" (p. 1). She becomes representative of Black girls' civic activism as she enters the public sphere to address environmental racism in Flint in the current context.

To understand the impact that Little Miss Flint has had on drawing attention to systemic racism in her community, Logan and Mackey (2020) highlight how Mari calls out the racist and classist structures that resulted in poisoned water. As they write, "Little Miss Flint serves as a moniker for an intersectional civic identity that captures Mari's age, her gender, her immediate context, and the nature of her oppression" (p. xii).

There is little research on why Black girls are called to activism, however the research available suggests that addressing racism is a key motivator. In an analysis of applications to attend a leadership and empowerment conference, Garcia, Fernandez, and Jackson (2020) found that Black girls viewed their participation as an empowering outlet for challenging stereotypes that have both individual and collective impacts on the Black community. Because Black girls who are working toward social change are doing so within structures of systemic racism, working within these systems calls for alternative forms of action that look different than traditional youth activism, such as formal activities associated with schools and youth organizations (Garcia, Fernández, & Jackson, 2020). Media literacy programs, for example, can offer Black girls avenues for expressing their experiences of media while challenging gender and racial representations in media. McArthur (2016), for example, found in her analysis of a critical media literacy program that Black girls' participation allowed them to disrupt narratives of mainstream media and deconstruct dominant narratives that may frame them as deviant, aggressive, and victims. When Black girls were given the opportunity to create their own media, they told powerful stories of their own lived realities (MacArthur, 2016).

More recently, the diffusion of social media platforms like Twitter and Instagram, allow girls more communication channels to disrupt dominant narratives. In their study of Black girls' use of social media, Kaler-Jones, Griffin, and Lindo (2021) found that social media allows girls a space for creating a "counter-narrative by commenting on social injustice and Black identity in their communities, country, and the world" (p. 169). Their use of social media becomes a "clapback" (p.170). It affords Black girls a way to respond to public discourse about them and to "reassert their visibility in a news media space that erases, constricts, and polices their forms of activism" (p. 170).

Kelly (2018) studied Black high school girls' use of the social media platform Snapchat to express frustration with racist interactions and harassment at school and were then disciplined by school administrators for "aggressive online exchanges" rather than supported. Kelly's (2018) specific study of Black girls' digital resistance strategies used to navigate white supremist institutional practices revealed not only the importance of situating such scholarship within the history of Black feminist activism and the dynamics of contemporary Black women's leadership and thought, but also the importance of studying Black girls' activism as it can contribute to this knowledge. Like Kelly, we are interested in the way girls' activism shapes the girls themselves—their identities as well as making some difference in the world. As Kelly writes, "the struggle for equity and justice in U.S. society must rest upon an understanding of the experiences and critical resistance of black females" (p. 375).

Missing still in the research on Black girls and media activism is how they grow up on social media. Since this is a visual medium, what does it mean to follow Mari and see her grow into adolescence as she continues to grow into a community leader, public figure, and activist icon? We acknowledge here that we are white, middle-aged women situated far away and studying the digital life of a young Black girl and her community located in the midwestern United States. We necessarily rely on and honor Black feminist thought for our understandings. This is the backdrop that frames our analysis of how Mari and her activism shapes and is shaped by the interplay of technology, specifically social media, the forces of capitalism, and mainstream media coverage.

Unlike some of the other climate girls in our case studies, Mari has the most stereotypically feminine performance. She enters activism as a Black girl, which challenges the controlling image of Black girls as deviant and loud. As Collins (2009) points out, "portraying African American women as stereotypical mammies, matriarchs, welfare recipients, and hot mommas helps justify U.S. Black women's oppression. Challenging these controlling images has long been a core theme in Black feminist thought" (p. 69). Mari's fame originated in the combination of beauty queen and activist. As Fixmer-Oraiz and Wood (2019) write, "growing up and identifying as a girl in America in the twenty-first century generally means you learn to care about your appearance, care about others, you learn to expect negative treatment, and that you can be "superwoman" and have both careers and families" (p. 158). Yet, this is complicated by constructions of Black girls as hypersexualized and deviant. Mari calls out these constructions and resists them. She posts pictures of her in pink pleated skirts or cheer outfits, for example. She also posts photos of her community engagement, including delivering school supplies and water filters. And, she posts reminders of her activism from her early activism during the Flint water crisis to her current efforts.

FRAMING THE FLINT WATER CRISIS

Mari's activism can be contextualized through the vibrant activist community in Flint. The people of Flint are not new to environmental activism. Flint has been overrun with pollution since the 1930s as a result of the concentration of the auto industry, The story of the dying auto industry and its impact on Flint's economy was chronicled in Michael Moore's (1989) documentary *Roger and Me*. For decades, citizens fought against the construction of the Genesee Power Station that threatened to contaminate air around the Black neighborhood. While they lost the fight (the power station was permitted in 1992), in 2017, the EPA concluded that "the State Department of Environmental Quality discriminated against residents near the plant because of their race at the time the plant was permitted in 1992" (Fonger, 2019). The ongoing environmental activism in Flint exposes the limitations of the Environmental Protection Agency's (EPA's) framework of environmental justice, which the EPA defines as "the fair treatment and meaningful involvement of all people regardless of race, color, national origin, or income with respect to the development, implementation, and enforcement of environmental laws, regulations, and policies" (Butler et al., 2016, p. 96). According to the EPA, all communities should have the same level of protections from environmental health hazards. However, Flint's deteriorating water system reveals the biases in this system and the persistence of environmental racism. Indeed, several scholars identify these practices as racial capitalism, because of the ways in which capitalism "develops through the proliferation of social hierarchies based in the devaluation of racialized people" (Vasudevan & Smith, 2020, p. 1161).

The Flint water crisis led to localized activist efforts to address the poisoned water. The water crisis activism included Flint H20 Justice coalitions, town hall meetings, panels, and hearings. Community members distrusted water forums sponsored by officials and instead opted for more grassroots activism (Pauli, 2019). Through their efforts, Flint environmental activists "sought to democratize the epistemological realm, fighting to establish the legitimacy of popular knowledge and for a vision of 'citizen science' that insisted on residents setting the scientific agenda within their own community" (Pauli, 2019, p. 14).

However, the story framed in mainstream media was that it was not the Michigan government who was at fault, but Flint citizens themselves. Carey and Lichtenwalter (2020) found that coverage in national media outlets *The New York Times* and *The Wall Street Journal* framed Flint citizens as victims who were not able to do anything but wait for a solution. These frames reinforced a sense of urban pathology, rather than focusing on structural issues that contribute to environmental racism. Additionally, framing Flint residents as lacking agency is counter to the many activist efforts that were occurring locally. As Jackson (2017) found, there was a failure of national media outlet coverage of the Flint water crisis until late 2015 when the state of Michigan and President Obama declared an emergency. In her content analysis of the media coverage, Jackson (2017) found that comments of officials were prioritized and residents were portrayed as hopeless and downtrodden. Narratives of "heroes" who were addressing the crisis often excluded African American activists. A lack of diversity in the newsroom leads to media paying little attention to environmental justice in communities of color. It is only after harm is verified by experts, rather than in response to citizen concerns, that media coverage emerges (Jackson, 2017).

Understandably, residents still do not trust the water, mostly because of the failure of government to address these issues. Distrust of the government is endemic to systemic racism in which African Americans are often victims of public health violations, such as the Tuskegee Syphilis Study, the case of Henrietta Lacks whose cells were used unbeknownst to her or her family for cancer research, and more recently with the disproportionate number of African Americans being infected from COVID-19 and skeptical of vaccinations. As a result, research shows that African Americans and other minority populations tend to value information that comes from interpersonal or social networks. Local experts are seen as more credible for disseminating health information. Additionally, research has found that African Americans have lower trust in government authorities, and more trust when health information comes from African American sources (Day et al., 2019). It is in this context that Little Miss Flint rises as an environmental activist who gains credibility locally and nationally.

LITTLE MISS FLINT AND PLACE-BASED SOCIAL MEDIA ACTIVISM

Moors (2019) studied the social media activist practices of Flint's residents to figure out what difference "place-based activism" made amid the national and negative dominant narrative that emerged from the mainstream news coverage of the 2016 Flint water crisis. Like others who study place-based social media theory, Moors (2019) showed how place described on social media "extend the realm of a given physical location into the networked realm" (p. 811). Moors' (2019) case study illustrated the "connective, interactive, material impact of social media" insofar as Flint residents used platforms to add complexity to mainstream news accounts as well as to address local audiences. Social media affordances such as hashtags, specific tagging, requests to share, and embedding links, were valuable and contributed to residents' activist goals of telling a different story—a positive story of the people and place that is Flint. Moors (2019) detailed how the norms of journalism continue to center government perspectives even as these norms should have changed by now. "[P]rominent accounts of the water crisis negatively affects the perceptions of Flint as a place and contributes to the marginalization of its people" (Moors, 2019, p. 812).

Social media activism was an alternative form of storytelling that supplemented journalistic coverage of the Flint water crisis. Hashtags framed Flint's citizens as victims, but also filled with hope. Van Dijck and Poell (2013) write that social media logic of connectivity "equally emphasizes the mutual shaping of users, platforms, advertisers, and more generally, online performative environments" (p. 8). Social media creates new meaning and relationships. Moors (2019) found that the way people in Flint were using social media allowed them to challenge dominant media narratives to show their lived experiences. As Moors writes, "social media activism is not only a conscious use of online, connective, and technological affordances to make social issues known, but that it also draws on those affordances to affectively influence discourses and effect social change in a way that transcends spreadability and scale of stories" (p. 811). Users innovate to make content more searchable rather than relying on algorithms. People did not want to be defined by the water crisis and because of social media's connective affordances, Flint residents had a mechanism with which to contribute to wider discourses with their own experiences and stories. "By broadcasting their ordinary stories throughout the global network of the internet, the citizens of Flint call on others to not only become aware of the happening in Flint but to connect with them and re-assess their perceptions about them as ordinary, dynamic people not singularly defined by the water crisis" (p. 817).

Little Miss Flint also uses place-based social media activism in her Twitter postings. Her activism continues the trajectory among Black feminist activists who have strategically used Twitter for social change. Her Twitter posts are multidimensional and add a critical voice. She promotes her kid-oriented activism and has an event for almost every season: Easter, Christmas, back to school. These are the kinds of events that give kids hope and something to look forward to. At the same time, she calls out racism and draws attention to how racism impacts her life, through school curriculum to her awareness of how racism is targeted toward her. For example, in one of her Twitter posts she writes, "I made it 8 days into 2021 before I got called a racial slur" (Copeny, 2021a).

Her Twitter posts are a lasting reminder that the Flint water crisis is not over and will continue to affect generations to come. As she draws attention to other water crises around the U.S. and the world, she always connects these back to Flint. For example, at the beginning of the pandemic, on March 13, 2020, Mari tweeted,

> Are you upset about standing in long lines, prices on essentials being raised for profit, and stores running out of the items you need to survive? Flint residents have been dealing with this feeling for almost 6 years when it comes to water. #CoronaOutbreak #coronavirus. (Copeny, 2020a)

The tweet was accompanied by a picture of her looking up at a tower of bottled water. This post reminds audiences that scarcity and fear of having clean water to survive has been a reality in Flint.

This reminder of Flint is very present in her Twitter posts:

> This #WorldWaterDay comes as we approach the 7 year anniversary of the #FlintWaterCrisis, and the most heartbreaking thing is that Flint is not the only city still dealing with toxic water, its a national issue. Help me help those without clean water. (Copeny, 2021g)

In another Twitter post, she posts a photo of a near-empty aisle of water bottles and writes,

> This is what the water aisle at our local Walmart looks like. The water crisis is far from over. It's why I fight to get my filters to people that need it the most. #Flint #ThisIsAmerica. (Copeny, 2021b)

After a long period when kids had to shift to online learning because of COVID-19, many people were excited about the return to in-person learning. However, Mari continued to put the Flint water crisis front and center alongside this celebratory discourse as evidenced in her tweet, "And now kids are going into schools filled with lead lines that have been sitting for months. It's bad all around" (Copeny, 2021f).

As news about other water crises emerges both nationally and globally, she continues to connect these instances to Flint. For example, after extreme weather in Texas in 2021 left close to 400,000 residents without clean water, Mari tweeted,

> These water lines in Texas are all too familiar. The people there are suffering. As soon as we can, I will be getting filters for those in need in Texas. Want to help send filters to help? Donate below. (Copeny, 2021d)

And she tweets,

> What is happening in Texas is the biggest failure of the government to take care of its citizens since the Flint Water Crisis (which is still not resolved). (Copeny, 2021c)

MARI'S ANTI-RACIST ACTIVISM

In addition to drawing attention to the Flint water crisis, Mari's Twitter posts give her a platform to discuss intersections of gender and racism. Social media hashtags draw attention to issues that are often left out of the mainstream. For example, Williams (2015) documents how Black feminists used Twitter to draw attention to the sexual brutalization of Black women and girls. As Williams (2015) writes, "Black feminists' use of hashtag activism is a unique fusion of social justice, technology, and citizen journalism" (p. 343). Williams cites the example of hashtag activism related to the rape of Jada, a sixteen-year-old Black girl, who was photographed half-clothed while she was passed out. People mocked her on social media after this sexual assault, tagging themselves in a similar position with #JadaPose. In response, Black feminists created a counter-discourse with hashtags #JadaCounterPose and #JusticeForJada to create a narrative for social justice and call out racialized sexual violence. As Jackson et al.'s (2020) book on hashtag activism illustrates, hashtags are a "method to thread conversations, people, and movements together" because they "spread beyond the platform and [get] incorporated into other social media spaces such as Facebook, Instagram, and Tumblr" (p. xxviii).

Hashtags arising from Black feminist politics reflect the experiences and needs of a marginalized community and call on mainstream politics to listen and respond (Jackson, 2017). Black feminist thought has liberatory dimensions (hooks, 1994), and to use it means to consider the freedom that can come with sharing experiences as well as the importance that comes with wider learning from that experience. Collins (2009) argues that stereotypes of Black women make racism, sexism, poverty, and other forms of social inequality seem normal and inevitable, when in fact, they hide structural inequality. Social media and place-based activism offer one outlet for addressing these issues.

Mari uses her Twitter as a space to be an anti-racist activist. For example, she re-tweets the comparison of the 1955 acquittal of Emmett Till and the 2020 acquittal of Breonna Taylor. She is especially concerned about making sure people humanize her:

> Her life mattered then, it matters now and it will matter tomorrow. Justice for #BreonnaTaylor now and forever. (Copeny, 2021e)

This tweet includes a photo of Breonna as a baby.

Mari uses hashtags as Black feminist activism, connecting to larger cultural conversations and histories about gendered violence toward Black women. #Sayhername was a response to the overemphasis on racial violence toward Black men, showing that Black women are also under threat, and we need to honor them through knowing their names. She retweeted the following from Hip Hop Caucus,

This Saturday will mark one year since Louisville police murdered our sister Breonna Taylor in her sleep. To honor her and other women who's lives were senselessly taken by police violence, join us in a #sayhername challenge through this weekend. How to participate. (Hip Hop Caucus, 2021)

BRANDING: FROM LITTLE MISS FLINT TO MARI FUTURE PRESIDENT TO GLOBAL YOUTH ACTIVIST

Her community activism evolves as she ages, and in that process, she takes on different reputations. Taken together, we see this as her creating her brand as an activist. This brand shifts as she ages and gains notoriety.

As Little Miss Flint, her brand was focused on being both a beauty queen and an activist as her consciousness grew. Her early posts (mostly by her mother) were critical of the beauty industry. Her first Twitter post was on July 11, 2011. It read "You can by (buy, sic) your kids all the stop brands, that still don't mean you know how to dress em #imjustsayin" (Copeny, 2011).

As she navigates the space of becoming a public persona, she aims high in civic ways. Evolving from a beauty queen to a future president necessarily shifts her priorities. She reminds followers of her activist credibility through pictures of her interacting with leaders like Obama, Biden, and Harris. There is a post where she is teaching "Uncle Joe" (Biden) dance moves (Copeny 2020b). She has access that other community activists do not have. Her posts during this time include reminders that "Flint has a problem" while also pointing out "America has a problem" and she is "gonna fix this mess" when she becomes President. She uses her platform and growing brand as part of a networked public to help others. She posts about partnering with a group called Power to the Youth who aim to start a revolution through voting. At the same time, Mari helps them raise money through selling sweatshirts. She wears them oversized in a fashion similar to the VSCO girls' aesthetic.

More recently, the UN Commission on the Status of Women meets for two weeks to talk about solutions to problems affecting the lives of women. To represent the United States, the Biden-Harris Administration created a diverse 2021 delegation. On March 15th, the U.S. Mission to the UN (2021) released information about this year's delegation and wrote, "this is the first time the United States will be represented at the White House level at the Commission on The Status of Women and the first time two women of color have co-led the delegation" (para. 2). Delegations include members of civil society from around the world, and Mari was chosen for the Biden-Harris delegation. Mari's title is listed as Global Youth Activist. In her social media posts, she used the hashtag #IGotMySeatAtTheTable.

As her activist brand develops, she becomes more involved with being a brand influencer who is attractive to corporations that need to appear socially and environmentally conscious. She is called on to play the role of brand ambassador, too. For example, she is one of the youths featured in GapKids 2020: Be the Future campaign. This campaign is a call to action for youth, led by youth. This campaign promotes sustainable fashion through clothing that helps save water and reduce waste.

Like Greta, Mari is an iconic protagonist, but the way co-performing works is different. Mari's followers can become part of her philanthropy and/ or benefit materially. People from all over contribute to Mari's vision to fill Easter baskets, to purchase back-to-school supplies, to take kids to the movies and make them feel good. Being a kid herself, her ongoing work amplifies what kids find fun and how adults can help. These acts are continuous as they broadcast ordinary stories of these seasonal cycles and show Flint as a resilient community with kids enjoying aspects of childhood, despite the harm that has afflicted them. You can win a computer, or you can watch Mari deliver the books you purchased to Flint kids. In one post, Mari is pictured holding a laptop and smiling. She is wearing her rainbow shirt, blue jeans, and Converse and sitting outside on concrete steps. Scrolling across the top of her picture is "Paid Partnership with asususa." The caption below reads

> Balancing between being a student, an activist, a philanthropist, and a normal kid is hard sometimes. But having a versatile @asususa Chromebook Flip C434with up to an Intel Core i5that works with my on the go life makes changing the world so much easier. That's why I love my ASUS Chromebook. It's powerful enough to keep up with everything I do but compact enough to take with me on the go. NanoEdge touchscreen and 360 degree hinge gives me the flexibility I need to switch gears. (#sponsored)And what's even better, I'm partnering with ASUS and we will be giving away an ASUS Chromebook Flip C434with and Intel Core m3 to onelucky winner. (Copeny, 2020c)

Mari's success at using social media to draw attention to the Flint water crisis and her philanthropic efforts to raise money for Flint kids has gained her national recognition. She has won awards for her activism, including the Shorty Award in Activism in 2019. The Shorty Awards recognize influencers, creators, brands, and organizations for their social media work.

There is a doll of her created by the toy company Lottie. The doll, Meg, resembles Mari and comes with a tiara, a yellow "Kids Voices Matter" t-shirt, a green jacket with a "stand up" badge, and a megaphone, showing her activism. In promotional materials for the doll, Mari poses with the doll, wearing some of the same clothes, like a green camouflaged sweatshirt. A quote from Mari is used to sell Meg,

My friends and I believe kids' lives matter! There are many things that are important to us. Kids have so much to say, we just have to be brave and use our voices! If you care about something, you must let people know. That's the only way to make a change! (Lottie Dolls, 2022)

Mari as Brand Influencer

Looking at Mari over the years provides a more complete picture to the growing scholarship about the Flint Water Crisis and girl influencer activism. While her Twitter posts contribute to her image as an activist and allow her to be more critical of systemic racism and environmental injustices, her Instagram posts serve a different function in creating her brand. On her Instagram account, Mari's bio is similar to how she presents herself on Twitter. She has over 150,000 followers as of 2022. She uses Instagram in many of the same ways she uses Twitter, yet since it is more of a visual medium, she is able to draw attention to her image and brand. Instagram, launched in 2010 and was bought by Facebook in 2012. Instagram traffics primarily on images. It is the fastest growing platform worldwide (McCrow-Young, 2021), and its users are younger (Suárez-Carballo et al., 2021). Instagram's platform gives content creators choices and gives followers sharing freedoms. For example, users can use and make videos, write text, create hashtags, create images, take pictures, and record or reuse sounds. In addition, as Arthur's (2021) study of Black women's travel in the digi-sphere shows, Instagram has options for engaging. Instagram content is easily shareable, houses hashtags that organize larger conversations and narratives, which support activism and create digital publics.

Zulli (2020) describes the Instagram platform as one that promotes a "casual, authentic, and every-day life brand," (p. 18) which, according to her research, may not serve female-identifying politicians who have to work against gendered leadership stereotypes. For a girl whose activism promotes community health that sprung from a preventable water crisis and has continued to bring bright experiences for the kids in Flint, Instagram may work well.

Her name is on a water filter product (Hydroviv) that can be installed in homes. The filters are a form of techno-ecofeminism because they purify water and eliminate the need to use single use plastic water bottles. Thanks to her Little Miss Flint Clean Water Fund, these filters have been donated to low-income families across the country. Mari herself sells T-shirts with her logo of a water drop in red and blue with her name and vote for her for president 2020. And activists, dating back to the late 1800s when Sojourner Truth sold cards of her image to fund her speaking tours, need money (Blakemore, 2016). Should it matter that Mari sells products as a rising influencer-activist in a capitalist system? Is Mari's brand activism for her community a grassroots capital approach to what corporations have been doing since social cause marketing or Corporate Social Responsibility proved profitable in the 70s? Does selling clothing, water filters, and dolls increase the good work? To quote Kunda (2020), "politics and social justice are integrating with public image in the digital age" (para. 11). This combination of activism and commodification increasingly blend. In a discussion of Banet-Weiser's commodity activism, Kunda (2020) points out:

> Banet-Weiser states that, "whether challenging police brutality or questioning unattainable beauty norms, branding in our era has extended beyond a business model: It is now both reliant on and reflective of our most basic social and cultural relations . . . Individual consumers act politically by purchasing particular brands over others in a competitive marketplace, where specific brands are attached to political aims and goals." By purchasing from social justice-oriented organizations, consumers feel as though they are contributing to the greater good through their purchase decisions. (para. 6)

Mukherjee and Banet-Weiser (2012) argue that sticking to a discourse of a dichotomy between profits and politics is no longer useful. Instead, there is a "lurking promise of political resistance within the bounds of commodified popular culture and mainstream media" (p. 4).

It is still the case, based on Little Miss Flint's commodities, that wholesale structural change is down the road. Riordan (2001) studied the commodification of girl power and noted that such commodification does increase awareness, but it is "first co-opted, and co-optation tends to neutralize the radical potential of messages" (p. 295). Social justice messages Mari posts and re-tweets on Twitter and Instagram exist between the commodities, which could be a change to what Riordan (2001) found. Followers get to see her thank Kids Footlocker for sending her a couple pairs of Nike shoes now and again. Mari partnered with Abercrombie Kids to share her message.

Mari the Kid

Mari's ability to mobilize different identities for social change is part of her activist branding. We see this as a contribution to youth rhetorical studies. The way children have been studied in rhetorical studies suggests that the youthful position of children is an enabling mechanism to articulate body knowledge and community truths (Thomas, 2020, p. 224). Specifically, in Little Miss Flint's case, Thomas shows how her ephebic rhetoric was effective as it opened the childhood perspective on the crisis—for one, her letter to the President had both a child-like quality, as it would, but also an activist reality since she was with adults demonstrating to get safe drinking water and speaking to media outlets about what it is like to try to have a normal childhood when you can't play in water or drink water out of the tap (p. 223). Her experience reminds people of playing coupled with the signal, "that Flint's water crisis *is so bad* that it demands even children's attention and labor to resolve it" (p. 223).

Thomas (2020) used the case of Little Miss Flint to detail the struggles Flint citizens faced and the rhetorical strategies an eight-year-old used locally and nationally as she fought for the right to a normal childhood for herself and kids like her. Thomas's case study argues that while public discourse characterized Little Miss Flint as a victim, her activism tells a different story. "Flint's water crisis offers a chance to move beyond the notion that children are apolitical victims of environmental injustice and, instead, suggests that the traditional demands of institutional democratization are, in fact, child's play" (Thomas, 2020, p. 217). "While it is reasonable to dismiss Little Miss Flint due to her minimal life experience and lack of formal education, particularly on issues of urban water management, there is also an enabling mechanism embedded in Copeny's ephebic, childlike rhetoric that ennobles a legitimate perspective, clarity, and authority on the topic" (Thomas, 2020, p. 225). The Flint community along with Little Miss Flint had to disrupt the dominant media frames that created that public discourse.

Inaction from adults fuels Copeny's activism. As Mari states, "we have kids here starting school that have never known what life is like to turn on the tap to get a drink of water. If you told me five years ago that Flint would not be fixed, I would not have believed you. After all, when you're a kid and something bad happens, it's those in power's job to actually step up and fix it—and fix it fast. It's also those in power's job to tell the truth. But that did not happen in Flint, and those lies and cover ups cost my community" (Copeny, 2019).

This strategy was effective because she was able to communicate to adults about the harm that was being done to her community and especially the children. As Thomas (2020) notes, scholarship on rhetoric and children "focuses primarily on societal constructions of children and/or objects produced for children" (p. 220). Little Miss Flint's activism can be seen as ephebic rhetoric, or "symbolic action enabled and constructed by, from and for children and young adults" (p. 224). Young activists are often limited in what they can accomplish, but "may find sources of agency in those very constraints" (Thomas, 2020, p. 221). In the case of Little Miss Flint, she has extended her activism to protecting kids in her local community, not just related to the water supply but also in supporting the children of Flint through raising money for material goods like school supplies.

Her activism continues to center on helping Flint children and providing resources to them. She has raised over $500,000 for her Flint Kids projects, including backpacks stuffed with school supplies, Christmas toys, Easter baskets, and movie screenings. She also has given away over one million bottles of water. Other of her initiatives include Flint Kids Read, which provides books to local children and Dear Flint Kids campaign which provides letters of encouragement for Flint Kids. Mari's activism extended to care for all the children of Flint, which illustrated her sense of responsibility to her community. Her activism included joining the People's Climate March in 2017, raising money for the children of Flint to see the movie, *Black Panther*, to empower them, and organizing a national letter writing campaign, #DearFlintKids, to bring joy and needed visibility to the kids of Flint.

We also found an interesting trend in mainstream media features of Mari wherein she constructs and is constructed as a child-like persona. She appears as an adolescent girl making big impacts with a "why wait?" approach in line with more traditional gendered norms of caring and taking care. This tone is in stark contrast to her Twitter persona as critical and the landing page of her website where the quote says, "My generation will fix this mess of a government. Watch us." In interviews with mainstream media, Mari is solution-oriented and wants to empower other youth to become activists. For example, in a PopSugar article, she is asked what motivates her and keeps her positive? She responds "knowing that I am not sitting around and waiting for the government to fix it keeps me going. Knowing that I decided not to wait until I grew up to face the problem head-on and offering solutions to those living with toxic water right now" (Meredith, 2020). "My advice to girls is to always believe in yourself and in the work that you are doing, even if the work is hard and it sometimes feels impossible," she said. "You can do it. You can change the world right now. You don't have to wait until you grow up" (Murray, 2019). Mari's traditional media persona is exemplified in a Sept. 30th, 2020, episode of her as a guest on Dr. Phil. The episode opens with a video montage that shows her meeting with politicians (Obama, Maxine Waters) and shows her in action as Little Miss Flint, giving out her backpacks and standing in the street with a bullhorn and shouting "no justice, no peace" at a Black Lives Matter protest. The interview opens as Dr. Phil introduces her. The camera points up at Mari on what looks like a the top of a bunkbed. Next to her are comics she has presumably colored and taped to the wall. Dr. Phil thanks her for joining, and from her smile, she is tickled to be on his show. He explains how impressed he is with her ability to raise money and impact people and asks, "what got you so passionate to get involved in this kind of activism?" Her reply: "I just want to help and give back to my community because I really don't like seeing people suffer." Dr. Phil shows pictures of how Mari's activism has inspired members of his own family. He then advises his audience to find what they care about, which is important because "then it comes from the heart and then people know that it is authentic." He then has Nupol Kiazolu, a twenty-year-old Black woman activist speak about Mari. Nupol compliments her on "spreading her message of love and kindness and really bringing humanity together." She is proud of her. Aside from the opening montage, her appearance on Dr. Phil is a decontextualized story of young Mari as a change-maker improving her community.

Romper, which is part of the *Bustle* brand, covered a story of girl activists and the lessons they "were taught" from their moms. Already, the activists, through the wording of the headline, are put in a passive position, which often happens to girls. Two others in this article are young climate activists: Haven Coleman (founder of the U.S. Youth Climate Strike) and Jamie Margolin (founder of Zero Hour). The article notes that Haven has accomplished so much at such a young age that it is reasonable for her to be taking a break from activism and "prioritizing her . . . mental health" (para. 17). For Mari Copeny, the *Romper* article recounts her letter to President Obama as one where she "encouraged" him to visit Flint. Copeny's focus in this article is her goal to "make sure Flint kids have access to everything they need." She is a young black activist who fights like a mom. She fights to protect her community, and especially the children. Moreover, in the article, she credits her matriarchal line as women who were generous and "gave back to the less fortunate" in their lifetimes. Copeny reports that her mom and grandma taught her to "never take advantage of things being given to you." Even though she and the Flint community were poisoned and lied to, she doesn't highlight that. She continues with a positive tone and brings attention to her community's needs as she works to invite others to help her meet them. Her social media is where she expresses social justice issues and her anger and outrage.

WHAT IS THE FLINT GIRL EFFECT?

As we sift through Mari's social media presence as well as her success at branding herself as a Black girl activist focused on environmental racism, we identify the "Flint Girl Effect." The Flint Girl Effect shows the importance of place-based activism for drawing sustained attention to environmental racism. In her social media, she reminds people that the Flint water crisis is not over. There are long-term health effects of drinking contaminated water. Beyond drawing attention to the Flint water crisis, she uses her platform to bring resources to the children of Flint, to communicate to them that the world does care about them. She invites audiences to become a part of the local solutions in Flint.

At the same time, the Flint Girl Effect shows how branding oneself through activism can make a difference. For the last ten years her influence both through social and mainstream media, aided by her mother, converges to elevate her brand while also making material change in Flint and other communities entangled in environmental racism. She enacts her agency as a Black girl leader, promising that her generation will "fix this mess" and through her ambitions to become president in 2044. She enacts her agency as she fights for community alongside her family and within the tradition of Black feminist activism.

As mentioned in chapter 1, place-based social media activism shows the impact of the climate crisis locally, engages audiences, and provides a visual example of how to take on systems that are contributing to environmental racism. As the climate crisis gets more desperate, these forms of media become crucial for galvanizing publics and creating change. Images of melting glaciers and starving polar bears may not resonate with audiences. But, strategies like Mari's are about solution telling, offering hope and a set of options for youth who will inherit these problems.

The different affordances of social media allow Mari to navigate how she wants her activism perceived. On Twitter, which is a medium that provides a constant stream of information, she can be more critical and speak out against injustice. On Instagram, she is able to use the visual medium to show how her identities have multiple dimensions. In addition to being an activist, she is also a teen girl living in Flint and she shows us what that specific experience is like. She reminds us that people still don't trust the water and there are empty shelves in the grocery stores where water bottles normally are. In a recent TikTok video posted on her Instagram, she is pictured in her urban community skateboarding through Flint. She breezes by a giant mural of her image to the song clip that begins "I can fly." The social media ecology allows content creators to navigate these different media to present more nuanced versions of identity, while also integrating them across platforms.

Mari's climate activism fits within the bounds of dutiful dissent and disruptive dissent as her activism works within the system as she also challenges that system to make change. We argue this form of influencing provides the platform for consumers to make sustainable choices while also calling out problems with the status quo, which matters. Despite the Global North purchasing privilege this form of activism affords, we see this as a potentially positive contribution. Being able to feel some power through consumer involvement quells eco-anxiety, which for youth is important for resilience. As Khan-Cullors (2018), founder of Black Lives Matter argued, there is an absence of safe spaces for women of color who are activists and organizers. While we cannot make claims about Mari's experience, we see that she has a successful activist brand. She is celebrated in her community and at national and international levels as she continues the climate and racial justice conversations into her teen years. #IGotMySeatAtTheTable shows how she has been invited to represent the U.S. in global climate talks, which is unprecedented for a Black girl who is critical of government involvement in structural racism that has poisoned her community. And, as we are seeing with BIPOC female leaders, like Kamala Harris, Alexandria Ocasio-Cortez, and Ilhan Omar, they are being taken more seriously, even though they are subject to racist and misogynistic attacks. Mari brings an experience that draws on the intersectional oppression of climate justice in a way that is celebrated. She is still framed as spectacular. She is hopeful and doing the work and cleaning the water. Like other climate girl activists, she is not waiting for adults to solve the problem. She has lost patience with inaction and has had success with action. That is why she wants to empower other youth.

Chapter 4

Indigenous Climate Girl Effect

This chapter brings together different conversations related to biodiversity, Traditional Ecological Knowledge, the oppression frontline Indigenous communities face, and strands of settler colonial arrogance to situate Indigenous climate girl activism. Tara Houska (Couchiching First Nation) states, "The reality is that we're just 5% of the population globally, Indigenous people, and we have 80% of its biodiversity. We are the last holders of the sacred places all over Mother Earth. Despite this, our voices are almost entirely absent from the table of solving climate crisis" (Diamond, 2019, para. 8). Biodiversity is an important topic in climate justice discourse, partly because of the importance of biodiversity to a healthy ecosystem, and partly because of the urgency of the planet being on the verge of losing a million species (Shaw, 2018). Often, Indigenous ways of knowing emerge as an important voice in this conversation because it is clear that Indigenous "practices have sustained [I]ndigenous communities, economies, and resources for millennia" (Dockry & Hoagland, 2017, p. 339). Generally speaking, Indigenous cultures have an interconnected and reciprocal relationship with the living world.

The Indigenous Environmental Network (2021) describes it like this:

> Our lands, waters and territories are at the core of our existence. We are the land, we are the water and the land and the water is us. We have a distinct spiritual and material relationship with our lands and territories, water, ecosystems, and all life; they are linked to our survival. (n.p.)

Some have studied Traditional Ecological Knowledge (TEK), in contrast to Western Scientific Ecological Knowledge (WSEK), because integrating knowledges appropriately has potential (Bussey, et al., 2016) in the age of climate change. However, as Estes (2019) makes clear, "What has been derided for centuries as 'primitive superstition' has only recently been 'discovered' by Western scientists and academics as 'valid' knowledge. Nevertheless, knowledge alone has never ended imperialism" (p. 9). Biodiversity is part of the public discussion, though, and in many locations where Indigenous Peoples are making decisions, their ecosystems are healthier and more biodiverse. Too often, though, fossil fuel extraction fueled by global capitalist corporations threatens this balance.

Those at the tables of power are full of what Schuck described as a colonial arrogance that dismisses or trivializes Indigenous Earth wisdom. Colonial arrogance, he said, shows up in "a false kind of pragmatism," which expects solutions to the climate crisis to come from "hard-headed nonhuman technology" (School of Environmental Sustainability, 2021). Another set of voices increasingly invited onto international stages are from Indigenous climate justice activist girls. Many are on the frontlines, so they likely experience Earth's destruction earlier, and many face multiple oppressions, based on their age, gender, and geographic locations.

We look at Indigenous girls' environmental justice activism in the frontline communities of Ecuadorian Amazon, Aotearoa (New Zealand), Fiji, Samoa, Mexico, and Brazil. In North America, we look at Native American girls' climate activism as part of the Standing Rock protest and First Nations' Autumn Peltier's water activism. We examine the concerns they raise, what they bring to the table, how they are making inroads, their intersectional approach, what cultural obstacles they navigate, and in some cases, where they are on their journeys as climate activists. The chapter also brings scholarship on Indigenous girls and climate activism and survivance rhetorics into the conversation and ends with the context of the frontline realities of #MMIW (Missing and Murdered Indigenous Women)—the intensity of organizing to fight on behalf of the planet at the same time that Indigenous girls are going missing and thought to be murdered or trafficked by people outside their communities. We want to acknowledge that as white thinkers and women raised in settler colonial ideologies, we are outsiders. Our interest is in comprehending knowledges not our own, pulling together relevant scholarship to inform our analysis, and amplifying their ecofeminist and eco-centered voices. We also aim to add their activist strategies and interventions to the scholarship on girlhood studies which is why, to center their voices, in this chapter we have more extended quotes from the Indigenous girls.

Indigenous climate girls bring to light the issues related to transnational mediated girlhoods: transnational girlhoods, which include cross-border connections based on girls' localized lived experiences, intersectional analysis that privileges girls' voices from the Global South, recognition of girls' agency within structural constraints, and a global activist agenda for change (Vanner, 2019). We find Vanner's (2019) emphasis on cross-border connections especially relevant to analyzing Indigenous girls who live in sovereign nations that cross borders in North America as well. Transnational girls become publicly known through images and texts and their discourses, affects, and material consequences are circulated via global media networks (Keller, 2021). Transnational mediated girlhoods are especially relevant to understanding how Indigenous climate girls are invited to the global stage as well as how their stories are part of activist networks and public culture.

SPECTACULAR INDIGENOUS GIRL ACTIVISTS

To begin, we examine the spectacular Indigenous climate activists fighting from the frontlines against extractive industries and complicit governments. These Indigenous girls are telling localized stories of the climate crisis, nurturing young voices, training, educating, organizing, marching, and speaking out on national and international stages. And like climate activists throughout this book, these Indigenous girls are showing up and holding governments accountable and taking politicians to task for their inaction.

Helena Gualinga (Sarayaku) is from a small, remote location in Ecuadorian Amazon, accessible only by canoe or small airplane (Foggin, 2020). She and her community live on resource-rich land and therefore have had to protest the military, extractive industries, and their government (Foggin, 2020). Fossil fuels are the focus of Helena's activism. "This year, while juggling her school work, she is spearheading a campaign called 'Polluters Out'" (Foggin, 2020). Frustrated with world leaders at the UN COP 25, Helena called them guilty of "criminal negligence" for the damage they help support (AJ+). Helena also tries to center marginalized voices. She sees the importance of role models and speaking out, and, according to Foggin (2020), Helena hopes to "work and lead a normal life" someday.

India Logan-Riley (Maori) grew up in Aotearoa watching the land of her and her ancestors erode and their waters become polluted or vanish. She represented Aotearoa in 2017 at the first Indigenous youth delegation to the United Nations Climate Change Conference. In her activism, India "incorporat[es] kōrero on tino rangatiratanga (stories of Maori independence and self-governance) and Indigenous solidarity" (Te Ara Whatu, n.d). To India, combatting climate change looks like returning/allocating financial resources back to Indigenous communities, allowing each community to determine necessary steps and doing so in a way that remains true to their heritage. India also believes that educating children about climate change and working towards solutions will be impactful, especially as younger generations take ownership in changing their futures (Dobric, 2021).

Shalvi Sakshi (Fiji) was born and raised in Fiji. She won an oratory competition that landed her in Germany speaking on climate change at COP23 to both the Prime Minister and Attorney General of Fiji (Heinrich, 2017). Fiji has been hard hit by climate change and has experienced severe storms, higher ocean levels, and soil erosion, which ultimately means Fiji will vanish into the ocean (McCarthy & Sanchez, 2019). Shalvi encourages other kids to become climate activists by getting them to focus on the one thing they can do to contribute to a healthier Earth. Her work to "clean the environment" in Fiji is to plant flowers (Heinrich, 2017).

Brianna Fruean (Samoa) is the youngest chair of Samoa's 350.org chapter. She has been an environmental activist since she was eleven years old. By age fourteen, she was speaking at international climate conventions (Pacific Community). Brianna's activism was spearheaded by the realization that, although Samoa and other Islander communities contributed the least to environmental issues, they are impacted at significantly higher rates every year, such that every season makes it more likely that their islands will disappear into the ocean (Xue, 2020). Because of their experiences, Pacific Islander youths are in a better position to speak on the dangers of climate change and work towards resolutions (Gleason, 2019; Xue, 2020), which is why Brianna's strategies are to strengthen and amplify their voices and educate youth and incorporate their perspectives and voices in solutions (Xue, 2020).

Xiye Bastida Patrick (Mexico) is a seventeen-year-old Indigenous climate activist of the Otomi-Toltec Peoples and currently based in New York City because of the climate crisis. Mexico City pumps water away from her hometown, and as a result, droughts increased, and floods ravished the local economy (Riggio, 2020). Xiye works to educate youth about climate change, especially Indigenous youth, as a means for reconnecting with the Earth and their own spiritual journey. Xiye sees a time problem in the narrative used to describe what is happening as coming rather than here (Cimons, 2019). She works with existing movements (Fridays for Future and People's Climate Movement) and she coordinates Re-Earth Initiative (TED Radio Hour, May 22, 2020). According to Bagley's 2019 interview with her, Xiye thinks youth add urgency to a climate movement that has been going on for decades. Her answer to a question about how she sees the climate movement changing is this:

> The climate movement did start in Europe with Greta Thunberg, and a lot of people often say that it is a white movement. But there are all these environmental justice organizations, people on the front lines of the crisis who are fighting for their rights. I'm seeing those two sides starting to merge, because it is a common cause. The predominantly white, mainstream environmental movement starting to acknowledge all the [I]ndigenous, [B]lack, and [B]rown communities on the front line. These two are merging in an amazing way that is going to make the movement stronger. (Bagley, 2019, para. 19)

Artemisa Xakriabá (Xakriabá) is also an Indigenous nineteen-year-old climate activist from Brazil who shared a stage with Greta Thunberg in New York's Battery Park at the 2019 global climate strike. Artemisa detailed the "more than 25 million traditional and Indigenous communities" she represents from a global alliance in Brazil that together "protect 600 million hectares of forest" (Democracy Now, September 23, 2019). Her voice is their voice in the fight to stop the natural disasters in all five "Brazilian biomes" brought on by systems of greed and unchecked power. In her speech, she explains "We, the Indigenous Peoples, are the children of nature, so we fight for our Mother Earth, because the fight for Mother Earth is the mother of all other fights" (Democracy Now, September 23, 2019). At seven years old, Artemisa was helping reforest the land (Franciscans for Justice, 2019).

Autumn Peltier (Wiikwemkoong First Nation) rose to international prominence in 2016 when she was twelve years old. At that time, she was to present a copper water bowl to the Canadian Prime Minister at the Assembly of First Nations. Autumn was only to present the bowl to him, but in doing so, broke into tears as she spoke anyway. She asked him to keep his promises to her people and protect their water. She appeared in regalia. The Canadian Encyclopedia features a video made by Canada News Broadcast (CNB) about Autumn. The video begins with footage of her praying for the water with her family. She is portrayed by CNB as a regular kid who texts and makes slime with her friends, but also as exceptional. The news personality interviews Peltier's mom who explains that this daughter was born serious. The interviewer asks Peltier about her anger, the meaning of her clothing, and if she experiences being bullied (she does), and if that will deter her activism. The video shows her working with her mom and mentions that they don't profit. The CNB story ends with a news update about Canada's progress on reducing water reserves. Was it the juxtaposition of a young girl interacting with the Prime Minister on this stage that garnered international attention and curiosity? The environmental problem wasn't new. Was it that she wasn't supposed to address him but did? A twelve-year-old speaking truth to power, respectfully and emotionally? Was it social media that made this moment easily shareable and therefore more noticeable?

We see that the Indigenous girls involved in high-profile ways in the climate justice movement use a coalitional and intersectional approach in their activism. These Indigenous girls are united even as people try to split them apart. And the climate crisis is clearly interconnected to them. In Artemisa's words, "I am also here as a young woman, because there's no difference between an Indigenous young female activist like myself and a young Indigenous female activist like Greta. Our future is connected by the same threads of the climate crisis" (Democracy Now, September 23, 2019).

STANDING ROCK #NODAPL PROTESTS

The Standing Rock protest, "grew to be the largest Indigenous protest movement in the twenty-first century, attracting tens of thousands of Indigenous and non-Native allies from around the world" (Estes, 2019). Schuck asserted, "[T]he 2016 DAPL protest at Standing Rock will be remembered as the Pettus Bridge event of the environmental justice movement" because of the degree of non-Indigenous "learning from the Earth wisdom of Indigenous people in all history" (School of Environmental Sustainability, 2021). Standing Rock is considered significant in the recent history of Indigenous climate justice activism, even as it is "the latest move in a centuries-long conquest that has eliminated Native Peoples and erased histories and culture, often cloaking violence in extra-legal exigencies or by evoking public crises not grounded in fact" (Grey, 2018, p. 226). Native American girl climate activists were involved in the protest from the start using both new media activism and place-based activism.

These activists used social media in an already well-connected Indigenous digital network and attracted international support. Some activists were involved in founding Sacred Stone camp and were supported and transformed by that involvement (Estes, 2019).

The Standing Rock protest refers to the grassroots fight to block an oil industry's ability to ruin water supplies and destroy sovereign Native nations' sacred lands and rights. The activism caused the Governor to declare a state of emergency, which became "the largest mobilization of cops and military in the state's history since 1890" (Estes, 2019, p. 54). Standing Rock Reservation is in North and South Dakota. In 2016, the United States Army Corps of Engineers prematurely gave TransCanada Energy the green light to build an oil pipeline (Dakota Access Pipeline), which set the Standing Rock Sioux Tribe's resistance to DAPL construction in motion (Estes, 2019). A Native American girl, her cousin, and some friends were at the heart of this action. The story, according to *New York Times Magazine*, began in 2015, when a nineteen-year-old Indigenous girl named Jasilyn Charger (Cheyenne River Sioux Tribe), her cousin, and some friends became concerned about the high number of suicides, endemic drug and alcohol abuse, and feelings of desperation that were becoming commonplace among Indigenous youth. These issues are a result of the legacy of colonialism and the socioeconomic structures they create, which devastate reservations and communities. To meet their own and other youth's needs, they created One Mind Youth Movement for Indigenous youth. One Mind raised money to create a safe house for youth, yet the organization quickly pivoted to focus on political activism. One Mind had participated in Keystone XL pipeline protests at

"Spirit Camp" with the Indigenous Environmental Network (IEN) who then paid for "One Mind members to be trained as organizers" (Elbein, 2017). One Mind, empowered with knowledge and experience, turned their attention to the construction of the Dakota Access oil pipeline because they believed "that the Dakota pipeline was not only a threat to their drinking water but also a harbinger of the larger environmental crisis their generation was set to inherit" (Elbein, 2017). The youth from these nations were granted permission to set up a camp on the Standing Rock Sioux Reservation. This was not easy as One Mind faced some hesitation from tribal elders because in Lakota culture, youth are not considered leaders, elders are (Elbein, 2017). However, this is shifting. "In the past, youth followed the guidance of Indigenous elders, the old ones. But in these prophetic times, it is the old ones who are following the leadership of the young, the youth leaders of the #NoDAPL movement" (Estes, 2019, p. 14).

One of One Mind's early Standing Rock actions to draw more attention to the problem, according to *New York Times Magazine*, was the idea for a relay race. Based on their traditions, One Mind members designed a 500-mile run "to deliver a letter to the Army Corps of Engineers, asking it to deny the Dakota Access Pipeline permission to cross the Missouri River. The IEN created a social media campaign announcing the run and organized a blitz of calls and letters from tribal members on various reservations" (Elbein, 2017). One Mind specifically wanted the help of youth from other Sioux reservations, which was made easier "because the Native American community has become heavily networked on social media as a modern means to keep the bands united" (Elbein, 2017). From there, another run was organized. This time a video was circulated on YouTube to invite support along the way. The protests grew exponentially and internationally, and tribal elders involved themselves.

In a video that went viral, twelve-year-old Tokata Iron Eyes (Lakota Sioux) was instrumental in drawing needed attention and in-person support to Standing Rock. The video invitation "to anyone who wants to come help" was filmed at Red Warrior Camp. In the video, Tokata explains how her ancestors fought for the land that DAPL threatens and that these protests are uniting people in a beautiful way. She explains that "this is a wake-up call to everyone" because "everything needs water to live." In the video, piano plays, people hug, people ride horses and canoe, and a few people are pictured standing in a field holding protest signs. The video looks, sounds, and feels like an invitation from a girl to join her at summer camp for prayer. And it worked. Tokata and her friends also started a successful social media campaign to stop DAPL, called Rezpect Our Water. Rezpect Our Water was a key organization in mobilizing support and they encouraged solidarity in calling for the need to think of future and past generations (Presley, 2018).

To review, a group of Native American youth organized to take care of each other, and, in that process, they organized to defend the rights of their communities and resist what many refer to as Big Oil. The IEN supported them and eventually their tribal leaders supported them. They attracted thousands of Indigenous and non-Indigenous people through a variety of means, both on and offline, to help in the fight for recognition of their rights, their sacred land, and for clean water (Grey, 2018).

Studies of rhetorical strategies used at the Standing Rock protest have helped explain what made the Standing Rock protest exceptional. As Grey (2018) described, Standing Rock resisted through "demonstrating daily a vibrant, multi-faceted Native presence in alliance with others who 'stood with Standing Rock'" (p. 226). Kelly and Black (2018) argued that the protest at Standing Rock "exemplified the vibrancy and creativity of contemporary American Indian political and cultural life" in that "activists mobilized narratives of survival and continuity, crafting a usable collective memory from the fragments and recollections of the parallel struggle of their elders" (p. 2). The constant updates of the happenings through video and livestreaming on Facebook from the activists were a "fundamental component of the resistance activity" that contributed to different kinds of connectivity (Martini, 2018, p. 4036). Young (2018) studied the frontline activists' use of reflecting mirrors to act as both defensive shields and reflective messages to security forces to promote a colonial visibility and ambivalence. Young (2018) also studied other activists' strategies at a nearby prayer camp and their decision to resist DAPL through performance wherein people took the form of "Water Protectors." They created a visual physical barrier to protect the river by standing together and holding "mirror shields" to defend the land under attack. The artistic acts of peaceful confrontation grounded in care for the land and based in Lakota thought, according to Young (2018), unified large numbers through anti-colonial action and "offered a powerful mode of collective agency for the protestors" (p. 271).

THEIR ONGOING ACTIVISM

One question that motivates this book is what happens to these girl climate activists over time. In this case, through their use of social and conventional media they highlight their ongoing activism and their intersectional Indigenous activist identities. In Tokata's case, her twelve-year-old climate activist self (and earlier) gained attention as she participated in the resistance against oil pipeline construction on her sacred lands. At sixteen years old, she invited Greta Thunberg to South Dakota to help fight for climate justice. In the local news article, both girls are pictured standing close together smiling.

A YouTube video has footage from a gym in South Dakota of Tokata and Greta discussing the climate emergency with the audience. Tokata describes her activism as centered on Indigenous environmental rights and missing and murdered Indigenous women. Sitting with Greta in folding chairs, she explained that "at any age we can see that these things [yellow water] are wrong, and we have the right to protect those things." Tokata and Greta talk about how they are alike in their "commitments to saving the planet," and that they have discovered how not to let their 16-year-old selves be divided by conflict and jealousies. They lobbied Congress together. She sat next to Greta in the school gym and explained to their audience that

> as an Indigenous person, as somebody who's grown up on Standing rock on the reservation and having to come back to this struggle after going to these metropolises like DC, it's very personal ... so for me having to bare that part of myself to these people who I need to listen because they are in power, they are in leadership positions right now, that is a process of trying to get them to understand how personal and how great of a crisis this is, is a very long process and we shared that together. (Unicorn Riot, 2019)

The adult moderator points out how amazing that they are sixteen.

Marvel's Hero Project selected Tokata to be one of twenty heroes. The Hero Project is a reality series that features episodes of ordinary youth (age eleven to sixteen) who are doing extraordinary things (Associated Press, 2020). Her hero introduction on the cover of her Marvel comic reads: "Behold ... The Thrilling Tokata: Teller of the Truest Tales." Her Marvel comic story, however, is about standing up to Indigenous youth *in* her community and encouraging them to take seriously their cultural knowledge. The narrative is a respect-your-elders kind of teenage bravery. Nary a mention of Standing Rock protest issues. However, Tokata herself feels positively about Indigenous representation in the Marvel comic world. According to the *Lakota Times*, Tokata is excited about her story because of the lack of Indigenous representation. She sees her hero episode as one that "highlights the resiliency of Indigenous people and the value of young people's ideas" (Associated Press, 2020, para. 8). Tokata's Instagram page (as of this writing) reflects her excitement. Information about her comic appears on her page where her profile picture used to have the #MMIW handprint on her face. The picture of her in a traditional skirt with the #MMIW symbol on her serious face is the banner image on a story about Tokata's activism by Tess Thomas (2020) in *Assembly,* a Malala Fund Publication. The topics of the interview are what she is proud of, what it means for Indigenous youth to lead in the climate justice movement, the role education plays in her climate advocacy, what Tokata hopes people hear in her talks and if she has empowering public speaking tips to share, the message in her Marvel episode, and finally, her recent involvement in #landback—an Indigenous political movement to raise awareness of the betrayals that resulted in their stolen land (Gomez, 2020). We argue that the social media ecology makes Tokata's intersecting identity and broad-based activism available. Tokata's multitudes are sharable.

As far as Autumn Peltier's ongoing public life as a climate activist, in her later teen years, Autumn is interested in holding power-holders accountable. She has become a role model and influencer and uses her platforms to raise her voice as a water warrior. She works with corporations aligning with their social justice causes. In 2016, *Canadian Living* awarded twelve-year-old Peltier their Me to We Award in the Youth in Action category (Buchner, 2016). The feature story about her award described Autumn's water conservation advocacy, her Ojibwe values, her family, and her motivation to give her grandchildren a future and be a role model. At the Children's Climate Conference in Sweden, Autumn represented Canada and helped draft the list of demands to present to the Paris UN Climate Change Conference. In 2019, she was named woman of the year by *Chatelain*, which refers to itself as the leading resource for Canadian women, for her role as a "clean water warrior." In the living section (not in news, health, or food sections), reasons for this title include being named the chief water commissioner by the Anishinabek Nation following in the footsteps of her great aunt. *Chatelain* highlights that Autumn has been places like to Sweden's Children Climate Conference, she has met people like Prime Minister Trudeau where she "insisted" he work harder on ensuring all Canadian communities have clean water. In addition, Autumn delivered a speech to The Global Landscapes Forum and the United Nation's General Assembly. *Chatelain* supplied two points from her speech. One is the need to protect water for all "habitants" globally, and the other is that Autumn will eventually be an ancestor and wants her "descendants to know I used my voice so they can have a future." Powwow.com featured a story about Peltier as a "sixteen-year-old Environmental Activist Doing Great Things." The story explains that "the sacredness of water is of utmost importance to her" and embedded a video created by CBC's Kids News of Peltier that was used for National Child Day. Autumn's voice narrates that they are praying for the water because "the water is sick, it's contaminated." She tells the story of being at a First Nations water ceremony and seeing water advisory warnings in the washroom. She learned from her mother the meaning of water advisories and that that community has "been under a boil water advisory for more than twenty years." It was immediately clear to her that something is very wrong. The next story is about her speaking with the youth in a northern First Nation community that didn't have clean water. Images of the youth marching to ask for clean water come on the screen as we hear Autumn's observation that the stories she heard were of grandparents walking every day to carry clean water home in buckets, the stories were "really sad." She concluded that this Canadian community had to live in third world conditions in a first world country, "it should not be like this." The final segment is Autumn explaining how she sees her early iconic image at the First Nations Assembly. We hear her explain, "I guess you could say I told off the Prime Minister," when she told him she, "was very unhappy with the choices you made and the broken promises to my people." He responded. He said he understood and told her, "he would protect the water." Peltier said she felt she made an impact and said she plans to "hold him accountable as long as he is Prime Minister because that's a strong promise to make, especially to a person like me." She ends by saying "you know something is wrong" and "you have to do something to fix it" when "a child speaks up" because "we shouldn't have to be speaking up." Aside from the video, the article explains that, to Indigenous Peoples water has the same rights as people and is their life. For her positive impact in the environment, in 2020, Autumn was named an Eco-Maven by ECO-18, an organization whose mission is to change the discourse on climate crisis. Representation of girls in Canada center white girls and erase (or cast as ghosts) Indigenous girls (de Finney, 2015), so Autumn's awards and media coverage contribute to her as a spectacular and exceptional girl climate activist. Since so few Indigenous girls in Canada make it into media coverage (de Finney, 2015), Autumn's popularity is likely positive for many First Nation girls.

Autumn's early visual media representation was of her crying in front of the Prime Minister as she presented her gift. In an image of an older Autumn, credited to Martlet, she is not smiling. She wears a turquoise neckace over a turtleneck and is pictured against a non-descript background.The overall affect is serious. Her Instagram (127K followers) shows pictures of her early meetings with important people and her visits to climate events where she is often pictured with her mom. More recently, her pictures include her in a reflective pose, wearing traditional dress, sitting on the river. Autumn models make-up as an influencer. Also, she recently "joined forces" with Abercrombie & Fitch where she contributes to their Equity Project on their Instagram.

As for Indigenous climate activists from Standing Rock, Jasilyn Charger (Cheyenne River Sioux Tribe) from One Mind is leading in her community. She is breaking new ground and talking about it in Our Climate Voices. She describes the tensions between the young and the tribal elders wherein children are to listen to and obey their elders. At Standing Rock, roles were reversed as the elders came around to support the youth. In Jasilyn's words, "we want people to help us rather than govern us and try to lead us." Jasilyn speaks to the tensions that arise as Indigenous girls aspire to take on leadership roles:

Being an activist is hard, but being a woman activist is even harder, because you have so many constrictions of your culture and culture of America and the sexism that comes with that. It's really hard to be a leader and be seen as a strong, motivational person to young people in my community because it's so patriarchal. Our leaders our men, our Tribal Chairmen are men, or medicine men are men . . . to really be seen and to go into the ceremonial spaces in front of those leaders is intimidating. You have all this masculinity, but at the same time, you're still trying to be powerful, you're still trying to show that you are the woman and are making change. It's really hard for me because when I do community events, I have to apologize to my elders for speaking English in front of them or just to present myself in front of them because usually women don't do that. Right now I am a staff carrier, and in our culture women don't do that, because that signifies a leader position. Women don't hold them, they don't carry them, and they don't have that responsibility. I was presented with a staff. The person who had it before me wanted me to have it because they saw me as a leader. They told me to carry this for all the women that have been forgotten, for all the women who don't have men in their lives to protect them, and for the LGBTQ community . . . I have to fight for change in my own culture and the culture of America at the same time. I get put down a lot. I get torn down a lot by elders and that hurts, but I'd rather it be me being torn down than a twelve or thirteen year old who feels that same way as me. (Our Climate Voices, 2019b, paras 21–22)

SURVIVANCE

The constant decolonial work to tell their past and present stories, and to be presently perceived, is what White Earth Ojibwe scholar Gerald Vizenor termed "survivance"—wherein narratives incorporate themes of survival and resistance that include Native presence. "Native survivance stories are renunciations of dominance, tragedy and victimry" (Vizenor, 1999 as cited in Kelly & Black, 2018, p. 3). As Indigenous activism, survivance rhetoric is necessary because of "a really common perception about Native people is that we are people of the past, that we're the static footnote in history," and that "people seem to think that we didn't keep progressing after the 1800s." Founder of IllumiNative, Crystal EchoHawk (Pawnee Nation), says, "White supremacy has deliberately attempted to erase Native Peoples from the past and make them invisible today" (her Insta). Vizenor's concept of survivance is "a way of finding voice, proclaiming presence, and renewing Native identity" (Grey, 2018, p. 228). Presley (2018) describes Vizenor's survivance as "survival coupled with endurance and resistance" (p. 297) and what the Standing Rock Sioux contributed to. Studies of survivance include Grey's (2018) study of the activism of community groups in Louisiana "with Native presence at the center" who came together to resist construction of Bayou Bridge Pipeline. Incorporating Vizenor's survivance into the discussion, Grey (2018) located strategies of survivance and said, "in each case, however, survivance claims presence, history, and a richness or multiplicity of identity as the articulation or tracing of life in motion" (p. 240). Brigham and Mabrey (2018) describe examples of "survivance" in the "temporal sovereign counterclaim" of the popular culture image of four Native American men fighting terrorism since 1492—"telling a different story about how precisely homeland security has been attacked" post 9/11 and by whom in the service of decolonial resistance (p. 115). Wieskamp and Smith (2020) used the lens of survivance rhetoric to understand discourses used in Native communities to address the problem of sexual violence enacted against Native women and girls by outsiders "at the highest rate of any demographic in the United States" (p. 72). "Survivance directly challenges settler colonialism by asserting the vibrance and existence of [N]ative [P]eoples as part of contemporary culture. This visibility creates space for community coping and endurance" (Wieskamp & Smith, 2020, pp. 78–79). Finally, Clark and Hinzo (2019) studied social media as a platform for digital survivance of #NoDAPL. We find digital survivance as we examine the stories of what these Indigenous climate activists have continued to do. For example, Jasilyn shares about her experiences as a climate activist and as a Native American young person leading in her community in a time of change. There are stories about Autumn and her role in drawing attention to the water inequities in Canada. There are stories about Tokata as an Indigenous climate activist, public speaker, organizer, and stories about her cultural values, all swirling around are examples of her survivance practices so important to self-determination for many sovereign Indigenous girls who struggle nonetheless against the discursive and actual violence of settler colonialism (de Finney, 2015).

INTERNATIONAL INDIGENOUS YOUTH COUNCIL AND #MMIW

Indigenous climate activists from the International Indigenous Youth Council (IIYC) participated in a climate change conference in 2021. These youth leaders brought a variety of topics to consider. Xavier Colon (Taino Nation) talked about working on the IIYC chapters intentionally working locally to address what is happening in the communities "that we serve and protect." Settler colonialism has worked to obscure and dismantle their way of life, Colon explained, and IIYC is trying to heal these divisions and relationships. Colon chose to participate in the academic conference "to raise a sort of awareness, also an eco-consciousness." In his words:

> Today is a good day because we get to share our story that's historically been marginalized. Our very existence as Indigenous youth in today's society is our resistance, and our experiences intersects within the scope of climate change and colonialism simply because we are Indigenous in a settler-colonial state. (School of Environmental Sustainability, 2021)

Indigenous youth panelist Colon continued that Indigenous peoples have "already survived an apocalypse and are living in a post-apocalyptic time." Eleanor Ferguson of Oglala Lakota Nation spoke about her IIYC chapter's work, "we are group of Oglala Lakota youth who operate a nonprofit org. We're working together as a collective to restore our Lakota traditional ways of living." Ferguson also talked about her belief in the Earth as mother and how women have special knowledge:

> The women of this Earth, we have a deeper understanding of the power of matter. . . . Now this wisdom is needed for the regeneration of the Earth. For the Earth's awakening. In order, you know, for the Earth to heal itself, the women have to step forward and say no more. (School of Environmental Sustainability, 2021)

And Samantha Arechiga of Nahuas Nation spoke about the problems of human-centric approaches to climate change and the reality that those with power and privilege are starting to feel it, but: "you can't keep redlining your way out of climate change, you can't keep displacing your way out of climate change. It's coming for you, and it's inevitable." Arechiga discussed other connections. "I know that Indigenous women, we make up more than 35% of the missing women in the United States alone, and you know . . . that's a lot more than you could even imagine." She talked about the importance of making space in environmental activism to talk about #MMIW because it is the way to see the "grim" connections. In her words:

> At these construction sites [where companies build pipelines] they have these man camps where the workers stay . . . and these men with really awfully internalized hypersexualized views of Indigenous women take Indigenous women. . . . there is a connection there . . . the more construction projects we have, the more ways that we degrade the land and degrade women and we're allowing for threats to happen to women by having these camps full of men . . . with these problematic ideas, these hypersexualized ideas of Indigenous women and then governments who don't really care to cover these issues who don't care to actually find these women. (School of Environmental Sustainability, 2021)

Those invested in ecofeminism are working to alleviate these combined horrors. Ecofeminism, in broad terms, is grounded in Rosemary Ruether's (1975) seminal work that "the social structures that dominate women are the same structures that dominate nature. Therefore, women should align themselves with nature to transform a system that devalues and potentially harms them both" (as cited in Dobscha & Ozanne, 2001, p. 202). These Indigenous intersectional climate activist leaders are trying to save the Earth, their bodies, the sacred land of their ancestors, so life can continue, and they are being disappeared and killed at the same time. They are not safe. Indigenous women and girls go missing and turn up murdered at alarming rates wherever they live (Lee, 2020). As these Indigenous climate activist girls raise their voices, organize protests, and advocate through a variety of means and mediums to preserve their land and culture, a large number of Indigenous communities in North America are struggling with a femicide crisis, and governments are not responding. For example, "the Canadian government refuses to call a national inquiry into violence against Indigenous girls and women despite intensifying national and international pressure" (de Finney, 2015, p. 171). And the social movement that goes by #IdleNoMore is a response to that silence, and other abuses. In 2013, Indigenous women of Idle No More led a protest to draw attention to the workings of power exacted by Canadian governmental "abuses of Indigenous rights, privatization of Indigenous lands, and rollback of environmental protections to intensify fossil fuel extraction" (Estes, 2019, p. 30). Here again, we see the combination and opposition to gender violence and Earth destruction.

The common symbols that signal the femicide crisis known as #MMIW are a single painted handprint over a person's mouth or a red dress hanging by itself. A close-up image of 19-year-old Maya Monroe Runnels-Black Fox, president of the Standing Rock Youth Council, from the "Frontline to DC" pipeline protests in Washington, DC, in April is one example. Runnels-Black Fox wore a red COVID-19 mask with the black painted handprint over her mouth on this "day of action." The headline reads, "The Future Has Spoken." The connotation captures the reality that Indigenous youth have organized to pressure the Biden administration to keep its environmental promises, but there is more. Greenfield's (2021) reporting quotes Runnels-Black Fox: "As Indigenous Youth, we're taught to think seven generations down, so we're not only thinking about ourselves—we are thinking about the future" (Greenfield, May 24, 2021). #MatriarchMonday holds a weekly space for networked activists to honor and remember those women who fought before them. Indigenous communities, women, and girls, are fighting to stay alive and free from violence and have had to for a long time.

WHAT IS THE INDIGENOUS CLIMATE GIRL EFFECT?

Indigenous climate girl activists are working locally all over the world and are an important part of the intersectional transnational climate justice activist networks. Climate justice discourse includes biodiversity conversations, Indigenous communities at risk, and a lack of Indigenous voices at the tables of power that are dominated by settler colonial perspectives. As Indigenous climate activist girls advocate across platforms and media outlets, their stories are survivance. Indigenous climate girl activists are holding power to account as they are holding themselves together all within the context of a femicide crisis in Indigenous communities in North America known as #MMIW.

We add Indigenous climate activist girls' leadership to climate activist scholarship. This is important because Indigenous girls are part of the larger network of climate girl activists and bring their lived experience of settler colonialism and climate change to the larger discourse on how to address the climate crisis. The Indigenous Climate Girl Effect mobilizes more privileged climate girls to use their platforms to listen to them. The collaborations that flow from these actions become a stronger case. Greta accepting Tokata's invitation to Pine Ridge, South Dakota is a great example of their solidarity in climate justice activism.

The Indigenous Climate Girl Effect is also them bringing their whole intersectional activist identities to their work and calling for people to recognize that a large-scale shift has to occur in the way people relate to and care for the climate and frontline communities. "Many Indigenous girls are focusing their cultural contributions on their communal political and cultural futures, grappling with complex issues of treaty rights, colonial gender policies and cultural and territorial decolonization" (de Finney, 2015, p. 169) and our investigation supports this.

Their activism also calls attention to the predatory practices of power that manifest in corporate greed, quiet (il)legal extraction permitting, and outsider violence against their communities. At the same time, their creative networked activism through new media and media coverage, their contemporary climate activism based in traditional practices, and their willingness to speak up in different spaces over time is hopeful.

"Yet it is not enough for stories to be told. They must also be heard, and to be heard they must cross online and offline boundaries and silences, reach new audiences, and move on old and new media platforms" (Jackson et al., 2020, p. 123). These Indigenous climate girls are being recognized and invited to the global stage alongside other high-profile climate girls. And many think Indigenous knowledges and approaches are crucial to addressing the climate crisis. The Indigenous climate girl effect contributes to our framework of techno-ecofeminism because TEK is a practice that contributes to biodiversity and can help to create more sustainable systems or address environmental destruction.

Their activism is being spotlighted by some of the corporations that are trying to be socially responsible, yet we wonder how much these companies are culturally appropriating Indigenous climate girls' actions. In the case of Tokata, the Marvel hero story only tells part of the story, the one that is digestible to a Western audience that tends to be uncritical of Disney's racialized and gendered representations, such as Pocahontas and Mulan. The takeaway from her Marvel story is that youth should respect their elders, but yet we have shown in this chapter how youth, especially girls, struggle to be seen as leaders in their communities. In the case of Autumn, she is now collaborating with Abercrombie and Fitch as a clean water activist. As the fashion company takes actions to manage and reduce water in their supply chain, through actions such as installing low flow toilets in their stores and automatic sinks in their offices, Autumn can make a difference (even if small). She also helps the company promote conversations about race and equity. These are new platforms through which Indigenous climate girls are able to be changemakers. As shown in this chapter, Indigenous climate girls face both oppressions, from sexism within their communities that makes difficult their leadership, to bullying, to misogyny and racism in Western culture, which fails to remember they exist and ignores the crisis of violence in their communities inflicted by outsiders.

We can learn by following their lead. We can learn more about their fight for their rights to safety and self-determination and accompany them as they envision a different future. And we can help pressure politicians to change the current border policies that allow the cases of missing and murdered Indigenous women and girls to remain unsolved. Those who hunt women and girls should not be able to hide when jurisdictions end.

Chapter 5

Technofeminist Climate Girl Effect

The motto of Girls Who Code (2016), an all-girl STEM program, is "teach a girl to code and she'll change the world." Indeed, evidence of this shows up in the innovative digital projects that girls are designing to raise awareness about the environment, such as a video game about the search for alternative energy or an app that tracks how much water you use in the shower. These projects show great promise, not only because they add girls' perspectives to the public sphere, but also because they show the potential social and environmental impact of teaching girls to code.

In this chapter, we apply a technofeminist framework to examine girls' digital environmental projects. These projects were created by girls participating in girl-only science, technology, engineering, and mathematics (STEM) initiatives. In our analysis, we examine not only what concerns girls have about the environment, but also the variety of tools they use to inspire social change. By looking at the underlying messages in these projects, as well as the aesthetics used to get their point across, we highlight how girls' technofeminist activism can be another avenue for environmental social change. Additionally, this work broadens the scope of technofeminist research to include the work of girls.

GIRL STEM ORGANIZATIONS INSPIRING DIGITAL ENVIRONMENTAL PROJECTS

For this chapter, we looked at organizations that use computer programming to increase girls' participation in STEM fields: Girls Who Code, Google Play's Change the Game, and Technovation. Girls Who Code was founded in 2012 by Rehmas Suajani. The mission of Girls Who Code is to close the gender gap in technology while also changing the image of what a programmer looks like and does. As Saujani (2016) states,

> In our programs, we don't just teach girls how to code, we teach them how to impact the world through computer science. We encourage them to use problem-solving, collaboration, computational thinking, and their creativity to solve some of our nation's biggest challenges—from a game to help players understand racial bias in the criminal justice system and a website to promote thoughtful discussion of feminism and racism to a new approach to preventing lead poisoning inspired by Flint, Michigan. (para. 4)

Girls Make Games, created in 2014 by Laila Shabir and Ish Syed, offers a series of summer camps, workshops, and game jams which are intended to encourage girls to find pathways into the video game industry.

Google Play's Change the Game is an initiative to support and empower women as game players and creators. Launched in 2017, Change the Game values include promoting diversity in and of games, empowering the next generation of game players, and celebrating women who are changing the game. As part of this initiative, there is a game design challenge for girls.

Technovation was started in 2006 by Tara Chklovski who was an engineer at USC. She was frustrated by the lack of women and people of color in her program. Technovation Girls, launched in 2010, is a twelve-week program that encourages young women from around the world to learn to code and build apps that fix problems in their communities. In 2019, around 7,200 girls from 57 countries participated. Funders include Google, Salesforce, Oracle, and Uber.

In order to understand the impact of these organizations, it is important to see them in relation to the broader context of efforts to increase gender equality in STEM.

Girls and STEM

The problem is well-known: women are vastly under-represented in STEM fields, accounting for 26 percent of computing professionals and only 12 percent of engineers in 2013 (Corbett & Hill, 2015). It is predicted that by 2027, only 22% of computer science college graduates will be female. Research has shown that there are several structural, cultural, and social barriers that hinder gender equality in STEM. In 2000, the American Association of University Women (AAUW) published Tech Savvy: Educating Girls in the New Computer Age, which listed a number of barriers that girls face in computer education, including a lack of interest in the ways technological learning was conveyed in traditional classroom settings and a male culture of computing, which tends to emphasize competition and masculine metaphors. The report argued that it was not a lack of skill that kept girls from excelling in computer classes, rather they conveyed a "we can, but we don't want to" attitude

(American Association of University Women Educational Foundation, 2000). The study emphasized a key finding: the approach to computing that was presented in schools, with an emphasis on technical proficiency, did not appeal to the girls.

This report was influential in the development of all-girl informal education programs that introduced girls to computer programming (Barker & Aspray, 2006). These programs sought to change the way computing was approached in all-girl classroom settings, emphasizing 21st century skills, such as communication and collaborative learning, as well as making the curriculum relevant to girls' lives. For example, a Girl Scout program in Texas offered a class on video game design where girls designed clothes and accessories to drag and drop onto the central character, a girl (Cunningham, 2011). In this way, video game design featured two important components: the central character was a female and the type of gameplay, designing clothes and accessories, centered around feminine interests.

The recommendations of the AAUW are still relevant (Corbett & Hill, 2015). The representation of women in STEM fields has steadily declined in the past 30 years. Seventy-four percent of girls say they are interested in STEM, but they do not enroll in those majors (Girl Scouts Research Institute, 2015). And, the numbers are far worse for Hispanic, African American, and American Indian women (Corbett & Hill, 2015). These attitudes and behaviors contribute to the "leaky pipeline" wherein girls stray from the prescribed path and do not become adults in STEM. Stereotypes and gender biases continue to impact women's career choices, leading them to opt out of these fields.

Girl-only STEM programs aim to develop girls' "tech-savvy" identities (Cunningham, 2016). That is, they aim to increase girls' self-confidence in their technical abilities by engaging them in projects that appeal to their interests, creating all-girl spaces to experiment, and exposing them to female role models and teaching them about women's contributions to STEM.

One example of an all-girls STEM program is the Girlhood Remixed Technology Camp. The camp is intended in part to address the contradictory discourses of digital technologies being a gender equalizer versus discourses of the Internet as a dangerous place where girls encounter predators and harassment. Indeed, many of the climate girls in our case studies have experienced networked misogyny through cyberbullying and trolling. Thus, the camp is "an intervention to pique girls' interest in digital spaces while allowing them to explore how they define themselves as young women in and through media and technologies" (England & Cannella, 2018, p. 77). In the camp curriculum, technology was reframed from a feminist perspective, asking the question "what does it mean to be a girl in the digital age" (p. 77)? The curriculum aimed to develop girls' critical literacy about technologies as well as their rhetorical literacy which "allows girls to purposefully, skillfully, and reflectively use technologies to produce new digital artifacts that address complex problems" (p. 78). In the end, "by developing critical and rhetorical literacies, girls learn to counter-create discourses that reassert the value of female identities and female interactions with technologies" (p. 78). Projects included designing computer games with characters that were not hyper-sexualized, creating podcasts about girls' consumption of media, and creating films that included positive female characters.

Beyond feeling more confident and informed about pursuing STEM pathways, McCreedy and Dierking (2013) found that participating in all-girl STEM programs had a number of "cascading influences." Girls developed a sense of personal identity and agency, which is important as girls learn to navigate and challenge patriarchal systems. Women also reported that their participation in all-girl STEM programs increased their social capital, networks, and leadership and life skills. Finally, participating in STEM programs had an impact on girls' civic engagement in general. These cascading influences are especially important since, as we have shown in our case studies throughout this book, girls are enacting citizenship in a number of ways as they address the climate crisis.

While little research has examined the types of projects that girls produce, the research available suggests that they are interested in social change (Cunningham, 2018). Girls are not as interested in the technical ins and outs of coding, but rather what coding can allow them to do (Ni et al., 2017). Girls become excited when they can solve real-world problems and improve their lives and the lives of their friends. Following the direction of the AAUW report, many all-girl STEM programs emphasize the importance of using coding to make a social impact. One girl game designer, Dakota, echoes this in her discussion of game design. As she comments, "few activities can compete with the excitement of designing a game: it encourages you to blend logic and creativity into a device with the mission of helping people have fun . . . use game designing as a way to shed light on issues that affect our world" (Baig, 2018). This finding about using technologies to have a social impact is also reflected in an article published in the online publication Sustainable Brands in which Giselle Weybrecht explained that female students were more interested in video games about sustainability (Shayon, 2017). Thus, designing games and apps that allow girls to engage with issues related to the environment resonates with them and offers another avenue for climate activism.

Making Technologies Feminist

We see girls' participation in designing environmental apps and video games as a contribution to technofeminsim. A question in the research on technofeminism asks if technologies can be feminist. As Chan (2018) writes "technologies can be feminist if they are designed to make women's lives easier or their unintended consequences facilitate women's lives" (p. 299). Feminist technologies are those that improve women's social condition, promote women's equality, and work toward more equal gender relations (Johnson, 2010). Technofeminist scholarship provides some examples. Peng (2020) applied a technofeminist analysis to argue that when the Chinese app Alipay offered the option for (female) users to apply a beauty filter when using its face-to-scan app, it illuminated the patriarchal assumptions of technological design. Beauty filters, she argues, reinforces the male gaze while also increasing women's anxiety about their physical appearance. Peng's study is important because it offers a non-Western perspective on technofeminism. In fact, some taking up technofeminism are testing its suitability to non-Western contexts. Both Chan (2018) and Segers and Arora (2016), for example, used technofeminism productively in Chinese and Bangladeshi contexts.

Technofeminism offers a lens for understanding how technologies can further (or hinder) feminist goals of gender equality. One component of technofeminism is what Wajcman (2006) calls "interpretive flexibility." This means it is important to look at how the technology is used in context, who is using it, how it is given meaning, and if this meaning is useful for feminist goals. If a particular technology furthers gender oppression, knowing how and why is productive. "Interpretive flexibility" is a method to draw attention to the constructed and interpreted (rather than determined and given) nature of our understanding vis-à-vis technology and its affordances. In this framework, gender itself is conceptualized as relational, interactional, and performative (Wajcman, 2006).

An example of interpretive flexibility is Chan's (2018) study of Chinese dating apps. Applying a technofeminist perspective, he looks closely at the uses of dating apps among women and the ways in which they use these apps challenge social norms. He found that on the one hand, dating apps did afford Chinese women liberating experiences, such as exercising sexual agency, developing a specifically feminine gaze, and offering protection from sexual harassment. However, he also found that dating apps "hide the structural gender inequality embedded in the sexual double standard, marriage expectations, and state policies" (p. 311). In many ways, he found that these apps reinforced gendered expectations of marriage and family. In the end, he argues that while technological innovation can be favorable to women, changes in the sociopolitical environment are also necessary for increasing women's equality.

Following Chan's lead, we agree that technology alone cannot solve systemic inequities. This is important because addressing the climate crisis requires both systemic changes (such as battling racism, sexism, and homophobia) as well as technical solutions that challenge these systems (such as moving away from an extractive fossil fuel economy).

Technofeminist activism highlights women's participation in shaping digital architectures. Girls' technofeminist activism in this chapter shows the ways that girls are using coding to work toward environmental social change. From games that simulate the impacts of one's carbon footprint to apps that help people turn trash into household projects, these new forms of media can influence behavioral change and offer insight into a problem such as climate change that may be difficult or overwhelming to comprehend. Diversity in the sources of innovation can lead to more nuanced understandings of not only the scope of pressing environmental problems and their impacts on different groups of people, but possible solutions that may not have been imagined without diversity. Girls' technofeminist activism, through their use of coding to contribute their unique perspectives about the environment and climate change to the public sphere, can shed light on how to increase their participation in STEM fields more broadly, having systemic and lasting impacts on our built and natural world.

VIDEO GAMES AND CLIMATE ACTIVISM

Can video games make a difference in the climate crisis? Scholars have shown that video games have the potential for pro-social learning (Cunningham & Crandall, 2019; Passmore & Holder, 2014). Video games are persuasive because they allow players to engage in perspective taking, which can lead to empathy. As Davisson and Gehm (2014) found, video games can promote civic engagement. Video games are rhetorical mediums because they include narrative worlds, rules, and simulations. Bogost (2008) calls this "procedural rhetoric" because narratives are developed through the process of playing the games. As video game scholars have argued, there are many ways to analyze the ideologies in video games, including the narrative (setting and plot), goals (the action in the game), goal rules (what to do to win), and aesthetics (the look and feel of the game) (Crandall & Cunningham, 2018).

From a technofeminist perspective, it is easy to see why we might be cautious about the feminist potential of video games. One of the critiques of mainstream video games is that they often depict hyper-sexual representations of female characters. Female characters are largely absent in the top-selling games and when they do appear, they are often hypersexualized and take on passive roles in the games (Williams, Martins, Consalvo, & Ivory, 2009). As for the industry, women are vastly under-represented. In recent years, there has been growing attention paid to these gender disparities. Female game designers have spoken about their experiences in the workplace, either being victims of sexual harassment or discrimination, or not having their perspectives taken seriously (Chess & Shaw, 2015). That said, we see video game and mobile app design as an avenue for increasing accessibility into STEM fields and allowing girls to offer their solutions to the climate crisis.

Given the reach of video games, the gaming industry could be considered one of the most influential industries in the world. One in five gamers are under the age of twenty one. And young people are increasingly concerned about climate change. In September 2019, the largest video game companies committed to use their platforms to encourage action on the climate crisis, launching the *Playing for the Planet Alliance* during the UN Climate Summit. Members of the Alliance commit to actions like integrating environmental messages into their games, reducing their emissions in the production of their products, and supporting more broader-reaching actions like planting trees and reducing plastic in their products.

In March 2019, the United Nations Environment Program released a study titled "Playing for the Planet" which looked at how the gaming industry could influence the behaviors of youth to protect the environment. This report outlined three strategies that could be incorporated in gaming. First, youth must be seen as agents of change. They need to be involved in message delivery so that they feel empowered to be agents of change, which can lead to long-term behavioral change. A second topic discussed was the importance of helping to foster a relationship with nature among youth. In addition to integrating environmental messages into video games, youth also need to be encouraged to interact with nature in the off-screen world. As Inger Andersen commented, "we need to get people on screens into the green and the green onto screens" (Patterson & Barrat, 2019). Finally, video games should influence youth's behavior in a positive way, which they call "green nudges."

Gaming can be an immersive vehicle for encouraging people to be more environmentally friendly. It can be difficult for people to fully comprehend environmental impacts because they are not always visible and happening in real time. Video games, then, can offer players the opportunity to experience concepts related to sustainability and climate change in a new way. Video games show potential for sustainability because they are imaginative and exploratory with social interaction and problem solving (Kelly & Nardi, 2014). Video games encourage players to think outside the box to solve problems and engage players in simulations about potential outcomes. Additionally, since sustainability is about changing behaviors and a call to action, gaming can engage players in seeing solutions and testing out the consequences of different simulations or actions. As Abraham and Jayemanne (2017) point out, existing methods of dissemination of science, which rely heavily on information and raising awareness, are not leading to ideological and behavioral change.

As Kelly and Nardi (2014) write, commercial video games "narrativize scarce resources, promote competitive and collaborative social interactions, and foreground survival goals," all skills that will be necessary as climate change worsens. They argue for the development of "global futures games" that would draw on the skills of gamers to generate understandings of global environmental problems. They write, "futures of scarcity require people to think strategically about adaptation and redesigning life—what is important to us, how we make choices, and the tradeoffs with which we will have to contend." Thus, they advocate for the development of digital games as media that can help simulate what futures of scarcity might be like and offer the public a better understanding of what futures of scarcity may look like. As they write, "video games can be generative platforms to develop adaptive strategies, make the strategies visible and critiquable, and give members of the gaming community an entry point from which to begin and develop discussions about the future" (para. 45). In the end, they write, "not only can better science lead to more interesting challenges within games, but the creativity of games could lead to better science for understanding a complex global model of potential futures" (para.45).

Games about sustainability are beginning to take hold. For example, the Dutch city of Utrecht has the Utrecht Sustainability Game Jam in which students create video game prototypes with the aims of educating and engaging users on the topic of sustainable and creative futures, not only locally but globally (Dale, 2020). Topics included climate change skepticism, anti-vaccination movements, disinformation campaigns, and a general disbelief in science. Other topics included teaching about sustainable living topics and food insecurity. One of the games produced, *Harm to Table*, is a split-screen game where players play minigames on different sides of the food production process. On one side is a farmer trying to manage a sustainable farm in a developing nation. On the other side is a player in a supermarket. The choices made by each player impacts the next, such as overly high demand for certain farmed goods to low grocery stock availability.

GIRL-MADE VIDEO GAMES ABOUT THE ENVIRONMENT

In this section, we analyze the rhetorical strategies used in girl-made video games about the environment. We find the majority of the games had an overall hopeful message: that human intervention could save the planet. The games place the players in the position of agents of change. As players collected trash or planted trees, their actions in the game contributed toward a better planet. Overall, the goals of the games girls designed were to educate and raise awareness about environmental problems, like plastic pollution in the ocean or the impact of hazardous waste on local communities.

The Environmental Story

The video games took place in a variety of natural settings including the ocean and the forest. However, these natural settings have become polluted and it is imperative that players clean them up. For example, *Plastic Pollution*, created by girls attending Girls Who Code, opens with a cartoon turtle who tells us that her name is Lille and that she has had a bad life since she was separated from her mom. When she was reunited with her mom, she was so happy she jumped up and down and a plastic straw got up her nose and she couldn't breathe. Players work to clean up the ocean so that Lille and her mom can lead a healthy life.

Inland created by Team GG in 2019 as part of their participation in the Girls Make Games program, is about a boy named Lucas and his animal companion, Willow the Polar Bear. The game opens up with Lucas telling us that, "Willow told me some angry Lumber Johns are cutting down trees, destroying the environment and negatively affecting climate change." Throughout the game, the players need to avoid the ax-throwing Lumber Johns who are cutting down trees. However, there is a positive message as well. In the game trailer, the message is that, "The world can be cruel. Do what you can to change minds and save lives." Throughout the game, players convince the Lumber Johns to plant trees, rather than destroy them.

While many of the games took place in natural settings that seemed far removed from girls' homes, *Quibbit*, created by participants in the Girls Who Code program, is a game about environmental issues in New Jersey. The girls write that they took on this project because of environmental justice. They recognize that many low-income homes are located near factories that release pollutants, thus exposing residents to dangerous chemicals, which cause serious health problems. Similar to the efforts of Mari Copeny documented in Chapter 3, this place-based activism shows potential for making real change.

Unspecified locations like "the ocean" or "the forest" may not resonate as powerfully as specific locations where players can imagine themselves making real change.

Many of the games attempt to tell the story through the eyes of those living in the environment. For example, *FisH20*, envisioned by girls participating in the Technovation Girls program, is a game that allows users to understand the real effects of global warming through the eyes of game characters. The player takes on the perspective of a fish and navigates through multiple obstacles including oil spills, plastic debris, and discarded fishing equipment.

Telling stories from the point of view of the creatures living in these environments is intended to increase empathy toward the threat these animals face. Empathy is an important aspect of pro-social games (Harrington & O'Connell, 2016). Pro-social video games can also promote collaboration and cooperation, which are valuable to civic engagement.

While many of the games focused on real-life environments, *EcoVerse* created by fourteen-year-old Dakota from Encino, California, is a series of mini games in which players plant and bring animal life to planets as part of a Galactic Restoration team. *EcoVerse* strays from some of the dominant themes in mainstream video games about destruction. Instead, she was more interested in creating a game that would build environments and bring them to life (Baig, 2018). This genre of games, which includes *Minecraft* and the *Sims*, are appealing to players because they are based on creating, rather than tearing down. Indeed, as Gee and Hayes (2010) found, the *Sims*, which is a sandbox game where users create different life simulations, such as creating houses, characters, and accessories. Gee and Hayes argue these kinds of games show that women gamers are engaged in developing new technical proficiencies that help increase their emotional and social intelligence. Thus, a game like *EcoVerse* continues to show how this genre may be more appealing to female audiences.

Game goals

Many of the games had similar goals such as earning points while cleaning up trash. The reward, in addition to earning points, was that environments were restored through the process of playing the game. For example, in *Kaiyo*, players are introduced to the animated Kelvin the Kelpie God (who looks like a seahorse) and instructs players that Kelpie "needs your help in saving the planet." During the game, players control a dolphin that cleans up pieces of trash in the ocean, earning points along the way. Each animal that is saved says "thank you."

Some games also had an adventure-based plot, such as *What They Don't Sea*, created in 2019 by girls participating in the Girls Make Games program.

The description of the game tells us that "as a marine researcher with the Rachel Carson Research Organization, you have been sent to collect samples of a special kelp for an alternative energy project. Along the way, you meet creatures friendly and not so . . . friendly."

Girls participating in Technovation Girls developed *Tap Tap Trees*, which the girls hoped would raise awareness about the problem of air pollution and how it can be mitigated by planting trees to increase the amount of oxygen. During gameplay, players collect seeds with their basket. Once players pass different levels, trees are planted.

Another game goal was educational, and this includes facts about environmental problems that are interspersed throughout the narrative. After playing *Plastic Pollution*, players take a quiz about their environmental impact. At the end of *Kaiyo*, players can explore facts about the animals that they saved. *MAI Water* focuses on the problem of the United Arab Emirates water consumption, which is the highest of the twenty-two Arab League nations. The girls developing this video game argue that excessive water consumption will eventually lead to environmental conflicts. Thus, they designed an educational game targeting both children and adults with the message of reducing water consumption.

Aesthetics

While many of the games used animation as a backdrop for the game, some games also included real-life pictures so that players could make associations between the video game and the real-life context in which the game is being developed. These photos are often accompanied with text to communicate to the players how they should understand the context. *Kaiyo* opens with a photo of a floating plastic island in the ocean with the caption, "did you know every square mile of the ocean has more than 45,000 pieces of plastic floating in it?" A callout appears with the word "help!" *Trash up* also includes pictures of the iconic floating island of plastic.

Some researchers have found that dialogue in gaming can be persuasive. For example, *Climate Fortnite Squad*, a group of climate researchers, chat with players of the popular game *Fortnite* as they play the game. These scientists believe that because mainstream ways of communicating about climate change are not effective, that it would be more effective to communicate to kids directly. It is these kids, they argue, who are the ones who will inherit the problems brought on by climate change (Andrews, 2018).

MOBILE APPS

The accessibility of mobile app development, as well as the diffusion of mobile technologies, has led to many all-girl app development programs. Many programs use MIT App Inventor, which is a visual programming environment that uses blocks-based coding to create functional apps for smartphones and tablets. According to the website, "the MIT App Inventor project seeks to democratize software development by empowering all people, especially young people, to move from technology consumption to technology creation" (https://appinventor.mit.edu/explore/about-us.html). App development has become accessible and intuitive, opening up the possibility for diversity in the sources of design. As more diverse populations are creating apps, they offer more utility and creativity of what apps can do.

In this section, we look at the themes that were present in apps created as part of the Technovation Girls program in 2018.

Tracking the Change They Want to See

One strategy used by girls designing environmental apps was to integrate trackers that would measure users' consumption as a way to promote behavioral change. These trackers hold users accountable by not only letting them understand what their consumption is, but how this consumption contributes to negative environmental impacts. For example, *ShowerDuck* teaches children to save water. This app times children's showers, and tracks how much water they save and waste. *ShowerDuck* includes a reward system in which the more water users save, the more points they earn. With these points, kids can customize their own virtual duck.

Droughtout is an app created by girls living in Spain who have identified that there is not enough rain to support local communities' water consumption. Given the impact of global warming, many rivers are drying up leaving water reserves empty. Not only does the app allow people to track how much water they are using, but it also offers tips on how to consume less water. One added feature is an alarm that reminds the user when their targeted consumption of water has been reached. The alarm is designed to promote behavioral change.

Garbage Goodbuyers is an app that allows users to keep track of what materials they have recycled. As they track their recycling habits, they are rewarded with points to play minigames. *Happy Globe* calculates how much CO_2 users generate. *Sheshe* allows users to upload photos of properly disposing waste materials in different collection points as a way to not only record one's own activity, but also to share these actions with others.

An interesting use of trackers was present in *Kill Adlets*. This app allows users to report the littering of flyers to police. By providing this information, they designers of the app hope that the statistical analysis can be used to see patterns in where littering is most problematic, thus encouraging change on a broader level.

Knowledge is Power

While many apps included trackers to influence behavioral change, other apps were offered information about the environment to users as a way to raise awareness about environmental impact. One of the common themes in the apps were that the information that they were providing was not only accessible but should be part of common knowledge. In their description of the *CLEAN4U* app, the girls write, "it's obvious that no one wants to live in a stale and filth environment. Don't you get worried about managing your unlimited trashes? Do you look at things broader that, the waste that might harm your health at the same time has effects on the climate change globally? If these two questions apply to you, then consider using our product." *CLEAN4U* provides users with information about non-hazardous solid waste collection, conservation, and disposal services.

Making information easy to understand was also present in *Reciclamex*, whose tagline is, "Pollution is our doom . . . or it certainly can be." *Reciclamex* is designed to help users search for recycling centers and trash bins near them. Additionally, the app helps users categorize and sort their trash. As the girl designers write, "It's a simple way to make a big change, that we desperately need." Another informational strategy in the apps was to use statistics for persuasion. *Dump That* informs people about whether their materials are meant for the garbage, recycling, or compost. As the designers write, "our goal is to educate as many people as we can about the benefits of recycling and composting. Only 60% of recycling is actually recycled, we strive to raise that amount. . . . We aim to make the world healthier and cleaner for everyone."

Osea is an app created by a group of three high school girls who want to help others recognize the effect of water pollution on ocean environments. As they write, "we are all ocean lovers, and believe that every creature living on land or sea should live in an ecosystem free of harmful influences." Additionally, the app offers tips on how to prevent pollution from occurring. "We want you to Sea the Change!"

The underlying message in these informational apps is that people can make a difference by just engaging in small activities, like recycling. For example, *Happy Globe* includes recommendations on healthy habits to help the environment as well as tips for recycling. The app also includes information about how to support local businesses. *EcoDIY* is an eco-friendly app that allows users to find new and useful ways to reuse materials that typically end up in landfills.

Community-building

The third strategy used in the apps was that of event organizing or making community connections. This strategy is intended to encourage users to see themselves as part of their larger community, either through empowering people to share resources with others or through creating volunteer opportunities in their communities.

Tree Leaf is a mobile application that alerts users to volunteer opportunities to help the environment through the collection of solid waste in public spaces and green areas of Mexican communities. *Tree Leaf* also allows users to organize events in their community. The app also gives users the opportunity to become a "Green Ambassador" to help organize, monitor events, and share their experiences with others.

Boxed In is a mobile app designed to deal with the reality brought on by the increase of e-commerce and delivery services. E-commerce has led to a large quantity of cardboard boxes being wasted. This app, then, is designed to address this problem, through matching people who may be in need of cardboard boxes. "Our app is Boxed In, and is environmentally friendly. With the use of Boxed In, none of your boxes will go to the landfill again, and you will never have to buy a cardboard box again."

WHAT IS THE TECHNOFEMINIST CLIMATE GIRL EFFECT?

In this chapter, we examined ways in which girls are creating digital projects to encourage people to recycle, conserve water, reduce their carbon footprints, and imagine a world where they can make a positive impact on the environment. These projects invite often like-minded youth to participate in positive actions to make a difference in their communities. The Technofeminist Climate Girl Effect shows that girls are not just passive consumers of technology, but rather active participants in technological design and innovation. The projects featured here show that girls offer unique perspectives not only on what environmental problems are most concerning to them, but also their ideas about how to address them. These perspectives are desperately needed if we are going to utilize technologies to solve some of our most pressing social problems.

Additionally, the Technofeminist Climate Girl Effect shows how girls use coding to address pressing environmental concerns. Both video games and apps offer strategies that include behavioral change, increased awareness of one's own consumption, empathy building, and simulation, which are crucial to making long-term impacts on the climate crisis. Climate change and the resulting environmental problems can be both hard to grasp and overwhelming to understand. We see their use of technology for environmental action as also a form of techno-ecofeminism because they offer new forms for engaging people in how to navigate problems caused by the climate crisis. These technological interventions are necessary for broader impact.

The girl-designed pro-social and pro-earth games show the kind of games girls design—one important component of technofeminism. The other component is how these apps and video games shape gender and gender relations. Coding allows girls to challenge STEM as a predominantly male domain. Through coding, girls are providing local solutions, such as trash pickups, that can inspire other youth to act. Additionally, this form of coding, which happens outside of the gatekeepers of Silicon Valley (who we already know are not inviting to girls and women), allows girls to engage civically and propose their solutions.

While we are hopeful about the Technofeminist Climate Girl Effect, we also are cautious that, as Segers and Arora (2016) argue, women's empowerment with respect to digital technologies also requires challenging structures of inequality. Companies such as Google have taken on the challenge of creating gender-inclusive policies and initiatives to increase diversity in the workplace. One way that we can continue to advocate for girls' technofeminist activism is to lobby tech companies to continue in this direction and continue to support girl-only STEM programs.

Chapter 6

Grassroots Climate Girl Effect

Some girl activists are creating grassroots organizations to participate in the climate justice movement. Melati Wijsen started Bye Bye Plastic Bags *saying,* "Our generation . . . we don't have the luxury of time. So we're not waiting for permission, we're not waiting for regulation, but we're going ahead with the actions and solutions right at our fingertips and we're implementing them" (Gilchrist, 2020, para. 16). These climate girl-founded grassroots organizations serve a variety of purposes, ranging from creating educational programs about the impact of plastic pollution, providing seed funding for local environmental efforts, endorsing political candidates for office, and encouraging youth to create their own local chapters to support these larger efforts. By launching these organizations, girls are creating institutional interventions and avenues for increasing youth participation in the climate justice movement. Institutionalizing these efforts brings a sense of legitimacy to their activism. Institutionalizing these efforts also shows that girls want to be taken seriously for their perspectives. In this chapter, we take up the question of why the environmental justice movement has recently attracted high numbers of girl participants in these more institutionalized ways.

In this chapter, we analyze the efforts of girl-founded nonprofit organizations, including Kids Against Plastic, Zero Hour, Bye Bye Plastic Bags, the Sunrise Movement, and the Green Hope Foundation. We also look at Earth Guardians and Kids F.A.C.E because of their history as youth environmental activist organizations. We look at the central concerns of these organizations as well as the different actions in which they participate. While a handful of girl activists have become the face of the climate justice movement, their visibility and actions have inspired thousands of others to join them. Also of interest is the institutional and structural network of these organizations. We look at how these organizations organize themselves, how they encourage youth to get involved, how they use digital media to inform their members and their publics about their actions, and how they keep momentum. Each of these organizations sustain their efforts through ways to donate and through selling earth-friendly materials that have their branding, such as bamboo notebooks, T-shirts, and iPhone PopSockets. It takes money to support a movement, so their consumer-oriented positioning is not surprising. However, they are encouraging a different kind of consumption that promotes sustainability.

One of the unique features of these nonprofits is their use of digital media to garner support and mobilize youth to join their movements. Through innovative uses of digital media, including the creation of apps, podcasts, YouTube channels, and social media platforms, they are able to frame messages about their climate activism. This becomes especially important when mainstream media tend to downplay and distort their efforts. As we will show, media coverage tends to focus on girls as figure heads and as spectacular, rather than focusing on what the organizations are doing and how they are making real change.

WHY GRASSROOTS?

In this chapter, we use the term "grassroots" to refer to the many institutional efforts that girls are creating to participate in the climate justice movement. Grassroots can refer to formal nonprofit 501(c)(3) organizations, and 501(c)(4) organizations, which are civic organizations designed to promote social welfare through lobbying for legislation and can collect contributions. Outside of the U.S., these kinds of organizations have different designations and may be referred to as non-governmental organizations. The distinction we are making here is that these organizations do not aim to profit and together they create the way they organize themselves.

Beyond the institutional categorizations of grassroots organization, grassroots organizing emphasizes bottom-up (rather than top-down) mobilization of local communities to take action. There are few books available to teach girls how to start their own grassroots organizations. Lyn Mikel Brown's (2016) book *Powered by Girl: A Field Guide for Supporting Youth Activists*, draws on interviews with women and girl activists to support intergenerational coalition building to support girl activists on their own terms. Brown puts the rise of spectacular girl activists in historical context. As she writes,

> by all appearances, the stars are aligned for young feminists. Armed with a well-honed sense of irony, an inventive amalgam of online and on-the-ground activism, and an intersectional lens, girl activists are getting it done. There's no denying the feminist blogosphere or girls' and young women's use of a rich array of digital platforms to connect, rant, strategize, and land the movement. (p. 1)

It is in this context that Brown (2016) identifies a "enlivened and palpable sense of possibility" (p. 4) that has led to the rise of girl-founded grassroots organizations, programs, and campaigns across the country where girls are doing social change work online, in their communities, and in their schools. KaeLyn Rich's (2018). *Girls' Resist!: A Guide to Activism, Leadership, and Starting a Revolution* also offers guidance for girls interested in grassroots organizing. Rich, who identifies as a queer feminist and nonprofit leader, provides guidance on how to plan a protest, run conflict-free meetings, and raise money. Rich explains grassroots activism as the kind of activism that is run by a group, "grassroots movements use power in numbers to stand up to people or organizations that have institutional power, or power that comes through or with a job, positions, money, identity, or status" (p. 16).

The organizations profiled here are part of the larger historical context of grassroots organizing for environmental justice. Practices of environmental grassroots activism and political lobbying gained a foothold in public consciousness in America in the 1960s and 1970s. Earth Day, for example, started in 1970 by a graduate student and a U.S. congressperson and was designed to educate about the importance of conservation and sustainability. Earth Day remains a global celebration. According to a 1990 *TIME* article called "Eco Kids," environmental youth activists were gaining attention in the 1990s presumably as children of the 1970s activists as they were agitating for environmental clean-up and recycling and gaining media attention. Two organizations that centered and attracted youth from this era are Kids F.A.C.E. (formed in 1989) and Earth Guardians (formed in 1992). At this time, the Environmental Justice movement formed with the help of Dr. Robert Bullard and the work of BIPOC environmental activists who sought to halt the unequal distribution of toxic waste in their communities causing disease and death. Now, in a full-on climate emergency, as the Earth heats up and every year continues to break records; and as our interconnected digital lives make organizing across great geographical distance possible; and as young girls are the face of these movements, we showcase the importance of these organizations in creating a sustainable network of youth activism.

We have selected these organizations because they have either been created by girls or have attracted large numbers of girls. The organizations chosen in this chapter all have received media coverage for their efforts. These grassroots climate girls are winning awards, and rise to the top of the lists of notable youth organizations.

HOW GIRLS BECOME GRASSROOTS CLIMATE GIRLS

In 1989, Melissa Poe wrote to then-president George Bush: "Dear Mr President, please will you do something about pollution. I want to live till I am 100 years old. Mr. President, if you ignore this letter we will all die of pollution. Please help. Melissa Poe, age 9 Nashville, Tennessee." Poe's letter appeared on 250 billboards across the U.S. She started the environmental nonprofit, Kids For a Clean Environment (Kids F.A.C.E.) so that she could involve her friends in environmental actions such as writing letters, planting trees, and litter pickups (Kouzes & Posner, 2011). Kids F.A.C.E. grew to have over 2,000 club chapters in fifteen countries with over 300,000 members, claiming to be the largest youth environmental organization.

Kids F.A.C.E is one of the earliest girl-led nonprofits. The efforts of grassroots climate girls align with Alimahomed and Keeler's (1995) finding that as children become aware of environmental problems, they can experience fear and anxiety. Many youths report having climate anxiety as they feel overwhelmed by the reports about the state of the environment (Wu, 2020). However, research finds that when children feel they have some control over making positive changes to the environment, such as through recycling or becoming vegetarians, they are more hopeful. This action-oriented approach is what propels the girls in this chapter to start their own nonprofit organizations. Most of the girls who organize for climate justice are serious about what is at stake. They are not sure they will have a healthy future and they want to hold adults accountable for making policy changes to protect the environment. To that end, they are moved to plant trees or design apps that make environmental clean-up fun or help organize large protests. These young activists have evidence on their side as they face adults who are neither educated, motivated, or willing to help. With stakes high, no adult obligations (a certain amount of freedom and energy) and a digitally connected network of like-minded people, they are creating organizations to enact concrete change.

Many of the stories about how grassroots climate girls got involved in the environmental justice movement begin with their personal experiences with the natural world. For example, according to an interview with *Bioneers*, as a young girl growing up in San Francisco, Rose Straus had a passion for marine life (Mangan, n.d.). She discovered that animals were disappearing "faster than I could study them," so she started a community organization to save them called Bay Area Youth for Climate Action, which is still in existence. At that time, the goal was to get coal out of Oakland and educate youth about politics. When Rose went to college, she still wanted to politically engage, which is why seeing the group on Facebook called Sunrise Movement appealed to her. Soon thereafter, her activism gained national attention when she showed up at a town hall in Pennsylvania and asked the gubernatorial candidate a question about fossil fuel monies and his election. Rather than take her question as serious and answer it, the candidate called her "young and naïve" (Barrett, 2018) and asked the audience if they were there to elect a scientist or to elect a governor. His response echoes much of the rhetoric of politicians who downplay scientists' (and kids') concerns about climate change. His response was caught on video and went viral, which was empowering, according to Rose, because it made her aware of how those in power rely on an uninformed electorate. Here, she was educated about climate issues only to have her knowledge dismissed by someone in power. This was eye-opening for her and those like her fighting for a sustainable future. Rose currently works for Project Super Bloom, whose aim is to encourage young people to change the political landscape in California.

Moving to action after learning about human impact on the environment is common in many of the stories of grassroots climate girls. Nadia Nazar, one of the co-founders of Zero Hour, became an environmental activist after watching a People for the Ethical Treatment of Animals (PETA) video about the meat industry. She became a vegetarian and in her research into the environmental impacts of the meat industry, she learned more about how it contributed to climate change. Nazar came across Jamie Margolin's Instagram account, where Margolin was posting about climate change and together they joined forces to start Zero Hour, a youth-led organization that "creates entry points, training, and resources for new young activists . . . who want to take concrete action around climate change" (thisiszerohour.org). Margolin, who identifies as Jewish, Latinx, and queer, was frustrated by the lack of action by government officials and the fact that youth voices were ignored in discussions about climate change. Margolin is from Seattle, Washington, and she was inspired to start Zero Hour after attending the Climate Reality Leadership Training Corps in 2017. Margolin felt she had to do something, because, as she states, "I've always planned my future in ifs." For example, if climate change hasn't destroyed the earth, then she could move forward with future plans (Yoon-Hendricks, 2018).

Nazar and Margolin were also both inspired by more recent grassroots activism that included high profile marches, such as March for Our Lives, the largest youth-led anti-gun movement in history. One of the leaders of the rally was Emma Gonzàlez, which further inspired girl-oriented activism. Additionally, the Women's March, which was a response to President Trump's 2016 election and a way to draw attention to women's issue, is cited as a source of inspiration. Following in these large-scale and public events, Zero Hour's biggest efforts was the Youth Climate March in July 2018.

Grassroots climate girls also have a hopeful message. They believe that the actions they participate in directly contribute to a more livable world.

For example, Margolin states, "we are on the verge of something amazing. We're going to change history" (Yoon-Hendricks, 2018). She is also part of the lawsuit against Washington State for not acting on climate change, which we discuss further in chapter 7.

Sara Blazevik co-founded Sunrise Movement after taking a college study break and clicking on a friend's Facebook post that had a YouTube link to cellphone video from a helicopter about a flood (Our Climate Voices, 2017). Blazevik followed the devastation closely and realized this could easily be her family in Croatia's story and it would make nary a ripple in public consciousness. And Sunrise Movement leaders have witnessed devastation firsthand: fires, hurricanes, and floods (Nilsen, 2019). It is personal to them and shows the vulnerability of humanity in dealing with climate emergencies.

In another example of how girls feel a personal connection to the environment which then encourages them to act, sisters Amy and Ella Meek started Kids Against Plastic in 2016. They became passionate about plastic pollution after learning about the UN's Sustainable Development Goals. Sisters Melati and Isabel Wijsen were inspired to start Bye Bye Plastic Bags, whose mission is to eliminate single use plastic, after learning about the activism of Nelson Mandela, Mahatma Gandhi, and Princess Diana. The Green Hope Foundation was founded by Kehkashan Basu when she was twelve years old. Basu describes herself as an eco-warrior. She first became involved in environmental activism when she saw an image of a dead bird whose stomach was filled with plastic waste. As a result, she advocated for recycling programs as well as the reduction of the use of plastics. She also started tree planting campaigns. In our interview with Basu, she talks about being an eternal optimist and believing that youth can create a sustainable future through their efforts. Basu has faced many challenges along the way including death threats, stalking, and cyberbullying. Despite these, Basu's message remains hopeful.

While the stories of grassroots climate girls signal about creating institutional and structural networks for youth activism, girls taking initiative for social change face the timeless obstacle of adults' perceptions of them. The youth-run Center for Young Women's Development (known now as Young Women's Freedom Center) is a nonprofit that relies on young people to achieve its mission and goals. The organization's philosophy is driven by the belief that young people should be in charge of making decisions and solving the problems they confront. O'Neill (1998), a young woman who was part of the organization, argued that one significant problem youth face is adults who don't believe in or respect them. O'Neill's article is titled "No Adult is Pulling the Strings and We Like it That Way." For adults, they would like to see their own influence on youth, assuming youth in charge means that "they will push us to do more than we ever imagined we could" (O'Neill, 1998, p. 612). The youth in this organization see age bias clearly and "have no use for" the radical feminist paradigm because "no organization that has embraced feminism has worked respectfully with young women as colleagues" (O'Neill, 1998, p. 613). In 1998, this young person argued that obstacles facing young women organizers and activists are "bogus developmental models, paternalistic legal frameworks, and outdated moral views about what is right and wrong for young women" (O'Neill, 1998, p. 615). Thus, as Brown (2016) lays out, it is essential that adult women allow girls to be activists on their own terms, especially when they are critical of adults. She writes working with girls "requires that we engage their resistance to things we hold dear, that we consent to live unsettled lives for the sake of their health and their best work, which means, of course, for the sake of their imagination, curiosity, critical thinking and courage" (p. 5).

BADGES, BAGS, AND BADASS GRASSROOTS ORGANIZATIONS

Now that we have detailed what drew the girls to begin these organizations and the frustrations they encountered, we expand on each organization's mission, vision, and overall strategy to illustrate their range.

Kids Against Plastic

The aim of the organization is to encourage and promote action against plastic pollution. The organization has three main goals: education, action, and advocacy. Kids Against Plastic began in 2016 by sisters Amy and Ella Meek. The tagline for the organization is a "charity set up by kids, for kids." They frame themselves as especially concerned about what they call the "big 4" plastic polluters, which include coffee cups and lids, plastic bottles, straws, and plastic bags.

Bye Bye Plastic Bags

Bye Bye Plastic Bags was started in 2013 by sisters Melati and Isabel Wijsen when they were 10 and 12 years old respectively. Their efforts over six years helped contribute to Bali's decision to ban single-use plastic bags in 2018. While not a comprehensive plan yet, there are still hopes to decrease plastic pollution in Bali. Bali has declared a "garbage emergency" because of how much beach trash was washing up on her shores. Bye Bye Plastic Bags has global reach, with twenty-two chapters in eighteen countries, displayed on a map locating them in Vietnam, Indonesia, and Japan. They have a handbook that helps guide kids to start their own movements to ban plastic. Bye Bye

Plastic works for local structural change through promoting clean-ups and petition campaigns to ban plastic. That said, one of the challenges they have is having a coherent message.

This is Zero Hour

Zero Hour, founded in 2017 by Jamie Margolin and Nadia Nazar, have an intersectional platform that recognizes how capitalism, racism, sexism, and colonialism all contribute to climate change. Additionally, they support the Green New Deal political platform and call for a "just transition" in which efforts to create an environmentally sustainable economy includes an infrastructure that uses clean, renewable energy sources. This platform is also coalitional, connecting social justice with environmental justice. For example, Zero Hour calls for moving away from the unjust prison system and the school-to-prison pipeline. They also call for respecting the Treaty Rights of Indigenous nations, which would also protect intellectual property and food sovereignty.

The Green Hope Foundation

The Green Hope Foundation, founded by then twelve-year-old Kehkashan Basu, is described as a youth-led social innovation organization. Their activities include holding workshops about how youth can be involved in environmental justice as well as conferences to raise awareness. For example, in January 2018, members of the organization spent time in Syrian refugee camps on the border of Lebanon. As part of their work, they conducted environmental workshops for over 600 refugee children. The Green Hope Foundation sees social justice and climate justice as interrelated and intersectional. Thus, their message on their website engages with the UN Sustainable Development Goals. There are places that show direct connections between the goals and the actions that they are engaging in.

Sunrise Movement

In 2016, the Earth's temperature set a new heat record. It is the same year that Varshini Prakash and Sara Blazevik, who were in their early twenties, founded Sunrise Movement. Sunrise Movement frames itself as "the climate revolution." Their aims are to stop climate change, create jobs, eliminate the fossil fuel industry's involvement in political corruption, and back the Green New Deal through elections and public pressure. The Sunrise Movement is mostly focused on political action, and they participate in change through pressuring politicians. While their message is one of no-compromise, they are working within the system to change it. One of Sunrise Movement's actions is called Wide Awake. It is a strategy, as they describe, based in pro-abolition tactics where they make noise (e.g., yell, bang pots, and pans) to wake politicians from their literal and figurative sleep. It's a turn-about-is-fair-play strategy where those who are awake (Sunrise Movement) don't let those asleep (politicians) sleep—no one gets to be comfortable and relaxed. The sleeping politicians are described as "architects of this death economy." However, Sunrise Movement makes room for and values of every kind of action.

Earth Guardians

Earth Guardians started in 1992 at a high school in Hawaii. They describe themselves in three generations: from 1992–1997, from 1998–2004, and the current generation began in 2005. Of the 11 staff listed, ten are girls. Headquartered now in Boulder, Colorado, and located on six continents, they number in the thousands and report 22K youth leaders. Their tagline is "we inspire and train diverse youth to be effective leaders in the environmental, climate, and social justice movements." They frame themselves as an intergenerational group led by trained youth leaders in the climate justice movement. Inspired by the Black Lives Matter movement, Earth Guardians recognize the intersectional nature of activism insofar as BIPOC are part of the environmental justice work they do. They are working for a "regenerative future" and the arts and storytelling are every bit as important as planting trees, protesting, going to court, and working on divesting. They attribute the media coverage they receive as the reason they have been able to grow nationally and internationally.

STRATEGIES: GEN Z RADICAL

Here we examine why so many girls are getting involved in climate activism and what it is they find attractive about these grassroots groups. Nonprofit work tends to be dominated by women (although not at the leadership level) because of the caring nature of the profession. Therefore, envisioned by girls as a space to make change, it makes sense for girls who want to make a difference in the climate crisis to join nonprofits. Also, as we have seen throughout this book, participating in actions about the climate crisis, ranging from protests to litter pickups, allows girls to enact citizenship in a way that helps to relieve eco-anxiety and form community with other like-minded youth.

We begin by looking at the range of grassroots organizations these climate activists created and the ways they present themselves. Sunrise Movement has an Army aesthetic and uses revolutionary language, but their aim is elections and passing the Green New Deal, which is using the mechanisms within democracy to create change. Zero Hour also presents itself as revolutionary with website photos of the racially diverse (mostly) girls raising one arm in the air with fists elevated and yelling. There is a photo of Margolin in the rain at a march speaking into a megaphone, unsmiling youth behind her. Zero Hour and Sunrise Movement look, feel, and sound like serious "unstoppable youth" with no compromise attitudes about the need for social change. They are both panicked and fed up and their aesthetic and language reflect the urgency they perceive. Bye Bye Plastic Bags, Green Hope Foundation, and Earth Guardians, on the other hand, have a Peace Corps vibe. They appear like an NGO—a group of volunteers doing good work for the planet. Messages from these organizations are "our future is in our hands." There are pictures and slideshows of groups of volunteers with matching T-shirts and signs explaining their actions, participating in activities such as installing solar panels on roofs and planting trees. Finally, some grassroots organizations have more of an after-school club look and feel. Kids Against Plastic, and to some extent Bye Bye Plastic Bags, are the kinds of organizations that appeal to younger kids. Younger kids are featured, their goals are simple and targeted, and their bright colors resemble other clubs for kids like Girl Scouts of America.

While each are working within the system to change laws and policy and practices, they do so in ways that make sense to them. The groups that appear more revolutionary and disruptive offer a range of ways to participate, which is welcoming and inclusive. Milstein et al. (2020) argue that organizations attract youth in large numbers who are more interested in inclusive messages about "reimagining nature-society-spaces" (p. 4), which is different from past environmental direct-action activism. We recognize that much of this may be indicative of being Generation Z (at least for kids in the Global North), a new generation with a new vision. Generation Z tends to be more digitally connected and savvy. They have an intersectional awareness, especially in challenging normative ideas of gender and sexuality as well as a more nuanced understanding of privilege and power.

We also see a Gen Z radical in that these girls used their agency to start and run these grassroots organizations. They are finding a way to work toward the future they need and enacting citizenship. The organizations raise the money they need to do their work. Each of these girl-founded and heavily youth-forged and youth-involved environmental activist organizations have stores and donate buttons. Whether buying "earth swag," "swag," or "environmentally-friendly clothing," most explain to consumers where the money goes. Bye Bye Plastic Bags, Earth Guardians, Green Hope Foundation ("help us help the planet"), and Zero Hour ("Support the Movement") all mention their need of and use for money. Sunrise Movement and Kids Against Plastic do not. Kids F.A.C.E lacks a store but offers their logo should you need it. Sunrise Movement may not list what they do with the money they receive, but they do inform buyers that the merchandise is Union made, sourced in the USA, and manufactured in socially responsible ways. Zero Hour tells consumers to "Consume Different." and Green Hope Foundation directs buyers to "Choose Branded Merchandise." Apart from the Meek sisters' book, what people can purchase represents an activist organization rather than individual activists. Sunrise Movement's Green New Deal shirt sells itself with this message, "We know you're already a movement-building badass. But with this shirt, everyone will know, too," and when you buy and wear it, you will be helping to bring "down the GOP-Elite death cult." They are able to create an infrastructure to support their work, such as hiring full-time positions and applying for grants. They fund projects they create that are critical to their mission.

These organizations are uniquely organized, which is Gen Z radical. All of the organizations we studied offer training, ways to join and support the cause, and are invitational. Some provide structures for youth to start local groups or get involved locally. Bye Bye Plastic Bags has teams in places including Tanzania, Seoul, Korea, Singapore, and the United States. Kids Against Plastic has a club for kids ages six to thirteen to join. As part of their participation in the club, kids receive badges and certificates for completing challenges, including litter pickup, eliminating single-use plastic from their consumption, and encouraging schools to become Plastic Clever Schools. Zero Hour encourages youth to start "sister groups." Like so many other environmental organizations, Sunrise Movement has chapter "hubs" across America. Currently, there are over 400 hubs. Some Sunrise Movement members live together and strive for a zero-waste life.

One trend we see with these organizations is that they are providing blueprints for ways youth can get involved and a place for widely sharing inspirational stories about youth activists. For example, Kids Against *Plastic* claims that it is unrealistic to get rid of all plastic packaging. What they want is for kids to become "plastic clever." Plastic clever is about making informed choices about plastic consumption and waste and also advocating for more sustainable sources. Amy and Ella Meek published *Be Plastic Clever* in 2020. The book teaches kids about plastic pollution and climate change as well as offers practical solutions to how youth can rid the Earth of single-use plastic. This idea of sharing information to inspire girls to become activists resonates with the girls who started nonprofits. For example, Margolin published the book *Youth to Power: Your Voice and How to Use It* in 2020. The book is also a guide to how to participate in social change and addresses topics such as how to write op-eds, how to organize successful peaceful protests, how to manage your time as a student and an activist, and how to use social media to spread your message. In the book, she interviews youth activists, including those who participate in resisting the Dakota Access Pipeline and in supporting the Black Lives Matter movement. Margolin is particularly focused on offering advice on how youth activists can maintain their mental health while also engaging in intersectional activism.

The girls who are participating in these organizations argue that in order to combat climate change, there needs to be different values and different ways of *being,* so they are creating rules on how people in their organizations should act together. Earth Guardians have a youth council to guide the movement. Zero Hour has "guiding principles" that state that "youth leadership is transformational and visionary. Youth must lead because they have always shifted culture towards progress and collective liberation" (http://thisiszerohour.org/files/zh-guiding-principles-web.pdf). Other principles include being peaceful and nonviolent, being humble and learning from each other, and extending the hand of friendship. Bye Bye Plastic Bags allow youth in different locations to apply to be part of the network of teams. Green Hope Foundation trains youth to be leaders in their communities. Green Hope Foundation created a Children's Board to sustain a network of younger activists. These youth are learning how to lead projects. Green Hope is trying to change the top-down approach.

Sunrise Movement created principles for decision making that activists must follow. The twelve principles begin with stopping climate change and creating millions of good-paying jobs in the process. They "grow their power through talking to [their] communities. Diversity is a fundamental value in that they are people 'from all paths of life.' They 'are nonviolent in word and deed.' They tell and honor each other's stories. They give what they can and ask for what they need. They take initiative (action) 'in the name of Sunrise' in groups of three. The three are there to 'ask for advice, not permission' from each other. They 'embrace experimentation and learn from each other." They are to "take care of ourselves, each other, and our shared home." They "unite with other movements for change" (not join, not ally, not work with or coalition build)" they "fight for the liberation of all people," and finally, they "shine bright," which, to them, means showing joy and being positive.

GRASSROOTS DIGITAL ACTIVISM

Grassroots climate girls involve youth in digital networks such as their social media, their websites, and YouTube channels. This activism can be seen as a form of cyberfeminism, defined as activism that examines the connections between the Internet and the potential for gender equality. Early cyberfeminists, such as Sadie Plant (1997) and Donna Haraway (2006), saw the Internet as a space to liberate women from the social and physical constraints of the material world. More recent scholarship on cyberfeminism offers a critical view that interrogates the impact of power in assessing the democratic potential of online communities (Gajjala & Oh, 2012). That said, digital media is an important channel for activism, fundraising, and networking and we find these girls are capitalizing on connective action.

Grassroots organizations play an influential role in climate politics, especially because they can act as a mediator between scientific expertise and the public as well as use public relations tactics to gain news coverage and draw public attention to these issues (Vu et al., 2021). We see this in the organizations profiled here. One of the challenges of climate activism is that environmental issues are not often framed in a salient way for lay audiences to understand. Framing, or how information is organized to reflect everyday reality, can be a persuasive tool because it can help make sense of complicated topics as well as propose solutions to social problems (Entman, 1993).

Nonprofits increasingly use social media to draw attention to environmental issues, yet there is little research on how nonprofits are framing social media messages to make change (Vu et al., 2020). Snow and Bedford (1988) identified three framing strategies including diagnostic framing (a problem in social life that is in need of alteration), prognostic framing (proposing solutions to the problem), and motivational framing (a call-to-arms that moves people to action). In general, many climate activists use social media for prognostic framing, without including motivational framing (Wahlström et al., 2013). How audiences respond to social media messages related to climate change is key for understanding activism. O'Neill and Nicholson-Cole (2009) found that audiences became less engaged with climate change information after being shown images of the negative impact of climate change, such as polar bears jumping from melting polar ice caps to survive. Instead, Bilandzic, Kalch, and Soentgen (2017) found that "gain-negative" frames, which show how individual actions can curtail climate change, had the strongest influence because people felt like they had a sense of agency for making a difference.

While Vu et al. (2020) found that nonprofits are still focused on diagnostic frames, we see that the ways grassroots climate girls are framing social media messages is having an impact and resonating with youth. They use multiple forms of digital media to amplify their messages and appeal to different audiences.

All of the organizations featured in this chapter use multiple forms of digital media to spread their mission as well as garner support for their cause. This is significant because girls are techno-savvy and developing technological interventions to participate in the climate justice movement. Girls are under-represented in STEM fields, yet research shows that they are more motivated to become technological innovators when they can see the social impact of their endeavors (Girl Scouts Research Institute, 2015). We see the digital activism of grassroots climate girls as a form of techno-ecofeminism because they are using their lived experiences to develop technological interventions to address climate change. These technologies empower youth to get involved in the broader movement. For example, Kids Against Plastic created a Citizen GIS project that includes a mobile app that allows kids to log where they are picking up plastic waste, as well as how much waste they have collected. The app allows users to sort the waste into different categories (plastic water bottles, soda bottles, bottle caps, straws, pens, vaping equipment, etc.). Once the information is logged, it is loaded onto a website that has a map indicating the impact of these projects. Being able to track and visualize these efforts allows kids to feel connected to others working toward change.

In addition to their app, Kids Against Plastic have launched a hashtag activism campaign titled #PACKETin, which is an advocacy project where kids collect packaging, either from their own consumption or through trash collection. They sort the packaging based on brands. Then, they put the packaging in an envelope and mail it back to the company to encourage them to use more sustainable packaging. The website includes the addresses of some of the most popular brands. The rationale of the project explains, "just as it is our responsibility as a consumer to dispose of our waste responsibly, shouldn't manufacturers take some responsibility for the post-use of their products?"

Bye Bye Plastic Bags used what they called a "name and shame" initiative to get businesses in Bali to ban plastic bags. Those who have banned plastic bags get a sticker and a shout out on social media platforms. Thus, consumers can put pressure on those businesses who have not banned plastic bags. An example of their techno-ecofeminist activism can be seen in their Mountain Mamas project, which trains women in Bali to make reusable bags from recycled materials. Not only does it increase the technological knowledge of rural women, but it also helps contribute to their economic development, since they sell the bags locally.

Bye Bye Plastic Bags has teams or chapters located throughout the world. Each of the different teams has their own social media accounts, primarily Instagram and Facebook. These platforms allow the chapters to share what they are doing in their location as well as build support for their larger efforts. For example, the Instagram feed of the Bye Bye Plastic Bags Denmark team, has pictures that support individual actions, such as how to cook a sustainable holiday meal or instructions on how to make a reusable mask. Additionally, many of the posts engage users, either through challenges such as picking up three pieces of plastic on your way home from school and sharing photos or asking users to submit photos of how they separate their trash. The Bye

Bye Plastic Bags Nepal team posted a comic of a person at a market buying a fish. When he asks the cashier for a plastic bag, she says "it's in the fish, sir." This comic draws attention to how plastic pollution is damaging to sea life. On these social media posts, teams are encouraging individual action, which as mentioned earlier in the chapter, can be an effective strategy for engaging youth who might connect more to lifestyle changes than marching in a protest.

In an interview with Tasya, communication director of Bye Bye Plastic Bags about how the organization uses social media, she commented, "we hope to use our platforms to spread the message of the urgency and yet the opportunities that exist! We really believe that through sharing knowledge and sharing solutions we can empower everyone to make a difference. And that is also part of the message we try to show by leading by example" (Tasya, email communication, January 21, 2021).

Kehkashan Basu posts on her Instagram account to promote the Green Hope Foundation. She posts about the talks she gives, awards she receives, as well as actions the foundation participates in, including planting indigenous trees and installing toilets in the villages of Bangladesh. In our interview with her, she talked about how she uses social media to show the work of Green Hope, since mainstream media don't always get it right. In our interview with her, Basu also spoke about the strategic way she has learned to use social media accounts for Green Hope Foundation. She uses Instagram, Facebook, Twitter, and LinkedIn because those are the social media channels that are most frequently used by international organizations and those at the highest level of policymaking decisions. Basu told us about her social media strategies. She says she never posts where Green Hope will be doing actions, because they are concerned about the safety of the marginalized communities where they are doing their work. For example, in 2018, they did some sustainability workshops in a Syrian refugee camp on the Lebanon-Syria border which is a war zone. In her strategy, Basu emphasized that safety is the priority—not creating actions for publicity. She uses social media channels to highlight the work that Green Hope is doing. As she says, "the work speaks for itself." Basu is hopeful that the photos of the work they are doing will spread and draw attention to the different solutions that are occurring around the globe, not just the "hegemonic Western way of thinking."

Zero Hour is active on social media. They have a medium page: https://medium.com/@thisiszerohourmedia. Medium is an open platform that allows people to publish articles on a variety of topics and encourages conversation and interactivity. Their profile on their Instagram page states, "we are an intersectional movement of youth activists fighting for a livable planet for all!" (https://www.instagram.com/thisiszerohour/). Posts are photos in celebration of Latinx heritage month, Indigenous People's Day, March against environmental racism, migrant justice=climate justice, definition of ableism, endorsements of political candidates.

Zero Hour also has a podcast called Zero Hour Talks and is produced by Goal 17 Media (storytellers for the common good). As of January 2021, they have produced eleven episodes around forty minutes long on topics ranging from keeping the climate movement active during coronavirus quarantine to "real talk about racism" to discussions of pride and misogyny, and how art can inspire activism. They also have a YouTube channel and had a panel on immigration. During the pandemic, they hosted webinars on patriarchy, environmental racism, and the Black Lives Matter movement. Through this strategy of having multiple communication channels to interact with audiences who may be interested in their message, they can have a greater impact.

Earth Guardians has developed an app called, EarthTracks, which people use to receive "gamified challenges" to change behavior. They describe it as "a Fitbit for the planet," because it quantifies individual and collective impact, but it is also an educational tool to teach people how to "reduce our personal footprint on a day-to-day basis, while also connecting Earth Guardians' global community of 300+ Crews."

These multiple forms of digital media, from apps to podcasts, show the innovative ways these organizations spread their message. This is important for connective action, in which youth feel part of the larger global youth community working for climate justice. For example, Sophie Gutheir, social media manager for Sunrise Movement, says, "I first learned about Sunrise after seeing the sit-ins at Nancy Pelosi's office while scrolling through Facebook. The actions were so powerful to me and the visuals of them were something that I had never seen before." She goes on to state, "Posting a meme may not seem that impactful, but if we have a tweet or a meme that gets retweeted or shared a lot, that means it's going to get on a lot of new people's feeds," she explains. "When this happens, new people who haven't seen our page before might look more into us and see all of the organizing we're doing and want to get involved" (https://billmoyers.com/story/tweet-for-climate-truth/).

Digital activism by these organizations increased during the pandemic of 2020. As Basu tells us, she has been able to reach a broader audience through high level webinars and, as a result, are able to reach and communicate with people and audiences that they couldn't have before (K. Basu, personal communication, February 22, 2021). Given these girls' ability to innovate using digital media to reach audiences, we anticipate that these kinds of opportunities will continue.

GRASSROOTS CLIMATE GIRLS ON THE STAGE

Many of the leaders of these grassroots organizations have participated in TED Talks. In this section, we look at how they speak about their experiences being girls and activists. TED Talks are committed to spreading innovative ideas and they feature inspiring speakers. Many of the girls in this chapter have delivered TED Talks. These talks have two purposes. While they raise awareness about these grassroots organizations to a global audience, they also give a voice to girls' innovative approaches to solving environmental problems.

For example, in their 2018 TED Talk, sisters Amy and Ella Meek begin their talk by stating, "We may just be kids, but we have something important to say, so please listen up." Throughout their talk, they address both adults, who they see as culpable for environmental problems, and children, whom they want to inspire to get involved. The sisters speak to the very slow progress being made, stating that by the time these plans are put into place, they will be middle-aged adults. Addressing kids, they state, listen up kids, we all have a huge potential. If we say the right things, we can have the loudest voices. We are the future, but we are also the present. If we want change to happen, we have to be brave enough to make it happen."

Margolin's talk is titled "Patriarchy, Racism, and Colonialism Caused the Climate Crisis." She traces the evolution of colonialism as a system of oppression and global environmental devastation. She names the institutions that need to change and she identifies what we, the audience, need "to speak truth to power, call out these systems of oppression, and demand the livable earth that we all deserve." Rather than highlight her age, she is committed to involving everyone in the movement.

In their TED Talk, sisters Melati and Isabel Wijsen begin their talk by posing provocative questions: Bali—a green paradise? Or a paradise lost? Bali—an island of garbage? A photo of plastic trash appears on the screen. This juxtaposition between what we imagine Bali to be and what these girls experience appeals to the audience's emotions. They detail the steps they took to launch the ban plastic bags campaign in Bali. The story involves humor and persistence. When they were told they couldn't, it inspired them more. For example, they went on a food strike to demand that Bali's governor meet with them about their campaign. In describing the action, Isabel tells, "we knew we didn't make the governor look good by doing this food strike, we could go to jail. But hey, it worked." She shrugs her shoulders and the audience laughs, recognizing her innocence.

These TED Talks are just one way that grassroots climate girls are gaining access and legitimacy with adult audiences.

MAINSTREAM MEDIA COVERAGE

One of the themes related to these girls' grassroots activism is that they want to hold adults accountable for their inaction when it comes to climate change. When we look at mainstream media coverage of these organizations, however, the story veers to them as spectacular. For example, a *Vox* article describes Sunrise Movement as "Disproportionately" young.

Most of the organizations we studied provide links to their mainstream media coverage, so we see the importance of media coverage to them. Media coverage in prominent outlets like the *New York Times* increases their legitimacy and credibility. We were curious about the differences between how the organizations represent themselves and how they are featured in the more mainstream.

One of the themes that emerges in the media coverage of these girls is that they are just trying to be kids, but they feel the need to also be activists. They are often framed as organizing marches and then coming home to do their homework (Engelfried, 2020). For example, Madelaine Tew, who is from Teaneck, New Jersey, is the director of finance for Zero Hour. In a *New York Times* article, she speaks about having to navigate activism while also going to school (Yoon-Hendricks, 2018). She tells the story about trying to meet a grant deadline and telling the school nurse that she was having menstrual cramps. So, she took that time to finish and submit the grant, which they were successful at securing $16,000.

Media coverage also tends to focus on the leaders of these organizations and their exceptionalism, rather than what they are trying to achieve or what their organizations are actually doing. In this way, mainstream media outlets do not take them seriously. Many of the stories repeat the same information and why they were called to act. The girls are seen as exceptional—they are profiled, and the same origin stories are repeated. For example, in media coverage of Zero Hour's march, there were profiles of youth in the movement. *The New York Times* described Zero Hour as "creatively minded and technologically savvy" (Yoon-Hendricks, 2018). However, there is little focus on what the group aims to do.

As Tasya comments on the media coverage of Bye Bye Plastic Bags, "We've been very lucky that the media has been very positive towards our work. But also sometimes very limiting to a specific storyline: 'The two sisters' 'The clean up efforts'—but we feel that we are so much more as a youth led movement and we try and convey that through our many different actions together with our team!" (Tasya, email communication, January 21, 2021).

Media have also granted awards to these girls because of their efforts, further framing them as exceptional. For example, the Wjisen sisters were named as among the world's most influential teenagers by *Forbes*, *TIME* magazine, and CNN. Melati has given four TED Talks in three years.

At the same time, girls are writing op-eds in high-level media outlets to frame their own messages. In an editorial published on CNN on Earth Day in 2018, Margolin writes, "please save your phony Earth Day tweets and Facebook posts, I don't want to see them. Put those in a bag along with your toothless 'thoughts and prayers' tweets for hurricane victims and dump them in the ocean just like you permit corporations to dump their waste" (Margolin, 2018). She signs the editorial "a teenage girl who has had enough and is not alone."

In interviews and editorials, Margolin continues to emphasize the connection between oppression and climate change. She becomes a spokesperson for other children who she says are so anxious about climate change it is as if it has become normal that the world will be ending. And it makes sense that she is a good person to lead the charge because youth are tired of the inaction from adults. In one interview she states, "the world is literally ending, you need to be thinking of the youth, putting the youth first, thinking about front-line communities, communities of color who are being impacted first and stop this self-congratulation" (Scheinman, 2018). In an interview with Pacific Standard at the Global Climate Action Summit in San Francisco, she states, "you can't just slap a solar panel on this issue and say 'done'" (Scheinman, 2018).

CHALLENGES

While these organizations are trying to use media coverage to their advantage, there are also some limitations in how media cover organizations like Green Hope Foundation. Basu speaks about the limitations of the Western media for only focusing on what she calls "one solution." She uses the example of the climate strikes. There has been so much focus on these strikes as a way for youth to draw attention to the movement, yet, as Basu tells us, climate strikes are not applicable to those living in the most marginalized communities. School climate strikes do not resonant for girls in places where they are not allowed to go to school. Basu relates a story where she partnered with the National Youth Parliament to speak at a school about sustainability. When she came out of the school, she saw an eight-year-old girl holding her baby brother. She could no longer go to school because her mom had to work. In other words, school strikes assume the same positionality of kids in school to be able to strike.

Basu would like media to cover the many different solutions that are being found all over the world. As she comments, different regions and locations face different challenge so media should instead highlight these efforts. Instead, Western media promote a single narrative, one that singles out girls as spectacular without mentioning the range of ways that youth are addressing climate change in their local communities (K. Basu, personal communication, February 22, 2021).

In addition to the challenges grassroots climate girls face with media coverage, they also struggle to find a clear and coherent message as they respond and adapt to the changing needs of their communities. Grassroots organizations necessarily evolve based on community need and funding sources, but this can make it more difficult to communicate to broader audiences. In discussing the challenges that Bye Bye Plastic Bags face, Tasya tells us,

> perhaps like many other startups, our challenges lay in resources such as funding, access to networks and mentorship. However, on a more general note, we have learned that a big challenge when it comes to changemaking is a lack of clarity in the goals we want to reach. We have worked with government bodies, large corporate and realize that the goals and the roadmap is not clear enough and without consequences / accountability measures. This was one of the frustrating barriers we came across through our work. (Tasya, personal communication, Janaury 21, 2021)

One of the challenging issues raised by Basu is the tokenization of youth within the larger environmental movement. Youth are invited to speak at climate conventions, but there is usually just one youth voice. And that voice stands in for all youth, even though there are a diversity of perspectives among youth. Basu's comments speak to the larger issues in youth-led activism. On the one hand, having alliances with adult organizations shows the legitimacy of their actions within the larger landscape of environmental organizations, so grassroots climate girls' organizations are not easily discredited. There is a mutually beneficial relationship because youth-led organizations can benefit from being associated with these long-standing and far-reaching environmental organizations. They can amplify their voices and even raise money to support their operations. On the other hand, though, there is the concern that adults may not take them seriously.

As Basu told us,

> Yeah there is a problem of dismissal I think that a lot of people don't view us as experts or recognize our unique lived experiences and that's definitely the case but at the same time a lot of the organizations that I work with now provide that same respect to young people and I think that's really important but definitely I think the dismissal of young people is just it's still very much rampant and

again we need that mindset shift to like really happen now. (K. Basu, personal communication, February 21, 2021).

WHAT IS THE GRASSROOTS CLIMATE GIRL EFFECT?

In our analysis of grassroots climate girls, we see that they are participating in what O'Brien (2018) terms "dutiful dissent." They are working within established systems to bring about the change they want to see. In Indonesia, that means banning plastic bags that have plagued them. For the Green Hope Foundation, it is about creating youth leaders who can propose local solutions and create a sustained leadership pipeline. For the Sunrise Movement, that means putting pressure on politicians to adopt the Green New Deal. Through creating organizations, they have a structural mechanism to raise money and choose which projects to fund. They communicate their messages and grow their networks through many different forms of digital media.

The Grassroots Climate Girl Effect refers to the range of tactics and engagement that resonate with youth and give them many ways to participate. They can make lifestyle changes, join a litter cleanup, or lobby politicians. Narratives of grassroots climate girls show how they came to this work because of their connection to the Earth and their dismay at the abuse that was caused by humans. That inspiration, which is to create non-profit organizations, led to the Grassroots Climate Girl Effect.

Similar to our other case studies, media frame grassroots climate girls as spectacular, which eclipses the overall impact of what they are doing. While media attention is one way to increase their credibility and legitimacy, it does not draw attention to the many ways girls and youth are making real change in their communities. As Avery McRae tells us in Chapter 7, when media focus attention so much on "eco-warriors" like Greta Thunberg, it may make youth feel like a small action might not make a difference. We anticipate that these grassroots organizations will evolve as the need to address the climate crisis intensifies.

This case centers on the agency of grassroots climate girls who have pulled up their sleeves and gotten to work on solutions. They ignore people who are either ignoring them, or who don't believe in them enough to take them seriously. They have laid the groundwork to confront climate problems with like-minded people. The Grassroot Climate Girl Effect shows how to use traditional methods of organizing in ways new and inclusive.

Grassroots activism is an effective way to bring about change, which is why it survives. One way to support these grassroots climate girls is through donations. What we have learned in this case is that, with more resources, these organizations, designed and run by passionate, intelligent girls, could make substantial progress in the larger climate justice movement. Giving money to these organizations and joining them is a way to support global local efforts. These girls have the vision and infrastructure in place to move their local initiatives forward or apply more political pressure. They have solutions, they have created the materials needed to do the work, (writing books, making videos, making tool kits) and they have built a way to be supported by anyone. We have what we need to re-invent our systems.

Chapter 7

Lawyer Up Climate Girl Effect

For this chapter, we take as inspiration the words of climate girl activist, Kelsey Cascadia Rose Juliana who said, "It's going to take more than one girl with a megaphone. See you in court, government" (Cooper, 2021). This sentiment brings us to the story of seven-year-old Rabab Ali, who in 2016 sued the Pakistani government for violating her rights to a healthy life. Ali argued that coal mining is dramatically increasing Pakistan's carbon dioxide emissions, polluting the air, and contributing to global warming. The lawsuit challenges the government's plan to develop coal fields in the Thar region, which would lead to more greenhouse gas emissions. This development would displace the already marginalized residents living there and have a negative impact on water quality as well as the atmosphere. In this lawsuit, Ali argues that these emissions violate her rights and rights of her generation.

Ali's case invokes the Principle of Public Trust Doctrine, which states that resources like water, air, and the ocean have to be protected because they are common to everyone and cannot be damaged by one generation or sold to the private sector. This case extends the public trust to the atmosphere. As Julia Olson, lawyer with Our Children's Trust, stated, "[Ali] basically lives in an area that is so polluted that she can't access the kind of natural resources she would like to spend time in" (Mitchell, 2016).

Ali's case is significant because it established that minors could file a legal petition in Pakistan. And in the past ten years kids have been entering a movement to sue their governments. Although a long process, climate litigation cases are fast becoming an effective means to hold governments and corporations accountable for the harm that they are knowingly doing to the planet. Cases have been filed in places including Canada, India, Pakistan, Colombia, and the United States. While so far only a handful of cases have been successful, this strategy establishes that the atmosphere can be considered a "public trust" that needs to be protected. Climate litigation cases also have other social and cultural impacts, including contributing to rhetorical debates about legal concepts such as human rights, mobilizing and sustaining the climate justice movement, and increasing the public's involvement in the fight for a livable future (Kempf, 2021; Rogers, 2016).

One of the rationales behind these cases is that governments have known that burning fossil fuels is the leading cause of climate change and that they have permitted and even subsidized private corporations' extraction of resources to support the fossil fuel industry. This infrastructure has created a situation in which the damage is widespread, threatening many ecosystems, contributing to deadly weather events, and impacting kids' future. Because the current legal and political system does not protect young people's rights to a livable planet and since young people can't vote, interventions through lawsuits are a strategy to protect their interests.

It is significant that young people are bringing these cases forward, since they suffer more harm than adults. Physically, they are still developing, and the health impacts of pollution will have long-term effects. They will bear the burdens of climate change, physically and financially, as they grow into adults. We know that girls are especially vulnerable to climate change because of their gender and cultural positioning, including reproduction, domestic duties, sexism, and misogyny. It is compelling, then, that girls are playing a central role and becoming the "face" of these legal movements. What happens when girls sue governments and corporations for creating a world that threatens their future and what motivates girls to participate in legal action, especially when this strategy has proven a long and unfair fight? In this chapter, we look at girls as spokespersons for these legal battles, the nature of the cases, the form of arguments gathering momentum, and their techno-ecofeminist activism. We see that girls' involvement in these cases evoke both agency (because they are exercising their rights) as well as creating a legacy (their stories are getting written into the legal documents).

CLIMATE LAWSUITS AS TECHNO-ECOFEMINIST ACTIVISM

Do governments have a right to ruin the planet and bio-futures? Climate change cases have been filed in at least twenty-eight countries, with 75 percent filed in the United States (Setzer & Byrnes, 2020). Climate lawsuits draw on the concept that a right to a healthy environment is guaranteed through constitutions, which also establish the importance of protecting the life, liberty, and freedom of a nation's people (Parker, 2019). These cases are intended to compel governments to develop more aggressive climate policies or enforce existing ones. In these cases, plaintiffs enter what communication scholar Goodnight (2012) terms the technical sphere of argument. Palczewski, Ice, and Fritch (2016) describe Goodnight's three spheres of argument, which are personal, technical, and public spheres. Each sphere delineates different rules, reasons, and judgements. Technical spheres, such as courts of law, are distinct because they are specialized through expertise and jargon, and they are often preserved through documentation. Additionally, law is highly technical, making it the realm of the elite. The legal system is a form of technology because it requires specialized knowledge and is a practical application of knowledge. Indeed, Moses (2007) reminds us that the term technology can refer to "technique," or the study of knowledge about things. The public sphere is where arguments happen that matter to a plurality—many people with different positions try to come to agreements together about how to move forward as communities and publics. In the case of climate lawsuits, technical arguments are matters of science and human rights, so increasingly they are public sphere arguments, too.

When girls are involved in the legal system, then, they are involved in both the technical and public spheres. They are entering into a space that is traditionally reserved for those who have specialized training in legal theory and access to the legal system. Girls' participation in climate lawsuits is a form of techno-ecofeminism because they are participating in the mutual shaping of technology, society, and environment. They are helping to write the technical aspects of the law through sharing their stories about the impact of climate change on them. They are also challenging the binary ways in which rights are afforded only to humans. In this way, they are enacting their political agency. In discussing youth activism, O'Brien et al. (2018) writes,

> [W]e explicitly recognize youth as political agents who may be engaging in activism in a diversity of ways. In other words, youth are neither in a state of "becoming" future citizens nor training to be participants in the sphere of formal politics; they are citizens with agency. (n.p.)

In the stories of how girls have come to participate in climate litigation, they often speak of a sense of injustice. First, they argue that governments are supposed to protect them, yet they are instead doing harm against them. Because they do not have voting rights, it is up to those in power to use technical means to make changes. At the same time, girls are putting forward arguments about the natural world based on their lived experiences in that technical space that are adding to the forms of knowledge that are accepted.

Another way that girls' involvement in climate litigation is a form of techno-ecofeminism is how they challenge and engage with scientific evidence, which is also a traditionally masculine and patriarchal space. As Sikka (2018) argues, these masculine ways of knowing, which tend to emphasize the interdependence of efficiency and economics, exclude alternative solutions which have relied on local knowledge and women as scientific experts.

Climate lawsuits emphasize both human rights and scientific evidence and add this element to public discourse (Setzer &Byrnes, 2019). This combination is proving effective since human rights arguments are resonating with judges and causal links between emissions and climate-related harm are gaining traction. This is important for cross-over influence, as Nosek (2017) argues, since climate change litigation is important for influencing both public debate and social norms, making political culture and public debate more climate-informed, galvanizing grassroots climate campaigns, and increasing public understanding of scientific concepts. Also, these lawsuits put a human face on the victims of climate change, since they don't appear distant in time and space or abstract in any way. Using youth (and girls) as plaintiffs also allows for publics to increase their affinity and identification with future generations. Girls' participation in climate litigation makes legible girls' proposed solutions to address the climate crisis. As these lawsuits bring technical arguments into the public sphere, a diversity of voices and perspectives are heard and taken seriously.

Rogers (2016) argues that climate litigation is a form of cultural performance. Climate change activism generates a paradigm shift when it highlights instabilities in established structures, institutions, and stereotypes, which is a key tenet of technofeminism and, by extension, techno-ecofeminism. Through her look at climate lawsuits, Rogers asks what the meaning of lawfulness is in the context of climate change. She draws on Blay and Piotrowitcz's (2000) concept of the "awfulness of lawfulness" to interrogate the subversiveness of climate litigation because it challenges existing social and political structures and presents alternative frameworks. Through her analysis of the lawsuits brought forth through Our Children's Trust, she shows how these lawsuits become effective symbolism. They provide an embodied representation of intergenerational equity and the expression of personal grievance and deprivation through sparking guilt and responsibility in adult bystanders. While many of these lawsuits have yet to be successful, they are successful at challenging an unjust and unsustainable system. Climate litigation leads to public argument debates about the meaning of key legal concepts which Rogers (2016) argues can be more effective in systemic change.

Techno-ecofeminism seeks to uncover assumptions and biases built into accepted systems. In the case of climate litigation, Morrow (2021) argues that it is important to include the framework of gender justice. Climate change disproportionately affects girls and women because it reinforces and exacerbates socially constructed relations of power and norms. In some of the worst affected areas, gender roles and responsibilities often confine women's activities and mobility to the home and sometimes traditions and laws limit women's access to natural resources, as well as financial and social capital, resulting in little ability to adapt and cope with climate change and natural disasters. Additionally, norms that inhibit women's access to information, knowledge, skills, and capacity-building limits their ability to adapt to climate change. Women as a vulnerable population whose human rights need to be protected was a strategy in the KlimaSeniorinnen case in Switzerland (Morrow, 2021). The case argued that older women were the most affected by heat waves. They demanded that the government should target emissions and develop mitigation measures to meet these targets. While the case is still ongoing, it shows how scientific knowledge can be used to advance gender equity and climate justice.

Women's mortality rates are higher than men's during climate-related disasters. At the same time, women also experience human rights abuses, human trafficking, sexual violence, disruptions to health services (family planning, maternal, or postnatal care), and interruptions in income generating activities. For girls, they are more at risk of being pulled out of school and taking on domestic duties during natural disasters. There is the impact of early pregnancy as well as a lack of access to information. Indeed, girls may be married off to offset a family's financial burden in times of crises. As Kwauck et al. (2019) writes,

> it is important to note that in most discussions of gender and climate change, attention to girls has been absent. This is in part due to climate policy-makers failing to adequately consider children as important stakeholders, beneficiaries, agents of change, or communicators of good practice—a state of affairs that is then replicated by climate decision-makers in climate policy and action. (p. 7)

Kwauck et al. (2019) found that the narrative of climate change places women as passive recipients of support rather than active providers of solutions. Climate strategies ignore girls and overlook the role of children and youth in solutions. However, research on girls' education shows linkages between empowering and transformative education for girls, fulfillment of girls' rights, and social change needed to reverse global warming trends.

HISTORY OF OUR CHILDREN'S TRUST

Many of the more recent climate lawsuits have been supported by Our Children's Trust, a nonprofit public interest law firm that was started in 2010. Our Children's Trust provides strategic legal services to secure legal rights to a safe planet. According to their website, they are the world's only non-profit public interest law firm "dedicated exclusively to securing the legal rights of youth to a healthy atmosphere and safe climate, based on the best available science" (Our Children's Trust, 2021). They represent young people and help them secure their future in a livable world. To do this, they have a strategy that includes targeted media campaigns, education, and public engagement.

Julia Olson, Executive Director of Our Children's Trust, became interested in representing young people and elevating their voices after becoming a mom. After having children, she saw climate change as the biggest threat not only to her own children, but children everywhere. Children are inheriting a climate system that they did not have a hand in creating and they do not have the power to make change because they can't vote. So, Olson is committed to using the justice system to step in to protect constitutional rights of individuals.

Olson likens climate lawsuits to the significance of *Brown vs. Board of Education* (Celebrating Ten Years of Our Children's Trust, 2020). She states that policymakers would have continued desegregation if there wasn't legal intervention. The U.S. Supreme Court ruling in *Brown v. Board of Education* ensured that school districts provided equal access to education, regardless of race. Just as that case protected the rights of children, so too do climate lawsuits. Olson argues that we have legalized "climate destabilization" and she wants the courts to declare the rights of young people to a stable climate.

The legal theory used in climate lawsuits is based on what Mary Wood (2013) identified as the "atmospheric trust." The atmospheric trust is based on the idea that just as other natural resources, such as water, are in the public trust, so too is the air. In this way, the goal is to hold governments accountable for not protecting the air. Governments are trustees for crucial resources that support the survival of our species. They need to handle these resources responsibly and so the concept of atmospheric trust provides a tool for lawyers to go to court and argue that governments are not doing their job and legal steps need to be taken for enforcement. Additionally, these lawsuits evoke guilt and a sense of responsibility in adult spectators (Rogers, 2016).

One of the first big actions of Our Children's Trust was to file a batch of lawsuits on Mother's Day, 2011. Actions were filed in all fifty states, as well as Ukraine and Uganda. The goal of filing these cases was to begin creating a body of law that allowed them to bring forth additional rounds of litigation. This action drew national attention, as youth were telling stories about how climate change was affecting them and participating in marches.

SOME OF THE KEY LEGAL ARGUMENTS

The first climate litigation lawsuits cases were brought in the 1980s primarily in developed countries around the time the United Nations Framework Convention on Climate Change (UNFCCC) and later the Kyoto Protocol were adopted. Then, there were a number of cases after the failure of countries to reach a global agreement at the 2009 Copenhagen Conference of the Parties (COP). The adoption of the Paris Agreement in 2015 marked the start of the current generation of cases. The Paris Agreement is designed as a legally binding agreement between countries to reduce greenhouse gas emissions to pre-industrial levels. In the following section, we highlight some of the salient arguments in these climate lawsuits to illustrate both arguments in these cases that are gaining traction and the impact climate girls are making in those legal battles.

Protection of Human Rights

One of the most successful climate lawsuits has been *Urgenda Foundation v. the Netherlands*. The Urgenda Foundation and 900 co-plaintiffs argued that the Dutch government was negligent in protecting its citizens by contributing to climate change. In 2015, the court ruled that the Dutch state had a responsibility to protect current and future generations from the danger posed by hazardous climate change and ordered the government to reduce greenhouse gas emissions by 25 percent by end of 2020.

In more recent climate change cases, a significant change is taking place. Human rights are gaining ground, especially since climate science is more persuasive. For example, Diaconu (2021) considers how the InterAmerican Commission for Human Rights (IACHR) can serve as a vehicle to pressure the United States government to take action on climate change and the potential for Indigenous people to lead the effort. Indigenous groups have framed their claims within an international human rights framework, such as the right to property. In 2005, Inuit from northern Canada and Alaska said they wanted relief from violations of their human rights caused by global warming and climate change from greenhouse gas emissions from the U.S. They argued that their hunting grounds were eviscerated as permafrost melted, sea ice thinned, glaciers receded, coastal erosion increased, and shorter winters and longer and warmer summers impacted their access to food. They claimed that U.S. acts, including withdrawing from the Kyoto Protocol, violated their human rights, especially the preservation of their health, right to life, right to security, right to a means of subsistence, and right to residence, movement, and home. The case was dismissed, but Diaconu (2021) argues that this case has the potential for providing groundswell for other cases. Further, Diaconu (2021) argues that the framework of 20th century human rights, which is state-based and protective of individual harms incurred at a fixed location within nation-state, are incompatible with twenty-first century challenge of climate change.

In September 2020, six Portuguese youth filed the first climate-related case with European Commission on Human Rights (ECHR). They argued that governments in 35 European countries are failing to protect human rights because they are not doing enough to address climate change. In the case, they argue that they are being discriminated against because they experience climate change more than older generations. They argue that they will experience the impact of rising sea levels, extreme heat, and extreme weather events for longer than older generations. One significant aspect of this case is whether or not the anxiety and anguish that young people experience in relation to climate change might also violate Article 3, which protects "freedom from torture and inhuman and degrading treatment." This speaks to the protection of human rights.

Protection of Earth Rights

Environmental personhood is also a legal framework for protecting natural habitats and has been used in climate change litigation. In 2017, the Māori tribe of Whanganui were successful in negotiating for the legal identity of the river Te Awa Tupua (Roy, 2017). In India, the Ganges and Yamuna rivers have been granted environmental personhood as a way to combat pollution in the rivers that are considered sacred to Hindu culture (Safi, 2017).

In April 2018, the Supreme Court of Justice of Colombia affirmed youth's constitutional right to a healthy environment. They agreed that deforestation of the Amazon and increasing temperatures are a threat to a healthy environment as well as a threat to life. Concurrently, the case was significant because it established that the Colombian Amazon has legal personhood status, and the Colombian government has a right to protect it. Because the Colombian government has not done enough to protect the rainforest or curb greenhouse gas emissions, the court ordered the Colombian government to create and implement climate mitigation plans and develop an "intergenerational pact for the life of the Colombian Amazon" with plaintiffs, affected communities, and scientific organizations.

Kids Have Rights: *Juliana vs. United States*

Juliana vs. United States began in 2011 in Oregon. At that time, Kelsey Juliana was fifteen years old, and she co-filed a suit against the Oregon State Governor asking for a climate emissions reduction plan that would protect the public trust of the atmosphere. By 2015, she filed a climate lawsuit against the U.S. government that also included twenty-one other youth plaintiffs, nine of whom are girls. The lawsuit argues that the government directly contributes to the climate crisis, through creating a fossil fuel-based system that is the major factor in causing injuries to the plaintiffs. The government knowingly violated their constitutional right to life, liberty, property, and the public trust and did not provide equal protection under the law. The United States does not have constitutional protections for a healthy environment. In the lawsuit, the youth argue that the production of fossil fuels and lack of policy related to greenhouse gasses threatens their right to life.

The fossil fuel industry and U.S. government have worked tirelessly to have the case dismissed. However, in 2016, Judge Coffin recommended that motions should not be dismissed. On November 10, 2016, U.S. District Court Judge Ann Aiken upheld Coffin's decision and issued an opinion and order that stated, "I have no doubt that the right to a climate system capable of sustaining human life is fundamental to a free and ordered society" (*Juliana v. US*). Her statement laid the groundwork for protection of the public trust.

In 2017, the Ninth Circuit Court of Appeals suspended all district court proceedings, but on July 30, 2018, the U.S. Supreme Court ruled in favor of the plaintiffs, denying the government's application for a stay and allowing the case to proceed. In February 2019, lawyers for the plaintiffs filed a motion for a preliminary injunction that would prevent the federal government from issuing leases and mining permits for extracting coal on federal public lands, as well as leases for offshore oil and gas exploration and extraction and preventing federal approvals for new fossil fuel infrastructure while the government's appeal of the case was being heard.

It was in February 2019 that grassroots climate girl activists in the networked public sphere exerted pressure. Zero Hour launched a nationwide campaign for young people to add their names to a Young People's amicus brief in support of the Juliana plaintiffs. By January 2020, the Ninth Court of Appeals issued an order that recognized the gravity of the evidence on the plaintiffs' injuries and acknowledged the government's role in causing them. However, two of the three judges said remedies should come from executive and legislative branches. At the time of this writing, the case is back in Judge Aiken's hands, and she is ordering settlement talks to proceed.

MEDIA COVERAGE

One of the strategies of the media coverage of these lawsuits is to have vivid descriptions of climate threats on children. In media coverage, many of the youth talk about their fear and anxiety related to how they experience the devastating effects of climate change. As Nosek (2017) writes, these harms are framed as intentional, resulting from the inaction from governments and corporations, especially when they know about the impact of climate change. These plaintiffs are framed as innocent victims who are experiencing dangerous threats.

Wonneberger and Vliegenthart (2021) studied inter-media agenda setting and political agenda setting to look at the salience of litigation cases on media and political agenda. In the *Urgenda vs. The Netherlands* case, they found that media attention led to parliamentary attention for the case and led to greater attention for climate policies and climate change in general. They found that climate litigation can serve as a focusing event that facilitates media and political attention to climate change. Because the parliamentary focused on climate policies, this influenced media attention about climate policies and climate change. In turn, this news coverage influenced parliamentary attention to climate policies in a reciprocal relationship. They conclude that public attention to litigation can be influential for societal influences of a lawsuit. This is a common practice in other social movements, such as LGBT and homeschooling. They call this "bottom-up agenda setting" (p. 13).

Despite the ability for media coverage to draw attention to these cases, media coverage of *Juliana v. U.S.* highlights the battle between kids and governments and corporations. In a panel discussion with the Northwest Alliance for Media Literacy about her experience with the lawsuit, Avery McRae, one of the plaintiffs, talked about media coverage of the case. As she says,

> there is a lot of really good media coverage and there's also a lot of kind of like almost condescending media coverage, almost kind of framing the story as youth fight government, right, and there's just some kind of weird connotation like, yes we are youth, but it's also like we're still doing the same job (as adults). (A. McRae, personal communication, August 9, 2021)

Avery goes on to say that framing of youth versus the government is problematic because it not only sets kids against the government, but it also can be dismissive of their ideas. In her words, this conflict frame,

> creates like this underdog sort of feel and it's like I'm not necessarily the underdog like that doesn't need to be the default, right. Like you don't need to necessarily be the underdog and I think that's oftentimes kind of how media displays it and I think that's off from my view. (A. McRae, personal communication, August 9, 2021)

Youth plaintiff Sahara Valentine agrees, stating "it kind of makes us to seem like we're powerless and it's amazing that we're given this opportunity to do this" (S. Valentine, personal communication, August 9, 2021).

LAWSUIT STORIES

One of the strategies of climate lawsuits is to tell the story of climate change through the eyes of those most affected. Nelson and Walker (2020) argue that law and media together are a good combination for furthering environmental justice. Kempf (2021) writes that climate change lawsuits have the potential to mitigate cognitive barriers, such as ignorance, uncertainty, mistrust, and risk discounting, that can get in the way of collective action on climate change. Thus, Kempf suggests that interventions should emphasize intuitive and experiential information, as well as scientific facts. Powerful narratives help to bring the issues to light. Additionally, Kempf speaks to the importance of vouchers, or those who are trusted members of a person's cultural group, to communicate about risk. Children are also a useful group to draw on because not only are they a vulnerable group who will bear the brunt of climate change, but they could engender a biological connection to future generations because kinship is a human value. Having kids tell their stories about climate change became powerful narratives for social change.

In this section, we draw out the themes that are present in the way girls tell their stories about their involvement in climate lawsuits. We see girls' lived experiences as a form of techno-ecofeminism through challenging dominant narratives of expert knowledge. Their experiences become part of the knowledge that is written into legal documents. Additionally, many of the girls put forth non-western narratives of climate science and expertise that challenge dominant paradigms. Finally, through their involvement with climate lawsuits, they are enacting their citizenship through the empowerment and conviction that critical consciousness brings.

In the case of the lawsuits brought forth by Our Children's Trust, the lawsuit is just one part of the story. The *Juliana* case is accompanied by a comprehensive media campaign. There is a social media campaign: #youthvgov. A book titled *As the World Burns* by Lee van der Voo (2020) tells the stories of the plaintiffs involved in the lawsuit. There is a documentary titled *Youth V. Gov* (2020) that has played on the film festival circuit. Plaintiffs' stories are told through short documentaries on the Our Children's Trust website as well as *Our Climate Voices*, a project aimed at humanizing the climate crisis through storytelling. In each of these media campaigns, telling the stories of climate change through the experiences of the plaintiffs is a key strategy for garnering public support for the case. Additionally, these stories allow us to see climate change through the girls' eyes.

Similar to place-based media activism that was present in Mari's activism in Flint, many of the stories about the *Juliana* case emphasize the importance of place for connecting to larger audiences. In each of the short films on the

Our Children's Trust website, the girls walk us through their environments. Kelsey Juliana takes us to the Mackenzie River in Oregon and the Kelsey creek, which is her namesake. Eshe Shirley lives in Boston, Massachusetts, and she shows us the impact of climate change on urban environments. Standing by the iconic Fenway Park, she tells us how it may be underwater as sea levels continue to rise. Ashley Funk takes us to her backyard in rural Pennsylvania, which is littered with gob piles, the remnants that fall off coal once it is transported. She tells us that "the coal industry has left me with this huge mound of toxic waste." Glori Dei Filippone's is filmed at the local farmers market in Iowa as she explains how the devastating floods are impacting the local economy.

Jaime Butler's video opens with the sound of Native American drumming and flute music. The camera pans on Arizona land and eleven-year-old Jaime speaks in her Navajo language. A title card explains that her family used to travel in the spring, but they can't do that anymore because the water has dried up. She first learned about global warming from her mom. Her mom explained that when it is too hot, the water dries up. The camera cuts to pictures of her house and she talks about how she doesn't have any running water in her house because of the severe drought. "Being Native American means I care about my culture and protecting the Earth. Our culture evolved over thousands of years in the world that we lived in. And if climate change happens, and the world that we lived in is taken away, then my culture is taken away. I think addressing climate change is the most effective way to protect my culture" (Our Climate Voices, 2019a).

In the *Youth v. Gov* documentary, we travel to Rayne, Louisiana, to learn about Jayden Foyntlin's community that has been impacted by floods and hurricanes. Jayden is an indigenous girl living in Rayne, Louisiana, and Olson begins her argument in front of the judge arguing that the government has threatened Jayden's life because of flooding caused by climate change.

Miko Vergun is a seventeen-year-old Marshallese climate advocate from Beaverton, Oregon, and plaintiff with *Juliana*. She was adopted from the Marshall Islands when she was three months old. The Marshall Islands are at risk because of rising sea levels. Not only do floods and hurricanes threaten the island, but also the debris that was left from U.S. nuclear testing in the 1950s would compound the environmental impact. Miko travels to the Marshall Islands and she tells us, "It would be devastating if the Marshallese have to move away because these are our islands. It's not fair that the Marshallese would have to move because of something to which they barely contributed" (Our Climate Voices, 2019c).

Each of the girls also talk about how they came to climate activism. Kelsey has always been an environmental activist. At age three, she stormed a kindergarten stage yelling "clear cuts are bad." In 2014, she spent four months on the Great March for Climate Change. In an interview, she argues that youth are especially effective climate activists because as they are developing a sensibility related to ethics, morals, and right and wrong, they become aware of how they are being harmed by the current way of doing things (Maynard, 2019).

Eshe states that, "you can't have all of the other kinds of justice if you don't have environmental justice." She goes on to state that racism and sexism aren't going to matter if we can't get our basic necessities. She describes her process of becoming an environmental activist, recounting how her parents stood up for civil rights and that made her want to fight for her rights. Eshe sees the interconnectedness of how the climate system supports every system and she makes connection with civil rights. She tells us her ideas about why people do not see protecting the environment as important and these include self-interest and following the status quo. She also talks about why the lawsuit is so important:

> In the civil rights movements, judges had to step into the unknown. They didn't know what it would be like to not have segregation be a part of the law. And that's scary. In the same way judges don't know what it's going to be like to have stronger laws to protect the environment than they have now. But the price of not doing it, just like the price of not enforcing desegregation, is too high. (Our Children's Trust, 2012)

She says that her goal is to "act like an upstander not a bystander."

One of Ashley's early actions was to organize a litter clean-up crew in her town. In one scene, she is painting the nails of an elderly lady, who tells us how the two met. She threw out trash from her car and Ashley stopped her and told her to pick it up. The lady reflects and says she had done it all her life and never thought about who was going to pick this up and now she understands the young folks are doing it (Our Children's Trust, 2012b).

Glori speaks about how her younger sisters got her thinking about how choices affect them. She saw the "cloud machines" from factories and wondered how they were affecting the environment. She decided to become a vegetarian and eat locally because it cuts down on her carbon footprint. She speaks about working at a farmers' market since she was eight years old. She shares a memory of a blind woman picking up apples and saying that they were beautiful, even though they couldn't see them. She makes the connection to climate change. "It's a lot like climate change. You can't just deny all of the evidence that climate change is there just because we can't see it" (Our Children's Trust, 2019a).

In addition to telling us about how they came to climate activism, they also speak about why they have engaged in climate litigation. Ashley filed a state lawsuit in Pennsylvania in 2012, asking that they enact carbon mitigation laws. She talks about the importance of making connections between the health of the environment and health of people worldwide. "I want them [policymakers] to speak with a child who has asthma because they have a coal plant in their back yard. What they don't realize is that environmental destruction is the destruction of human health" (Our Children's Trust, 2012b). She says people thank her for cleaning up litter, but when governments try to pass regulations to clean the air, people react negatively because they can't see how the atmosphere is harmed.

Jaime's climate action started with letters to President Obama. Although she lives and experiences drought in Arizona, her first letters to him were about the Arctic Wildlife Refuge and Gulf of Mexico BP oil spill. President Obama wrote to her after her sixth letter to him and encouraged her and her generation to stay involved. At eleven years old, Jaime filed a lawsuit against Arizona Governor Janice Brewer and the Arizona Department of Environmental Quality to compel the state to develop a plan to mitigate global warming by reducing carbon emissions. She did not want financial compensation but instead a climate recovery plan (Our Climate Voices, 2019). Despite the power of her message, Butler lost the court case.

Miko is Jewish and as part of her bat mitzvah project she researched climate change and did a fundraiser for a nonprofit organization working in the Marshall Islands. This led to her becoming an ambassador for Plant for the Planet which teaches kids how to talk about climate change for policymakers. She wanted to find her place, given that she is from the Marshall Islands. This process raised her awareness about environmental racism. As she tells us, "Dismissing people of color who are impacted by climate change like my own people in the Marshall Islands is a form of environmental racism. People of color are especially marginalized in the climate change movement, even by people who are trying to help us." She puts forward a non-Western view of addressing climate change. She recounts how many people believe that it is optional to live a "greener" lifestyle and reducing waste. However, for Marshallese, there are climate change classes in the schools, and they learn about the threat of their island going underwater. "I fight not only for youth empowerment and representation in the United States, but also for the representation and survival of my people in the Marshall Islands" (Our Climate Voices, 2019c).

Glori petitioned the Department of Natural Resources (DNR) in Idaho to lower emissions by 6% per year to help stop climate change. They denied her petition, but she talks about how she plans to appeal it. In her testimony, she asks judges to think about children and their future.

Participating in climate litigation allows climate girls to take on technical identities. Their individual experiences inform their perspectives as they form their arguments that are taken seriously in the legal system and potentially influencing systemic change. Technofeminism, importantly, is mutual shaping of gender and technology. As the legal system is a form of technology, and as girls' stories are written into climate litigation, they are also taking on techno-identities as they come to identify as experts with their own goals for their lives. For example, Eshe describes herself in the following terms, "I am a French horn playing, basketball playing, systems thinker" (Our Children's Trust, 2012e). Ashley describes herself as, "a future engineer and policy maker" (Our Children's Trust, 2012b). Jaime describes herself as a Navajo artist.

Glori enjoys acting and talks about what she has learned through the process of being involved in the lawsuit. She states that with acting, you don't always get the part the first time, so it important not to give up. "If you keep trying over and over again, someone will listen to you" (Our Children's Trust, 2012a).

In the story of Kelsey in *Youth v. Gov,* she talks about how she romanticized protest and imagined herself as a "one girl revolution" wearing hiking boots and speaking for the trees. Now, through her involvement in the lawsuit, she sees that she is defending her home and the homes of all the youth involved in the film. She speaks about being excited about the lawsuit because it is democracy in action. It allows people to challenge authority when it is clear that those in power are not doing the right thing.

LAWYER UP GIRLS TAKE ON "TRUTHS"

Documentary is a visual form of storytelling that adds another kind of legitimacy and truth to an issue. Also, documentary adds to the girls' activist legacy and ensures their story lives on in the public sphere. The audience is different than a legal audience and, as Goodnight (2012) specified, the form of argument in the public sphere is necessarily different. This form of storytelling creates an intersection between the legal system and the public. Public sphere arguments need to transcend matters of the personal and technical to become part of the collective. All publics have to deliberate to solve the problems they confront. As Goodnight (2012) writes, "deliberative rhetoric is a form of argumentation through which citizens test and create social knowledge in order to uncover, assess, and resolve shared problems" (p. 1).

Part of the story of the *Juliana v. U.S.* case is how knowledge is contested and there is a battle over what counts as truth. In one of the troubling scenes in *Youth v. Gov,* the youth plaintiffs are giving their depositions about the harms done to them because of climate change. The lawyers for the defendants ask them very technical questions about climate change, such as how do you know that the snowpack is less than in previous years? What are your qualifications to talk about climate change? Avery spoke to us about this experience,

> that was one of the most anxiety inducing experiences of my life because they very much made me feel like one wrong move and I was gonna just screw it up and there's these like three lawyers and their fancy suits and their like Chanel watches and they walk into this room and they set down their big binders full of questions and then the lady comes in with the typewriter and she's typing what everyone saying and the second that you messed up the lawyer says oh oh can we go back 'cause I I don't I don't understand . . . it's like very much like an interrogation but you've done nothing wrong. (A. McRae, personal communication, August 9, 2021)

In the film, we see how knowledge about the negative impact of carbon emissions was known by the U.S. government since the 1960s, yet much of the documentation was not available to the public. There is a point in the film where we are in the basement of a former government employee who shares their archive of scientific reports on the impact of the fossil fuel industry, which serves as evidence for the central argument in the case that the U.S. government is intentionally violating kids' rights to a livable future. This scene illuminates how scientific knowledge is wrapped up in politics and economics.

One of the outcomes of girls' involvement in climate litigation is the critical consciousness that girls encounter that fuels their activism. Girls are advancing scientific arguments based on their own understanding of climate change and challenging accepted ways of thinking. In the process, they are entering into a technical realm normally reserved for the elite.

Avery and Sahara talk about the experience of being a part of the lawsuit and how it developed their skills beyond just understanding the law. Sahara spoke about how the lawsuit taught her about the legal system and empowered her to use her voice to speak out against injustice:

> this whole lawsuit has just been such a big part of my life and it's obviously taught me a lot more about the judicial system and the government and taught me a lot about environmental policy and opened my eyes a lot more. I think one of the biggest things it's done to shape me in the future is public speaking because I was like 10 or 11 in the beginning of this and I was, you know, completely scared of public speaking as most super young kids are and I would do it only when I when I had to and if people asked me. I would usually make an excuse or to say no and then at one point I realized like you just gotta put yourself in

these situations and then you'll get better at it and so I think I was like hey like I would like to work on my public speaking and so if there are opportunities that come up please let me know . . . that's been like a really interesting and visible switch. (S. Valentine, personal communication, August 9, 2021)

Avery also spoke about how her involvement in the lawsuit contributed to her mental health. She says that knowing that she is in a challenging situation with other kids who are also going through it with her helped keep her going. She was able to form community with the other plaintiffs and felt empowered that she was on a good path.

WHAT IS THE LAWYER UP CLIMATE GIRL EFFECT?

The very phrase "our children's trust" positions adults as protectors of children in the future. These girls and youth are telling the world, they want in. It is not a "normal" part of childhood to file lawsuits against governments for the right to a future. Yet here we are. Girls are bringing their serious concerns to the technical legal sphere for action and answers. Their arguments are made from their experiences, which taken together comprise the Lawyer Up Climate Girl Effect.

The Lawyer Up Climate Girl Effect centers girls' stories in the public sphere. These stories fan out and take different forms in our digital networked public. The compelling stories are videos, they are bundled together in inspiring collections, they are the basis of news and feature stories, they are a documentary film. These girls are empowered through their experience in the legal system—shaped by their involvement in the technical sphere—participating in furthering the fight by sharing their stories broadly. They are vouching, in Kempf (2021) terms, to reduce cognitive barriers and show others that it is easy to be involved in climate justice and in a variety of ways. To consider Wajcman's (2002) technofeminist perspective is to uncover how "technology is both a source and consequence of gender relations and vice versa" (p. 356). These girls' experience hold governments accountable through storytelling as legal argument and as public debates. In these global legal spheres, girls are far away from the confines of "childhood." This configuration arouses attention in the public sphere. The Lawyer Up Climate Girl Effect adds perspectives and humanizes what can seem abstract and out of reach. Their actions increase public understanding as they broaden the legal debates. This fuels the success of these lawsuits, hopefully slowing the pace of the climate crisis globally. Environmental activism is but one part of their lives, and they are more than their fight. They are kids being kids, they are involved in their communities and participating in school and family activities. Their ambitions and investments and struggles are all part of the story. The Lawyer Up Climate Girl Effect is about the personal, social, and technical consequences of these lawsuits.

Girls are seeking legal standing to sue and are plaintiffs in the process. At the same time, girls are creating a legacy. Their names and stories are written into legal documents, and they are helping to frame the arguments about why the government needs to protect their rights to a livable planet. As these girls continue to exercise their rights and be spokespeople in legal battles for healthy air, water, and soil, they grow in conviction that comes from witnessing grave injustice. The systems may not be in their favor and the fight is overwhelmingly unfair, but they continue with their knowledge, conviction, and persistence. Little by little, their cases make the human rights and Earth rights arguments and gain more traction. Environmental personhood is a promising legal position.

The climate crisis quickens with the turn of each season. The Lawyer Up girls humanize the legal battles through their techno-ecofeminist activism. All legal fights, especially those against governments, corporations, and corruption, cost money and take time. We can help them by getting involved and spreading the word about these legal battles. We need to do a better job of listening to these citizens of Earth and ignore the allure to feelings of guilt, which can lead to climate defeatism and inaction.

Chapter 8

The Future of the Climate Girl Effect

We started this project asking questions about climate girls, and we ended this project inspired by them. They themselves are not always inspired, which is clear in climate girl activist, Kelsey Juliana's statement, "I'm scared shitless for my future" (Cooper, 2021). Nevertheless, they are doing research to understand scientific arguments and political institutions. They are listening to each other, showing up for each other, and holding those in power to account. Despite the formidable obstacles in front of them, they have gained momentum. These climate girls are innovative and networked. Through their engagement with media, their participation in global climate summits, and their advocacy for the planet, they are creating social change and clearing a path for others. Like Wildemeersch et al.'s (2021) research on young sustainability activists, we too found them enacting "a new kind of 'public pedagogy' . . . [wherein] the young both educate themselves and the wider public" (p. 11). This reflects the growing trend of training citizen scientists to be involved in local knowledge production. The climate girls in our case studies are likely the first generation of iconic protagonists in the climate justice movement. A second generation is sure to rise.

A framework for the future emerged from our analysis of their activism and their solutions. In this chapter, we highlight the insights and interventions that make up this framework. First, we discuss how these climate girls are enacting citizenship now rather than waiting until some magical adulthood when they can participate. They have an intersectional and coalitional approach to their leadership, which is important for addressing a complex global phenomenon. Their participation in the mediasphere creates inroads and influence and they invite audiences to co-perform with them as they fight for climate justice. Finally, their techno-ecofeminist activism challenges established systems of inequality while creating new systems to address the climate crisis.

In the end, we offer suggestions for the way forward to support them as they will be the ones leading the next generation through the climate crisis.

CLIMATE GIRLS AS CITIZENS ACTING FOR THE EARTH

Some girl studies scholars have argued that the concept of "empowerment" needs to be understood in terms of power dynamics (or how much power they do have in a patriarchal system), but we find these girls enacting sustaining change. Even though they are criticized by adults for their age and not having enough knowledge to know the "truth" about science and politics, they are finding a new way forward that gives voice to their truths: what it is like to be a girl who experiences the climate crisis in ways that adults will not have to grapple with. Their lived experiences, either as transnational girls, Black girls, Indigenous girls, or girls suing governments, bring them to activism and adds another dimension to the importance of acting and to their own critical consciousness—an idea based in Paulo Freire's (1972) work. Critical consciousness comes as these activists learn to question the complexity and workings of power. When these climate activists try to influence voting or protest the construction of oil pipelines, they are having formative experiences. They learn to understand and navigate systems, and they learn who is lying and why. Their activist experiences will continue to evolve.

The climate activist girls we studied are experiencing the challenges and opportunities of leading a youth movement as youth. They are empowered through the agency they can exercise in this capacity. Some girls see local problems and start grassroots organizations. Some take risks by refusing to carry on as usual. These climate activists are empowered as they learn to create technologies to solve the problems they encounter or raise the money to lift up their communities. Also empowering is the support of the United Nations and other established networks and organizations that come alongside of them and support their activism. They accept the invitations to speak, write, train, share, organize. They rise as public figures, and their spheres of influence enlarge. These climate activists are empowered and working together as networked transnational activists. Not only does their initiative make material and symbolic differences, but their initiative also fuels their hope. Through their activist digital networks and organizations, there is a sense of togetherness. They are not alone, they show up for each other, and they have each other's backs against the climate of hostility and ignorance they face. Finally, on empowerment and agency, these climate girls exert pressure on public agendas about climate crises.

These activists envision a way of being together in the world that is intersectional, cooperative, and inclusive. They are putting what they envision into action. Their strategies range from empowering other youth (e.g., you're never too small to make a difference), to speaking as youth (e.g., we are just kids who shouldn't have to be doing this work), to calling out adults for their lack of maturity and inability to take seriously the climate crisis. One theme we want to highlight is the ongoing importance of a strongly worded letter. It offers an avenue that allows girls to enact citizenship appropriate for their age, yet quickly instigated more action. Greta's school strike began with a letter to members of Swedish Parliament. Little Miss Flint wrote a letter to the President of the United States who responded with much-needed attention. A group of Indigenous girls organized a 500-mile run to deliver a letter to the Army Corps of Engineers about a flawed decision they needed to reverse. In 1989, a grassroots environmental organization began with a letter from a nine-year-old that was printed on a billboard. It read in part, "Mr. President, if you ignore this letter we will all die of pollution." The rhetorical form of a letter is still a successful way to raise awareness and start movements, especially for women. Letter writing has long been a form of women's expression and is considered a feminine form of communication that made possible their voice in the public sphere.

These climate girls take themselves seriously and are doing serious work. They are actors in the public sphere, pressuring politicians, asking questions, and researching the science and policy of the climate crisis. They are invested in a future they envision. Similar to Thomas (2020), we find climate girls acting as citizens now rather than waiting until they become adults, which offers new insights into how to honor and encourage youth in social movements.

INTERSECTIONAL GIRLHOOD STUDIES

Our case studies of climate girls offer several contributions to the field of girlhood studies. First, this generation of climate girls are consciously intersectional. They are aware of how systems of oppression, including racism, heterosexism, and capitalism, impact the climate crisis as well as their own lived experiences as girls. They recognize the limitations of their own positionalities and do not speak for others. Climate girls such as Greta Thunberg and Jamie Margolin advocate for those who are most impacted by the climate crisis.

These climate girls are coalitional and use their platforms to support one another. One thing we noticed was how many forces try to divide them and reinforce the gendered trope of girls as backstabbing and competitive. Yet, climate girls are savvy and staying focused on their overall message.

They are in a seemingly impossible situation of fighting the practices of the massive fossil fuel industry, the practices of global capitalism, and the ingrained misogyny that stem from patriarchy. #MMIW is a good example of how all three comingle and result in the femicide crisis plaguing Indigenous communities. Indigenous climate girls, and those who work in solidarity with them, are fighting on the frontlines of oil pipelines and mining and this form of activism is dangerous. They are in remote areas where their safety is threatened. The newer exploration into transnational girlhood by scholars including Vanner (2019) and Keller (2021) provide insight into how we should understand girls' participation in climate activism as they cross borders and engage with what Daggett (2018) calls "petro-masculinity." Climate girls are challenging patriarchal cultures and are subject to misogynistic attacks.

The other contribution from climate girls are the ways they bring attention to how climate change impacts girls. Girls and women already face discrimination and inequality, and the climate crisis compounds these problems (Kwauck et al., 2019). They are at increased risk of violence, child marriage, dropping out of school, and food and economic insecurity. Climate girls see that there is no climate justice without social justice, and they center this message through their actions. This intersectional framework is essential for addressing the disparities that arise.

Because they challenge cultural stereotypes, climate girls' leadership carries a number of implications for challenging expectations of what constitutes being a girl. These challenges will differ by culture, necessarily, but these girls speak from a variety of subject positions, and they take on a variety of roles. As they demonstrate, they are more than their activism. They are models, heroes, teenagers, dolls, murals, artists, students, sisters, spokespeople for corporations. These multiple identities allow them to participate in activism in different ways and allow them to draw on their own experiences to make necessary change. For example, in her book *Youth to Power,* Margolin (2020) stresses the importance of self-care in order to avoid burning out.

These girls begin their activism at a young age and grow into teens and young adults. While we find a lot to be positive about, these girls face obstacles. First, they are girls, and their bodies argue nonverbally (DeLuca, 1999). However, bodies of young girls are the center of the images of media coverage and because of this, they are spectacular objects to be consumed in different ways rather than heard. Their bodies and their messages are used on international stages. They are interviewed for publications, they receive leadership awards, they are used to signal corporations' commitments to social change. This isn't surprising given what happens with adult women of influence. Their activism gets buried and downplayed, and they are commonly constrained by hate. Everything about how they show up, their appearance for example, is the subject of intense criticism. You can see in Mari's social media, that she has to call out the way her message is hijacked when her body becomes the focus of attention. Fat-shaming messages are directed at Greta on her social media. In the *Youth V. Gov* documentary, adult lawyers bully girl plaintiffs and question their credibility through using girls' own scientific arguments against them. Bullying also comes from within their activist circles. In our interview with Kehkashan Basu who started The Green Hope Foundation when she was twelve years old, she recounted her early experiences with bullying:

> I've faced so many challenges throughout my journey and the first thing that I started off so young and on top of that being a girl. I started by facing threats of physical abuse, stalking, I was a victim of cyberbullying, you know death threats, things like that, and it continues to this day, and even when I was twelve, I was elected as global coordinator for the United Nations environment program for children and youth and that made me the youngest person and the only minor to ever hold a position and very surprisingly I received tremendous harassment from older youth who literally organized like social media hate campaigns against me, who used to send horrible emails and gave me and my parents sleepless nights because it was supposed to be a safe space, but people not liking, the older youth and now that I think about it, all of whom were guys, not liking the fact that there was a twelve-year-old girl in a position of power. I think that, you know, there are tremendous challenges and when you try to do good work there are always going to be naysayers and obstacles. (K. Basu, personal communication, February 21, 2021)

Autumn Peltier of Wiikwemkoong First Nation is another example of a climate activist who experiences bullying as part of her climate activism. They are targets on social media and within their communities. As we have shown, these girls are bullied and vilified at the same time they are celebrated and revered.

These obstacles don't stop them. They are resilient and hopeful even as they fight climate defeatism and eco-anxiety in their own and each other's lives. In the end, the clock still ticks down to the tipping point and their choices are few. They can either back down or keep pushing forward together through these many obstacles. Avery McRae, a plaintiff in the *Juliana vs United States* lawsuit, talked about her epiphany about adults in this way:

> [being treated negatively] also really helped me kind of like just get over my need for validation from everybody that I was around because we live in a very liberal town but there's still people that did not agree with all your doing . . . they would tell me to go play with my Barbie dolls to get off the courts and like go do my own kid thing, right? And I very quickly learned that I do not need to be accepted by everyone, and I did not any validation from adults who weren't gonna do anything anyways and that was definitely like a weird thing for a ten

year old to learn because you kind of grow up with this mentality of adults know everything, they're the ones that support you, they're the ones that help you and that was quickly like ripped away from me. I was like, "oh that is not true," like I am very much in this with me and with the people who are actually going to support me . . . adults in the world are gonna lift up the youth like absolutely not. It's going to be where you were going to have to kind of push through this crowd of people who are like, "hey, what are you doing? Like, why are you doing that?" and you just kind of keep going, and I think that's something different that I was not prepared for going into this but I'm ultimately glad that I did. (A. McRae, personal communication, August 9, 2021)

What we learned through our research on these climate girls is that we need to honor and support the ways in which these girls are navigating these spaces. Additionally, we can learn from how they utilize intersectionality to understand and work for climate justice.

INFLUENCE IN THE MEDIASPHERE

The mainstream media systems these climate girl activists navigate is a corporate, profit-driven media system that doesn't value diversity on either side—journalists or sources. This situation leads to a narrow, Western-dominated neoliberal narrative of spectacular, harmless, eco-activists who are remarkable for their bravery but ignored in their calls to action (Grady, 2021). Many of these climate girls are trying to interrupt this problem of being constructed in spectacular ways, and they get frustrated with media frames of them. Media frames are wildly off base, too narrow, and often reinforce gender norms. Climate girls respond to media coverage about their activism and work together in a digital network to call out problematic coverage. Additionally, they call out media coverage for creating conflict that pits youth against government or fierce girls against the political establishment and men, where no conflict exists. For example, Vanessa Nakate, the Ugandan environmental activist, was cropped out of a news photograph about girl climate activists at the World Economic Forum. The optics betrayed the racial bias and structural racism at work at the Associated Press (AP). AP later apologized after public outcry. Climate girls show us the importance of pressuring media practitioners to reform their coverage of the climate crisis and the need to include solution-telling and non-Western narratives.

Also, the tendency for media coverage to highlight girl climate activists as extraordinary serves to disempower ordinary climate action. Sahara Valentine, a plaintiff in the *Juliana vs United States* lawsuit explains how the spectacular is an obstacle to ordinary climate activism. In her words,

I often see with media coverage a lot of like super awesome and inspiring people getting interviewed. They're doing these like really big things . . . you know that can be, maybe like suing the government or like Greta or a lot of these like sort of well-known climate warriors or what have you. And I think that for everyday readers can be hard because then you read, or you look at these articles or see this media coverage and it makes it seem difficult if you want to make a difference. It kind of portrays it as like you need to be doing this whole huge things like suing the government or missing like every Friday school day to go sit out. . . . and that can make it super difficult. A question we often get is like what can other folks do that aren't suing government? I think that is something that the media can work on is trying to also share stories of folks who aren't doing these whole huge things to make it more maybe like accessible or for folks who aren't suing the government for them to see what they can do. (S. Valentine, personal communication, August 9, 2021)

This kind of media coverage creates a sense that these lone climate warrior girls are taking care of it, and they will save us. In many cases, we see the climate girl activists use the language of unity as part of their activism. Their constant message is that they are not against each other, but against the system that leads to extinction. There is strength in unity. Many social movements of the past lost strength through fracture. Sometimes these fractures appeared from internal strife—a common challenge of plurality. Sometimes social movement fractures were engineered externally and imposed as a strategy of division. We find these climate activist girls have anticipated this threat. For example, Tokata and Greta both speak about their work together in Washington, D.C., and the strategy not to let jealousies divide them. Artemisa Xakriabá is another who doesn't see different climate activists' work as distinct because "the fight for Mother Earth is the mother of all other fights." Xiye Bastida explains that "we refuse to let attempts at division affect our purpose" (Johnson & Wilkinson, 2020, p. 5). Across difference and different actions, these climate activists work together. They consciously refuse to be divided by media and culture, and they come from a position of strength in their resistance. These climate activist girls use social media to create counternarratives, yet social media isn't a safe haven for them. Social media has accelerated the spread of information but also has pitfalls, such as disinformation, weaponization of social media, networked misogyny, all of which serve to undermine climate girls' activism.

Social media platforms and their connective affordances connect humanity now more than ever. We can now bear witness to different climate struggles, resistance, and progress toward taking down massive corrupt industry and governments all over the world. Through the affordances of social media, climate girl activists put a continuous flag on the issues. Adults created Earth Day in the 1970s. These climate girls can and do make every week an Earth

Day. For example, Mari's #WednesdaysforWater posts spread weekly awareness about places that need clean water. Greta's #FridaysforFuture is a weekly reminder of how climate activism is routine. And #MatriarchMonday's are reminders of the need to shift narratives about Indigenous women's lives for a more useful future.

TECHNO-ECOFEMINISM

Techno-ecofeminism has the potential to contribute to long-term change because it harnesses knowledge from those who are left out of the sphere of design and challenges established systems, advocating for more equitable ones. It makes transparent the mutual shaping of gender and technology, and through this transparency, offers insight into how to make it better. These climate girls use technologies to resist as well as to critique established systems while creating new ones through their techno-ecofeminist activism. They are designing technologies to address a range of social equalities as they fight for a healthy, unharmed planet. Their activism necessarily challenges patriarchal ways of knowing, showing the gendered and racial implications of established ways of doing things. In their interventions, they are advocating for technological design that can lead to better solutions, such as apps to track litter cleanups. Mari's branded water filter, for example, addresses the structural racism of failing infrastructures in poor communities of color, while attune to sustainable options. The legacy of girls' stories of climate destruction that are written into climate litigation and in legal spaces traditionally reserved for those with access to the legal system is a different example of techno-ecofeminist interventions.

The use of technologies for protection is another form of techno-ecofeminism these climate activist girls used. Green Hope Foundation's founder, Basu, recognized the importance of safety on the ground. As a practice, Green Hope does not advertise the locations of their youth training. It is only after an action is complete that they share their successes and experience on social media. Avery McRae uses technology for protection as she shields herself from comments on social media:

> There's definitely part of me that is tempted to go online and like scroll through those comments and be like OK, what are people saying? And then I have to be like, no, it doesn't matter what they're saying. It does not affect me in the slightest, like has nothing to do with me and I'm not gonna let that affect me 'cause that's dumb. And I'm like a very sensitive person. If I read something rude, I will be very very hurt by it for a long time, and so I've kind of had to like

train myself to not do that 'cause it's not productive at all. (A. McRae, personal communication, August 9, 2021)

A final way we see techno-ecofeminist strategies is through greentrolling, which is a climate activist response. climate activist girls expose corporations who are engaging in greenwashing. Greenwashing is the term used to describe corporations' attempts to create environmentally friendly public impression. For example, Greta talks about greenwashing and the fashion industry,

"Many are making it look as if the fashion industry are starting to take responsibility, by spending fantasy amounts on campaigns where they portray themselves as 'sustainable,' 'ethical,' 'green,' 'climate neutral' and 'fair.' But let's be clear: This is almost never anything but pure greenwashing. You cannot mass produce fashion or consume 'sustainably' as the world is shaped today. That is one of the many reasons why we will need a system change" (Pattinson, 2021, para. 11).

These climate activists respond to greenwashing by making fun of the phony corporate logic and thereby undoing bogus and expensively produced corporate claims (Telford, 2021).

Since climate girls are developing innovative and local solutions and interventions based on their experiences, there are many opportunitites to learn from their techno-ecofeminist activism. Additionally, since research on gender equality in STEM fields shows that girls are more interested in coding when they can see the social impact of their actions, finding ways to encourage techno-ecofeminism can be a useful strategy for including more climate girls in these efforts.

FORWARD THINKING

Climate girls give us hope, yet the hope projected on them is not enough. We note the importance of their resilience as they realize adults are failing them and that they stand to inherit insurmountable problems. We know that kids paying attention to the climate crisis suffer eco-anxiety and struggle with an impulse to opt out. Margolin recently acknowledged the reality of climate defeatism among her generation. Some young people feel like it is hopeless to do anything to help the planet. One way adults can be allies is to help them navigate these feelings so that young people can continue to adapt to what projections tell us will only get worse. We have to be able to deal with the realities of the climate crisis with them. This is where we need a better connection between scholarship and activism because we cannot keep pinning our hope on a few activist girls. Different relationships and a different set of values is required to deal with the climate crisis.

Relationally speaking, we question why adults are threatened and distanced from climate girl activists. What nerve are they hitting? What will girls' environmental activism look like in the future as environmental degradation continues to be an issue as they grow up? bell hooks (2013), in her critique of Sheryl Sandberg, chief operating officer of Meta platforms and author of women's leadership book, *Lean In*, encourages us to dig deep, change unjust systems and work in a coalitional way to build an alternative world, not rely on "faux feminism" that encourages girls and women to "lean in" rather than challenge structural oppression. According to Brown (2016), "digging deep demands self-reflection; that we consider how and why we participate in behaviors and systems we know can be harmful to ourselves and to others" (p. 4). Climate girls are asking us to challenge these systems, yet few people are. Instead, we are relying on their hope and energy to lead the way. At the same time, Brown urges that "if we really want more girls who speak up and act out in the face of injustice in our schools and communities, we have to understand and invest in the conditions that support them" (p. 5). Some of these climate activists talk about their relationships with adults who want to protect them and pretend everything is going to be fine. These climate girls see right through these attempts to placate them because they are paying attention to science and educating themselves, talking with each other and facing adults who do not change. Affectively, their trust turns to anger. Climate girl activist Avery McRae asks that adults show up differently. In her words, we need:

> Parents showing their own emotion towards the climate crisis because it's . . . so strong that it's like overwhelming, and [parents are] like, "I don't want my kids to see that I'm that I'm struggling with this," but like one of the most powerful moments in my entire life was my parents both breaking down with me—like full on emotional crying because of something in the lawsuit because of just climate change in general. Like there are so many moments where you kind of have to let yourself be like emotionally raw with her kid because your kid knows what's going on and if you're trying to just hide it [and] be like, "Oh no it's fine, it's fine, like, yes, it sucks but it's OK, like I'm fine," like that doesn't do anything 'cause they know that something's not right. Like they understand you know? Pick up on energy. And I think that there's often times . . . like, oh, well, you know, my kid can cry about it, but I can't cry, that like I need to be strong for my kid but you both can. (A. McRae, personal communication, August 9, 2021)

Avery is asking for family alliances. These girls often call for intergenerational activism. The risk is always that adults take over in a negative cycle based on protection or superiority. Being ready and willing to listen will help create the intergenerational alliance needed. For this to work, a more realistic kind of affective labor is needed, especially in the areas of trust and truth-telling.

Examples of inclusive and diverse communities engaging the climate crisis exist. In those places, where everyone is working together to mitigate harm, where people are climate action planning, where people are working toward creative solutions, where people are attending to Indigenous knowledges for biodiversity and life, solution telling strategies are emerging. Important to this type of response is radical empathy at any age. "Radical empathy requires taking actions that will not only help that person but will also improve our society" (Givens, 2020). Peschau (2021) argues that radical empathy could be a key difference to effectively responding to the exigence we have to face to continue to live as creatures on Earth. "Radical empathy allows us to overcome cultural and societal divides while acknowledging our different dispositions and experiences. Rather than conceiving of ourselves as one humanity, it reminds us of our many humanities" (Peschau, 2021).

COVID-19 has shown us the beauty and the beast of human potential. We see that through crises, communities can support each other and offer crucial networks for survival where possible. COVID-19 makes visible how human life is vulnerable and fragile, yet the collective intelligence that can come from creative local and global interventions to deal with this crisis shows the potential of resilience. Yet, there has also been a dark side to the crisis: hoarding resources, blaming anti-vaxxers, disinformation campaigns, and nativism and xenophobia are just a few of the things we have witnessed over the past eighteen months. We have also seen increased public protests related to racial and economic injustice. Through this moment, climate girls are even more convicted in their activism. They continue to show up virtually and in person for Fridays for Future, they hold online panels and webinars to train youth activists, and they refuse to be stopped in their tracks. If anything, they are even more energized by their work because of the experience of living through the pandemic and what being connected has done for their work.

The climate crisis is bigger than we are, so we need everyone's time, energy, and activism, and everyone recognizing the devastation of capitalism and neoliberal logics. To do that, we have to become critical of systems that cause the crisis. Capitalism is a major part of the climate crisis, so moving as fast as we can away from extractive economies and profit orientations, no matter how "green" they may appear, is the right way forward. We notice both a range of awareness among climate girls as well as a range of ways they are participating in capitalist systems. These climate activist girls create the materials they need to support and sustain their movement. They are writing books to help other activists, raising money through selling T-shirts and PopSockets, becoming brand influencers with companies. They are raising awareness as they raise money. Through purchasing, people take on climate activist identities and have climate-related conversations. One problem is that commodities are part of the problem, so purchasing ignores the harmful ways in which capitalism exploits the environment. In this way, commodity activism is both helpful and problematic. The climate activist girls are also creating trainings and educational materials and offer them through their grassroots organizations, which broadens the scope of how climate activists can act and sets the agenda for what they think needs to be done.

In the end, it is important to move beyond Western binary thinking that sees Earth as separate from humans and idolizes capitalism as the most efficient system. Indigenous scientists such as Robin Wall Kimmerer of the Potawatomi urge us to see the reciprocal ways in which humans and the natural world intertwine to learn how to restore and protect ecosystems, work toward sustainable development, and develop climate resiliency as we navigate the climate crisis. We offer this quote from Kimmerer (2013) as a North star, "Even a wounded world is feeding us. Even a wounded world holds us, giving us moments of wonder and joy. I choose joy over despair. Not because I have my head in the sand, but because joy is what the earth gives me daily and I must return the gift" (p. 327).

References

ABC News Australia (2019, September 30). The Greta Thunberg helpline [Video]. YouTube. https://www.youtube.com/watch?v=KIP2vukNOPc

Abraham, B, & Jayemanne, D. (2017). Where are all the climate change games? Locating digital games' response to climate change. Transformations. 30, 75–94

Aguilar, L., Granat, M., & Owren, C. (2015). *Roots for the future: The landscape and way forward on gender and climate change.* IUCN & GGCA. https://wedo.org/wp-content/uploads/2015/12/Roots-for-the-future-final-1.pdf

Ahmed, S. (2017). *Living a feminist life.* Duke University Press.

Ahmed, S. (2009). Embodying diversity: Problems and paradoxes for Black feminists. *Race Ethnicity and Education, 12*(1), 41–52.

Alimahomed, S., & Keeler, B. (1995). The youth role in creating a healthy future for the earth: An examination of the link between collective action for the environment and the emotional health of children. *Environmental Health Perspective,* Suppl. 6, 63–6. https://10.1289/ehp.95103s663

American Association of University Women Educational Foundation. (2000). *Tech savvy: Educating girls in the new computer age.* American Association of University Women.

Anshelm, J., & Hultman, M. (2014). A green fatwā? climate change as a threat to the masculinity of industrial modernity. *Null, 9*(2), 84–96. https://10.1080/18902138.2014.908627

Arthur, T. O. (2021). Been exploring the globe: Black women's internationalism and race and gender and counter-power and truth in the Instagram digi-sphere. *Florida Communication Journal, 49*(1), 47–75.

Associated Press. (2020, January 30). Pine Ridge's Tokata Iron Eyes turns superhero in Marvel show. *Lakota Times.* https://www.lakotatimes.com/articles/pine-ridges-tokata-iron-eyes-turns-superhero-in-marvel-show/

Bagley, K. (2019). *Meet Xiye Bastida Patrick, the New York version of Greta Thunberg.* Bulletin of the Atomic Scientists. https://thebulletin.org/2019/11/meet-xiye-bastida-patrick-the-bronx-version-of-greta-thunberg/

Baig, E. C. (2018, November 11). Google girl gets girls into the game but designing apps for your mobile phone. *USA Today.* https://www.usatoday.com/story/tech/

talkingtech/2018/11/08/teen-girls-design-android-games-you-can-now-get-google-play/1920479002/

Banet-Weiser, S., & Miltner, K. M. (2016). #MasculinitySoFragile: Culture, structure, and networked misogyny. *Feminist Media Studies, 16*(1), 171–174. doi:10.1080/14680777.2016.1120490

Banks, A. [@Arron_ banks]. (2019, August 14). *Freak yachting accidents do happen in August.* [Tweet]. Twitter. https://twitter.com/arron_banks/status/1161747086616010752?lang=en

Barker, L. J., & Aspray, W. (2006). The state of research on girls and IT. In J. M. Cohoon, & W. Aspray (Eds.), *Women and information technology: Research on underrepresentation* (pp. 3–54). MIT Press.

Barrett, V. (2018, August 2). "You're the naive one": Youth activist's open letter to a candidate for governor. *The Guardian.* https://www.theguardian.com/us-news/2018/aug/02/climate-youth-activism-scott-wagner-naive

Bashi, G., Martellotte, L., Modungwa, B., & Olmos, M. E. (2018). Young feminists' creative strategies to challenge the status quo: A view from FRIDA. *Gender & Development, 26*(3), 439–457.

Bennett, W. L., & Segerberg, A. (2012). The logic of connective action: Digital media and the personalization of contentious politics. *Information, Communication & Society, 15*(5), 739–768.

Bent, E. (2020). This is not another girl-power story: Reading Emma González as a public feminist intellectual. *Signs: Journal of Women in Culture & Society, 45*(4), 795–816. https://10.1086/707796

Bernier, M. [@MaximeBernier]. (2019, Sept. 2) *@GretaThunberg is clearly mentally unstable. Not only autistic, but obsessive-compulsive, eating disorder, depression and lethargy, and she lives in a constant state of fear.* [Tweet]. Twitter. https://twitter.com/MaximeBernier/status/1168579736278380547

Bernier, M. [@MaximeBernier]. (2019a, Sept. 2). *I'm also concerned about all the children that @GretaThunberg has irresponsibly encouraged to skip school, or who have become more anxious, distressed, and in some cases suicidal because they believe they have no future.* [Tweet]. Twitter. https://twitter.com/MaximeBernier/status/1168580699869384709

Bernier, M. [@MaximeBernier]. (2019b, Sept. 2). *She has become an influential figure in a movement that is a threat to our prosperity and civilisation. If she wants to play that role, she should be denounced and attacked.* [Tweet]. Twitter. https://twitter.com/MaximeBernier/status/1168581010340089858

Bilandzic, H., Kalch, A., & Soentgen, J. (2017). Effects of goal framing and emotions on perceived threat and willingness to sacrifice for climate change. *Science Communication, 39*(4), 466–491. https://doi.org/10.1177/1075547017718553

Binnie, I. (2019, December 19). *Activist Thunberg turns spotlight on Indigenous struggle at climate.* Reuters. https://www.reuters.com/article/us-climate-change-accord-greta/activist-thunberg-turns-spotlight-on-indigenous-struggle-at-climate-summit-idUSKBN1YD1J5

Biswas, S. (2020, February 15). *Disha Ravi: The jailed Indian activist linked to Greta Thunberg.* BBC News. https://www.bbc.com/news/world-asia-india-56068522

Blakemore, E. (2016, July 28). How Sojourner Truth used photography to help end slavery. *Smithsonian Magazine*. https://www.smithsonianmag.com/smart-news/how-sojourner-truth-used-photography-help-end-slavery-180959952/

Blay, S., & Piotrowitcz, R. (2000). The awfulness of lawfulness: Some reflections on the tension between international and domestic law. *Australian Yearbook of International Law, 21*, 1–19.

Bogost, I. (2008). The rhetoric of video games. In K. Salen (Ed.), *The ecology of games: Connecting youth, games, and learning* (pp. 117–140). MIT Press.

boyd, d. (2010). Social networking sites as networked publics: Affordances, dynamics, and implications. In Z. Papacharissi (Ed.), *Networked self: Identity, community, and culture on social network sites* (pp. 39–58). Routledge.

Brigham, M. & Mabrey, P. (2018). "The original homeland security, fighting terrorism since 1492": A chrono-controversy. In C. R. Kelly & J. E. Black (Eds.), *Decolonizing Native American rhetoric: Communicating self-determination* (pp. 104–124). Peter Lang.

Brockington, D. (2009). *Celebrity and the environment: Fame, wealth and power in conservation*. Bloomsbury Publishing.

Brough, A. R., & Wilkie, J. E. B. (2017). Men resist green behavior as unmanly. *Scientific American*. https://www.scientificamerican.com/article/men-resist-green-behavior-as-unmanly/

Brown, L. M. (2016). *Powered by girl: A field guide for supporting youth activists*. Beacon Press.

Brown, R. N. (2009). *Black girlhood celebration: Toward a hip-hop feminist pedagogy (vol. 5)*. Peter Lang.

Buchner, J. (2016). 2016 me to we winner: Autumn Peltier. *Canadian Living*. https://www.canadianliving.com/life-and-relationships/community-and-current-events/article/2016-me-to-we-winner-autumn-peltier

Bullard, R. D., & Johnson, G. S. (2000). Environmentalism and public policy: Environmental justice: Grassroots activism and its impact on public policy decision making. *Journal of Social Issues, 56*(3), 555–578.

Bussey, J., Davenport, M. A., Emery, M. R., & Carroll, C. (2016). "A lot of it comes from the heart": The nature and integration of ecological knowledge in tribal and nontribal forest management. *Journal of Forestry, 114*(2), 97–107. https://doi.org/10.5849/jof.14-130

Butler, L. J., Scammell, M. K., & Benson, E. B. (2016). The Flint, Michigan, water crisis: A case study in regulatory failure and environmental injustice. *Environmental Justice, 9*(4), 93–97.

Carey, M. C., & Lichtenwalter, J. (2020). "Flint can't get in the hearing": The language of urban pathology in coverage of an American public health crisis. *Journal of Communication Inquiry, 44*(1), 26–47. https://10.1177/0196859919833794

CBC News (2018, March 21). The teen fighting to protect Canada's water—meet Autumn Peltier [Video]. YouTube. https://www.youtube.com/watch?v=xqdE_7OZaqE&t=4s

Cerny, B. L. (2021). *16-year-old environmental activist doing great things*. PowWows.com. https://www.powwows.com/sixteen-year-old-environmental-activist-doing-great-things/

Chan, L. S. (2018). Liberating or disciplining? A technofeminist analysis of the use of dating apps among women in urban China. *Communication Culture & Critique, 11*(2), 298–314.

Chazan, M., & Baldwin, M. (2019). Granny solidarity: Understanding age and generational dynamics in climate justice movements. *Studies in Social Justice, 13*(2), 244–261.

Chen, H. (2021, May 21). *Chinese media just tried to fat-shame Greta Thunberg*. Vice. https://www.vice.com/en/article/5db3g3/china-climate-change-greta-thunberg

Chowdhury, R. (2019, November 29). Woman of the year 2019: Autumn Peltier. *Chatelaine*. https://www.chatelaine.com/living/autumn-peltier-woman-of-the-year-2019/

Cimons, M. (2020, September 19). Meet Xiye Bastida, America's Greta Thunberg. *The Peril and Promise*. https://www.pbs.org/wnet/peril-and-promise/2019/09/meet-xiye-bastida-americas-greta-thunberg/

Citron, D. (2014). *Hate crimes in cyberspace*. MIT Press.

Clark, L. S., & A. Hinzo, (2019) Digital Survivance: Mediatization and the sacred in the tribal digital activism of the #NoDAPL movement. *Journal of Religion, Media and Digital Culture 8*(1), 76–104

Clinton, H. R. (2017). *What happened*. Simon and Schuster.

CNN (2018, February 17). Florida student Emma Gonzalez to lawmakers and gun advocates: 'We call BS.' CNN. https://www.cnn.com/2018/02/17/us/florida-student-emma-gonzalez-speech/index.html

Cohen, C. J., & Jackson, S. J. (2016). Ask a feminist: A conversation with Cathy J. Cohen on Black Lives Matter, feminism, and contemporary activism. *Signs: Journal of Women in Culture and Society, 41*(4), 775–792.

Cohen, R. (2021, October 20). Prominent NYU activists publicize sexual assault allegations against each other. *Washington Square News*. https://nyunews.com/news/2021/10/20/jamie-margolin-emma-tang-sexual-assault-allegations/

Collins, P. H. (2009). *Black feminist thought: Knowledge, consciousness, and the politics of empowerment* (2nd ed.). Routledge.

Cooper, C. (Director). (2021). *Youth V. Gov*. [Film]. Barrelmaker Productions.

Copeny, M. [@LittleMissFlint]. (2011, July 11). *You can by your kids all the stop brands, that still don't mean you know how to dress em #imjustsayin* [Tweet]. Twitter. https://twitter.com/LittleMissFlint/status/90658871256940544?s=20

Copeny, M. (2019). The Flint water crisis began 5 years ago. This 11-year-old activist knows it's still not over. *Elle*. https://www.elle.com/culture/career-politics/a27253797/little-miss-flint-water-crisis-five-years/

Copeny, M. [@LittleMissFlint]. (2020a, March 13). *Are you upset by standing in long lines, prices on essentials being raised for profit, and stores running out of the items you need to survive? Flint residents have been dealing with these feelings for years when it comes to water. #CoronaOutbreak#Coronoa* [Tweet]. Twitter. https://twitter.com/littlemissflint/status/1238700429183201280

Copey, M. [@littlemissflint]. (2020b, October 4). *Who can guess the dance move I'm teaching Uncle Joe? This pic is from the last day the world was open back in March* [Photograph]. Instagram. https://www.instagram.com/p/CF8c0vbnd5t/?utm_source=ig_web_copy_link

Copey, M. [@littlemissflint]. (2020c October 30). *Balancing between being a student, and activist, a philanthropist, and a normal kid is hard sometimes. But having a versatile @asususa Chromebokk Flip C434* [Photo]. https://www.instagram.com/p/CG_Jiawnmpd/

Copey, M. [@LittleMissFlint]. (2021a, January 9). *I made it 8 days into 2021 before I got called a racial slur* [Tweet]. https://mobile.twitter.com/LittleMissFlint/status/1348089645981175808

Copey, M. [@LittleMissFlint]. (2021b, January 15). *This is what the water aisle at our local Walmart looks like. The water crisis is far from over. It's why I fight to get my filters to people that need it the most. #Flint #ThisIsAmerica* [Tweet]. https://twitter.com/LittleMissFlint/status/1350265094207381506

Copey, M. [@LittleMissFlint]. (2021c, February 18). *What is happening in Texas is the biggest failure of the government to take care of its citizens since the Flint Water Crisis (which is still not resolved)* [Tweet]. https://twitter.com/littlemissflint/status/1362542173506445315

Copey, M. [@LittleMissFlint]. (2021d, February 19). *These water lines in Texas are all too familiar. The people there are suffering. As soon as we can, I will be getting filters for those in need in Texas. Want to help send filters to help? Donate below* [Tweet]. https://twitter.com/LittleMissFlint/status/1362932139633897472

Copey, M. [@LittleMissFlint]. (2021e, March 13). *Her life mattered then, it matters now and it will matter tomorrow. Justice for #BreonnaTaylor now and forever* [Tweet]. https://twitter.com/LittleMissFlint/status/1370941221133242369

Copey, M. [@LittleMissFlint]. (2021f, March 15). *And now kids are going into schools filled with lead lines that have been sitting for months. It's bad all around* [Tweet]. https://twitter.com/LittleMissFlint/status/1371551130266767365

Copey, M. [@LittleMissFlint]. (2021g, March 22). *This #WorldWaterDay comes as we approach the 7 year anniversary of the #FlintWaterCrisis, and the most heartbreaking thing is that Flint is not the only city still dealing with toxic water, it's a national issue. Help me help those without clean water* [Tweet]. https://twitter.com/LittleMissFlint/status/1374020523051614209

Copey, M. (2021). *About Mari*. Mari Copey. https://www.maricopeny.com/about

Corbett, C., & Hill, C. (2015). *Solving the equation: The variable for women's success in engineering and computing*. AAUW. https://www.aauw.org/app/uploads/2020/03/Solving-the-Equation-report-nsa.pdf

Corsaro, W. (1997). *The sociology of childhood*. Pine Forge Press.

Cowan, R. S. (1983). *More work for mother: The ironies of household technology from the open hearth to the microwave*. Basic Books.

Crandall, H., & Cunningham, C. M. (2016). Media ecology and hashtag activism: #Kaleidoscope. *Explorations in Media Ecology, 15*(1), 21–32.

Cunningham, C. M. (2011). Girl game designers. *New Media & Society, 13*(8), 1373–1388.

Cunningham, C. M. (2016). She designs therefore she is?: Evolving understandings of video game design. In K. D. Valentine, & L. J. Jensen (Eds.), *Examining the evolution of gaming and its impact on social, cultural, and political perspectives* (pp. 147–169). IGI Global.

Daggett, C. (2018) Petro-masculinity: Fossil fuels and authoritarian desire. *Millennium: Journal of International Studies, 47*(1), 25–44. doi:10.1177/0305829818775817

Dave, A., Ndulue, E. B. & Schwartz-Henderson, L. (2020). *Targeting Greta Thunberg: A case study in online mis/disinformation online.* German Marshall Fund of the United States. https://www.jstor.org/stable/pdf/resrep26753.pdf

Davisson, A., & Gehm, D. (2014). Gaming citizenship: Video games as lessons in civic life. *Journal of Contemporary Rhetoric, 4*(3/4), 39–57.

Day, A. M., O'Shay-Wallace, S., Seeger, M. W., & McElmurry, S. P. (2019). Informational sources, social media use, and race in the Flint, Michigan, water crisis. *Communication Studies, 70*(3), 352–376.

de Finney, S. (2015). Playing Indian and other settler stories: Disrupting Western narratives of Indigenous girlhood. *Continuum, 29*(2), 169–181.

DeLuca, K. M. (1999). Unruly arguments: The body rhetoric of Earth First!, ACT UP, and Queer Nation. *Argumentation and Advocacy. 36*(1), 9–21.

Democracy Now. (2019, September 23). 19-year-old indigenous climate activist Artemisa Xakriabá: "We fight for mother earth." Democracy Now. https://www.democracynow.org/2019/9/23/brazil_indigenous_climate_activist_artemisa_xakriaba

Diaconu, L. C. (2021). The time is now for the IACHR to address climate action as a human right: Indigenous communities can lead (again). *American Indian Law Journal, 9*(2), 215–241. https://digitalcommons.law.seattleu.edu/ailj/vol9/iss2/2

Diamond, G. (2019, August 1). Tara Houska on building justice and equality in era of climate change. *Skoll.* https://skoll.org/2019/08/01/tara-houska-on-building-justice-and-equality-in-era-of-climate-change/

Dobric, R. (2021). How to effect change. *AKO Journal.* https://akojournal.org.nz/2021/01/13/how-to-effect-change/

Dobscha, S., Ozanne, J. L., (2001). An ecofeminist analysis of environmentally sensitive women using qualitative methodology: The emancipatory potential of an ecological life. *Journal of Public Policy and Marketing, 20*(2), 201–214.

Dockry, M. J., & Hoagland, S. J. (2017). A special issue of the journal of Forestry—Tribal forest management: Innovations for sustainable forest management. *Journal of Forestry, 115*(5), 339–340. https://doi.org/10.5849/JOF-2017-040

Driscoll, C. (2002). *Girls: Feminine adolescence in popular culture and cultural theory.* Columbia University Press.

Driscoll, C. (2008). Girls today: Girls, girl culture, and girls' studies. *Girlhood Studies, 1*(1), 13–32.

D'Souza, D. [@DineshDSouza]. (2019, September 22). *Children—notably Nordic white girls with braids and red cheeks—were often used in Nazi propaganda. An old Goebbels technique! Looks like today's progressive Left is still learning its game from an earlier Left in the 1930s.* [Tweet]. Twitter. https://twitter.com/DineshDSouza/status/1175848457191510016?s=19

Elbein, S. (2017, January 31). The youth group that launched a movement at Standing Rock. *The New York Times*. https://www.nytimes.com/2017/01/31/magazine/the-youth-group-that-launched-a-movement-at-standing-rock.html

Engelfried, N. (2020). *How generation Z is leading the climate movement*. Waging Nonviolence. https://wagingnonviolence.org/2020/01/youth-climate-movement-zero-hour-jamie-margolin-greta-thunberg/

Entman, R. M. (1993). Framing: Towards clarification of a fractured paradigm. *Journal of Communication, 43*(4), 51–58.

Epstein, R., Blake, J., & González, T. (2017). *Girlhood interrupted: The erasure of Black girls' childhood*. https://www.law.georgetown.edu/poverty-inequality-center/wp-content/uploads/sites/14/2017/08/girlhood-interrupted.pdf

Estes, N. (2019). *Our history is the future*. Verso.

Fairclough, N. (1995). *Critical discourse analysis: The critical study of language*. Routledge.

Field, C. T., Owens, T., Chatelain, M., Simmons, L., George, A., & Keyse, R. (2016). The history of Black girlhood: Recent innovations and future directions. *The Journal of the History of Childhood and Youth, 9*(3), 383–401.

Fixmer-Oraiz, N., & Wood, J. T. (2019). *Gendered lives: Communication, gender, and culture* (13th ed.). Engage.

Foggin, S. (2020, January 31). Helena Gualinga is a voice for Indigenous communities in the fight against climate change. *Latin America Reports*. https://latinamericareports.com/helena-gualinga-voice-indigenous-communities-fight-climate-change/4192/

Fonger, R. (2019). *EPA says state allowed discrimination during creation of flint-area power plant*. Michigan Live. https://www.mlive.com/news/flint/2017/01/epa_says_genesee_township_powe.html

Franciscans for Justice. (2019). Activist spotlight: Artemisa Xakriabá. *Franciscans for Justice*. http://www.franciscansforjustice.org/2019/12/28/activist-spotlight-artemisa-xakriaba/

Frazer-Carrol, M. (2019, September 25). *On environmentalism, whiteness and activist superstars*. Gal-Dem. https://gal-dem.com/on-individualism-whiteness-and-activist-superstars/

Frerie, P. (1970). *Pedagogy of the oppressed*. Continuum.

Fridays For Future. (2022). *Strike statistics*. https://fridaysforfuture.org/what-we-do/strike-statistics/

Gajjala, R., & Oh, Y. J. (Eds.). (2012). *Cyberfeminism 2.0*. Peter Lang.

Gandhi, L. (2020). *Climate activists of color are being erased by the media*. Supermajority. https://supermajority.com/2020/02/climate-activists-of-color-are-being-erased-by-the-media/

Garcia, P., Fernández, C. H., & Jackson, A. (2020). Counternarratives of youth participation among Black girls. *Youth & Society, 52*(8), 1479–1500.

Gee, J., & Hayes, E. R. (2010). *Women and gaming: The Sims and 21st century learning*. Palgrave.

Gelin, M. (2019). *The misogyny of climate change*. New Republic. https://newrepublic.com/article/154879/misogyny-climate-deniers

Gilchrist, K. (2020, August 20). *She got plastic bags banned on Bali by 18. Now she wants to mobilize other young activists.* CNBC. https://www.cnbc.com/2020/08/20/plastic-pollution-gen-z-activist-melati-wijsen-mobilizes-others.html

Girl Scouts Research Institute. (2015). *Generation STEM: What girls say about science, technology, engineering and math.* Girl Scouts Research Institute. https://www.girlscouts.org/content/dam/girlscouts-gsusa/forms-and-documents/about-girl-scouts/research/generation_stem_full_report.pdf

Girls Who Code. (2016). Teach a girl to code and she'll change the world. https://girlswhocode.com/wp-content/uploads/2017/01/GWC_Clubs_VolunteerFlyer_Nov2016_compressed.pdf

Givens, T. E. (2020, June 8). *A time for radical empathy.* TransformingSociety. https://www.transformingsociety.co.uk/2020/06/08/a-time-for-radical-empathy/

Gleason, E. (2019). Girl you need to know: Brianna Fruean is a Pacific climate warrior. *New Zealand Fashion Quarterly.* https://fq.co.nz/girl-you-need-to-know-brianna-fruean/

Gomez, A. R. (2021). *Indigenous People's Day comes amid a reckoning over colonialism and calls for return of native land.* The Conversation. https://theconversation.com/Indigenous-peoples-day-comes-amid-a-reckoning-over-colonialism-and-calls-for-return-of-native-land-147734

Goodnight, G. T. (2012). The personal, technical, and public spheres of argument: A speculative inquiry into the art of public deliberation. *Null, 48*(4), 198–210. https://10.1080/00028533.2012.11821771

Grady, C. (2021). *Who runs the world? Not teen girls.* Vox. https://www.vox.com/the-highlight/22352860/teenage-girls-pop-culture-tiktok-olivia-rodrigo-addison-rae

Gramenz, J. (2020). *Greta Thunberg reacts to Canadian oil company's logo on explicit cartoon.* New Zealand Herald. https://www.nzherald.co.nz/world/greta-thunberg-reacts-to-canadian-oil-companys-logo-on-explicit-cartoon/VVAWRYZYMIDCX2LQT6OTXAADWM/

Green, L. (2020). Confident, capable and world changing: Teenagers and digital citizenship. *Communication Research & Practice, 6*(1), 6–19. https://10.1080/22041451.2020.1732589

Greene, D. T. (2021). (W)rites of passage: Black girls' journaling and podcast script writing as counternarratives. *Voices from the Middle, 28*(4), 38–42.

Greenfield, N. (2021, May 24). *The future has spoken: It's time to shut down DAPL and stop line 3.* NRDC. https://www.nrdc.org/stories/future-has-spoken-its-time-shut-down-dapl-and-stop-line-3

Grey, S. H. (2018). The tail of the black snake: Social protest and survivance in South Louisiana. In C. R. Kelly & J. E. Black (Eds.), *Decolonizing Native American rhetoric: Communicating self-determination* (pp. 285–302). Peter Lang.

Griffin, C. (1993). *Representations of youth.* Polity Press.

Haraway, D. (2006). A cyborg manifesto: Science, technology, and socialist-feminism in the late 20th century. *The international handbook of virtual learning environments* (pp. 117–158). Springer.

Harrington, B., & O'Connell, M. (2016). Video games as virtual teachers: Prosocial video game use by children and adolescents from different socioeconomic groups is associated with increased empathy and prosocial behaviour. *Computers in Human Behavior, 63*, 650–658.

Harris, A. (2003). *All about the girl: Culture, power, and identity*. Routledge.

Harvey, A. (2021). *Feminist media studies*. Polity Press.

Heinrich, C. (2017, November 15). Shalvi Shakshi's diary from COP23 in Bonn. *UNICEF*. https://www.unicef.org/pacificislands/stories/shalvi-shakshis-diary-cop23-bonn

Hesford, W. S. (2013). Introduction: Facing Malala Yousafzai, facing ourselves. *JAC, 33*(3–4), 407–423.

Hesford, W. S. (2014). The Malala effect. *JAC, 34*(1–2), 139–164.

Hip Hop Caucus [@HipHopCaucus]. (2021, March 11). *This Saturday will mark one year since Louisville police murdered our sister Breonna Taylor in her sleep. To honor her and other women who's lives were senselessly taken by police violence, join us in a #sayhername challenge through this weekend* [Tweet]. https://twitter.com/HipHopCaucus/status/1370146991875969026

Hirji, Z. (2019). Teenage girls are leading the climate movement—and getting attacked for it. *Buzzfeed*. https://www.buzzfeednews.com/article/zahrahirji/greta-thunberg-climate-teen-activist-harassment

hooks, b. (1994). *Teaching to transgress: Education as the practice of freedom*. Routledge.

hooks, b. (2013). Dig deep: Beyond lean in. *The Feminist Wire*. https://thefeministwire.com/2013/10/17973/

Horeck, T. (2014). #AskThicke: "Blurred lines," rape culture, and the feminist hashtag takeover. *Feminist Media Studies, 14*(6), 1105–1107.

Houdek, M., & Phillips, K. R. (2020). Rhetoric and the temporal turn: Race, gender, temporalities. *Women's Studies in Communication, 43*(4), 369–383. https://10.1080/07491409.2020.1824501

Indigenous Environmental Network. (2021). *Just transition*. https://www.ienearth.org/justtransition/

Jackson, D. Z. (2017). *Environmental justice? Unjust coverage of the Flint water crisis*. Harvard Kennedy School Shorenstein Center on Media, Politics and Public Policy. https://shorensteincenter.org/environmental-justice-unjust-coverage-of-the-flint-water-crisis/

Jackson, S., Bailey, M., & Welles, B. F. (2020). *#HashtagActivism: Networks of race and gender justice*. MIT Press.

Jackson, S. J. (2016). (Re) imagining intersectional democracy from Black feminism to hashtag activism. *Women's Studies in Communication, 39*(4), 375–379.

Jane, E. J. (2017). *Misogyny online: A short (and brutish) history*. Sage.

Jenkins, H., Purushotma, R., Weigel, M., Clinton, K., & Robison, A. J. (2006). *Confronting the challenges of participatory culture*. MIT Press.

Jenkins, H., Shresthova, S., Gamber-Thompson, L., Kligler-Vilenchik, N., & Zimmerman, A. (2016). *By any media necessary: The new youth activism*. NYU Press.

Johnson, A. E., & Wilkinson, K. K. (Eds.). (2020). *All we can save: Truth, courage, and solutions for the climate crisis*. One World.

Jung, J., Petkanic, P., Nan, D., & Kim, J. H. (2020). When a girl awakened the world: A user and social message analysis of Greta Thunberg. *Sustainability, 12*(7), 2707.

Kaler-Jones, C., Griffin, A., & Lindo, S. (2020). The clapback: Black girls responding to injustice through national civic engagement. In G. Logan, & J. Mackey (Eds.), *Black girl civics: Expanding and navigating the boundaries of civic engagement* (pp. 159–174). Information Age Publishing.

Kangujam, L. [@LicypriyaK]. (2020a, January 26). *Dear Media, Stop calling me "Greta of India." I am not doing my activism to looks like Greta Thunberg. Yes, she is on of our Inspiration & great influencer. We have common goal but I have my own identity, story. I began my movement since July 2018 even before Greta was started.* [Tweet]. Twitter. https://twitter.com/LicypriyaK/status/1221628420611698689

Kangujam, L. [@LicypriyaK]. (2020b, January 26). *If you call me "Greta of India," you are not covering my story. You are deleting a story.* [Tweet]. Twitter. https://twitter.com/LicypriyaK/status/1221632355644760064

Kay, J. B. (2019). Introduction: Anger, media, and feminism: The gender politics of mediated rage. *Feminist Media Studies, 19*(4), 591–615. https://10.1080/14680777.2019.1609197

Kay, J. B., & Banet-Weiser, S. (2019). Feminist anger and feminist respair. *Feminist Media Studies, 19*(4), 603–609. https://10.1080/14680777.2019.1609231

Kearney, M. C. (2009). Coalescing: The development of girls' studies. *NWSA Journal, 21*(1), 1–28.

Keller, J. (2021). "This is oil country": Mediated transnational girlhood, Greta Thunberg, and patriarchal petrocultures. *Feminist Media Studies, 21*(4), 1–5.

Kelly, C. R. & Black, J. E. (2018). Introduction: decolonizing Native American rhetoric. In C. R. Kelly & J. E. Black (Eds.), *Decolonizing Native American rhetoric: Communicating selfchec-determination* (pp. 1–24). Peter Lang.

Kelly, L. L. (2018). A snapchat story: How Black girls develop strategies for critical resistance in school. *Learning, Media and Technology, 43*(4), 374–389.

Kelly, S., & Nardi, B. (2014). Playing with sustainability: Using video games to simulate futures of scarcity. *First Monday, 19*(5). https://doi.org/10.5210/fm.v19i5.5259

Kempf, C. (2021). Why did so many do so little? movement building and climate litigation in the time of *Juliana v. United States. Texas Law Review, 99*(5), 1006–1040. https://texaslawreview.org/why-did-so-many-do-so-little-movement-building-and-climate-change-litigation-in-the-time-of-juliana-v-united-states/

Khan-Cullors, P., & bandele, A. (2018). *When they call you a terrorist: A Black Lives Matter memoir*. St. Martin's Press.

Kimmerer, R.W. (2013). *Braiding sweetgrass: Indigenous wisdom, scientific knowledge and the teaching of plants*. Milkweed.

Koerner, C. (2019). *Fox news apologized to Greta Thunberg after a pundit called her "mentally ill."* BuzzFeed News. https://www.buzzfeednews.com/article/claudiakoerner/fox-news-apologized-greta-thunberg-mentally-ill

Koffman, O., & Gill, R. (2013). "The revolution will be led by a 12-year-old girl": Girl power and global biopolitics. *Feminist Review, 2013*(5), 83–102.

Koffman, O., Orgad, S., & Gill, R. (2015). Girl power and 'selfie humanitarianism.' *Continuum: Journal of Media & Cultural Studies, 29*(2), 157–168. https://10.1080/10304312.2015.1022948

Kouzes, J. M., & Posner, B. Z. (2011). *Leadership begins with an inner journey.* https://10.1002/ltl.464

Kunda, L. (2020). Ben & Jerry's, Black Lives Matter, and the politics of public statements. *Flow*. http://www.flowjournal.org/2020/07/ben-and-jerrys-blm/

Kwauck, C., Cooke, J., Hara, E., & Pegram, J. (2019). *Girls' education in climate strategies.* The Brookings Institution.

Lee, K. (2020, January 31). Native women are vanishing across the U.S. inside an aunt's desperate search for her niece. *Los Angeles Times* https://www.latimes.com/world-nation/story/2020-01-31/murdered-missing-native-american-women

Lesko, N. (2012). *Act your age! the cultural construction of adolescence* (2nd ed.). Routledge.

Logan, G., & Mackey, J. (2020). Towards an emergent theory of Black girl civics. In G. Logan, & J. Mackey (Eds.), *Black girl civics: Expanding and navigating the boundaries of civic engagement* (pp. xi-xxvii). Information Age Publishing.

Lottie Dolls (2022). Mari Copeny / Kid Activist Doll / Little Miss Flint. https://www.lottie.com/products/kid-activist-doll-mari-copeny

Loyola University Chicago. (2021). *Climate change conference.* Climate Change Conference: School of Environmental Sustainability: Loyola University Chicago. https://www.luc.edu/sustainability/initiatives/climatechangeconference/

MacKenzie, D., & Wajcman, J. (Eds.). (1999). *The social shaping of technology.* Open University Press.

Mangan, A. (n.d.). *Young climate activist dissed by gubernatorial candidate: An interview with Rose Strauss.* Bioneers. https://bioneers.org/young-climate-activist-dissed-by-gubernatorial-candidate-an-interview-with-rose-strauss-zmbz1808/

Marchese, D. (2020). Greta Thunberg hears your excuses. she is not impressed. *The New York Times*. https://www.nytimes.com/interactive/2020/11/02/magazine/greta-thunberg-interview.html

Margolin, J. (2018). *Dear leaders: You've failed your children on climate change.* CNN. https://www.cnn.com/2018/04/22/opinions/jamie-margolin-climate-change/index.html

Margolin, J. (2020). *Youth to power. Your voice and how to use it.* Hachette Books.

Martín, M. (2021). Time's up for a change of political focus: Katniss Everdeen's ecofeminist leadership in The Hunger Games film series. *Journal of the Spanish Association of Anglo-American Studies, 43*(1), 89–109.

Martini, M. (2018). Online distant witnessing and live-streaming activism: Emerging differences in the activation of networked publics. *New Media & Society, 20*(11), 4035–4055.

Marvel. (n.d.). Marvel's hero project season 1: Thrilling Tokata. Marvel HQ. https://www.marvelhq.com/comics/marvel-s-hero-project-season-1-thrilling-tokata

McArthur, S. A. (2016). Black girls and critical media literacy for social activism. *English Education, 48*(4), 362–379.

McCarthy, J., & Sanchez, E. (2019). *12 female climate activists who are saving the planet*. Global Citizen. https://www.globalcitizen.org/en/content/female-activists-saving-planet/

McCreedy, D., & Dierking, L. D. (2013). *Cascading influences: Long-term impacts of informal STEM experiences for girls*. The Franklin Institute. https://www.fi.edu/sites/default/files/cascading-influences.pdf

Meade, A. (2019, August 1). Greta Thunberg hits back at Andrew Bolt for 'deeply disturbing' column. *The Guardian*. Retrieved from https://www.theguardian.com/environment/2019/aug/02/greta-thunberg-hits-back-at-andrew-bolt-for-deeply-disturbing-column

Mendes, K., Ringrose, J., & Keller, J. (2019). *Digital feminist activism: Girls and women fight back against rape culture*. Oxford University Press.

Merchant, C. (2005). *Radical ecology: The search for a livable world (2nd edition)*. Routledge.

Meredith, K. (2020). *Little Miss Flint wants to run for president in 2044, and she hopes America evolves by then*. Pop Sugar. https://www.popsugar.com/news/mari-copeny-gap-be-the-future-campaign-interview-47686191

Meyer, K. (2016, April 27). *Asked and answered. President Obama responds to an eight-year-old girl from Flint*. Obama White House Archives. https://obamawhitehouse.archives.gov/blog/2016/04/27/asked-and-answered-president-obama-responds-eight-year-old-girl-flint

Meyer, R. (2019). Why Greta makes adults uncomfortable. *The Atlantic*. https://www.theatlantic.com/science/archive/2019/09/why-greta-wins/598612/

Milstein, T., McGaurr, L., & Lester, L. (2020). Make love not war? radical environmental activism's reconfigurative potential and pitfalls. *Environmental Planning and E: Nature and Space, 4*(2), 296–316.

Mitchell, T. (2016). *Seven-year-old Pakistani latest to sue government over climate inaction*. New Matilda. https://newmatilda.com/2016/04/08/seven-year-old-pakistani-girl-sues-government-over-climate-inaction/

Mollusk, J. (2019, September 5). Greta Thunberg sings Swedish Death Metal [Video]. YouTube. https://www.youtube.com/watch?v=CLxpgRqxtEA&t=28s

Moors, M. R. (2019). What is Flint? Place, storytelling, and social media narrative reclamation during the Flint water crisis. *Information, Communication & Society, 22*(6), 808–822.

Morgan, P. (2019, September 24). Grating Greta's a vulnerable young drama queen who should go back to school—but President Trump should stop mocking her and start listening—because she's right about climate change. Retrieved from https://www.dailymail.co.uk/news/article-7498719/PIERS-MORGAN-Gretas-young-drama-queen-Trump-stop-mocking-start-listening.html

Morrow, K. L. (2021). Tackling climate change and gender justice–integral; not optional. *Oñati Socio-Legal Series, 11*(1), 207–230.

Moses, L. B. (2007). Why have a theory of law and technology? *Minnesota Journal of Law, Science & Technology, 8*(2), 589–606.

Muhammad, G. E., & McArthur, S. A. (2015). "Styled by their perceptions": Black adolescent girls interpret representations of Black females in popular culture. *Multicultural Perspectives, 17*(3), 133–140.

Mukherjee, R., & Banet-Weiser, S. (2012). *Commodity activism: Cultural resistance in neoliberal times.* NYU Press.

Munro, E. (2013). Feminism: A fourth wave. *Political Insight, 4*(2), 22–25.

Murphy, P. D. (2021). Speaking for the youth, speaking for the planet: Greta Thunberg and the representational politics of eco-celebrity. *Popular Communication, 19*(3), 193–206. https://10.1080/15405702.2021.1913493

Murray, R. (2019). *How Little Miss Flint captivated the nation—and what she's up to years later.* Today. https://www.today.com/style/what-mari-copeny-aka-little-miss-flint-now-t159829

National Cable Satellite Corporation (Producer). (2021, April 21,). *House oversight and reform subcommittee hearing on fossil fuel industry and climate change.* [Video/DVD] C-SPAN.

Nelson, A. C., & Walker, J. (2020). A case of climate change. In B. Ghosh, & B. Sarkar (Eds.). *The Routledge Companion to Media and Risk.* Routledge.

Nevett, J. (2019, May 3). *The Greta effect? Meet the schoolgirl climate warriors.* BBC. https://www.bbc.com/news/world-48114220

Ni, L., Harunani, F., & Martin, F. (2017). Empowering middle school students to create data-enabled social apps. *Journal of Computing Sciences in Colleges, 32*(6), 88–100.

Nilsen, E. (2019, September 17). *The new face of climate activism is young, angry, and effective.* Vox. https://www.vox.com/the-highlight/2019/9/10/20847401/sunrise-movement-climate-change-activist-millennials-global-warming

Nosek, G. (2017). Climate change litigation and narrative: How to use litigation to tell compelling climate stories. *Wm.& Mary Envtl.L.& Pol'Y Rev., 42*, 733.

O'Brien, K., Selboe, E., & Hayward, B. M. (2018). Exploring youth activism on climate change. *Ecology and Society, 23*(3). https://doi.org/10.5751/ES-10287-230342

O'Neill, K. (1998). No adults are pulling the strings and we like it that way. *Signs: Journal of Women in Culture and Society, 23*(3), 611–618.

O'Neill, S., & Nicholson-Cole, S. (2009). "Fear won't do it" promoting positive engagement with climate change through visual and iconic representations. *Science Communication, 30*(3), 355–379.

Olesen, T. (2020). Greta Thunberg's iconicity: Performance and co-performance in the social media ecology. *New Media & Society.* https://doi.org/10.1177/1461444820975416

Our Children's Trust. (2012a, April 20). *TRUST Iowa* [Video]. Vimeo. https://vimeo.com/40756009

Our Children's Trust. (2012b, July 23). *TRUST Pennsylvania* [Video]. Vimeo. https://vimeo.com/46266101

Our Children's Trust. (2012c, September 21). *TRUST Oregon* [Video]. Vimeo. https://vimeo.com/49915241

Our Children's Trust. (2012d, September 30). *TRUST Arizona* [Video]. YouTube. https://www.youtube.com/watch?v=c97dQ_LpRu4

Our Children's Trust. (2012e, October 30). *TRUST Massachusetts* [Video]. Vimeo. https://vimeo.com/52495384

Our Climate Voices. (2019a). *Jaime Butler, Navajo nation*. Our Climate Voices. https://www.ourclimatevoices.org/2019/jaimebutler

Our Climate Voices (2019b, July 25). *Jasilyn Charger, Cheyenne River Sioux Tribe*. Our Climate Voices https://www.ourclimatevoices.org/2019/jasilyncharger

Our Climate Voices. (2019c). *Miko Vergun, Beaverton, Oregon*. Our Climate Voices. https://www.ourclimatevoices.org/2019/mikovergun

Our Climate Voices. (2017). *Sara, New York, New York*. Our Climate Voices https://www.ourclimatevoices.org/2017/sara

Owens, T. C., Callier, D. M., Robinson, J. L., & Garner, P. R. (2017). Towards an interdisciplinary field of Black girlhood studies. *Departures in Critical Qualitative Research, 6*(3), 116–132.

Pacific Community. *Brianna Fruean*. Pacific Community. https://www.spc.int/sdp/70-inspiring-pacific-women/brianna-fruean

Palczewski, C. H., Fritch, J., & Ice, R. (2016). *Rhetoric in civic life* (2nd ed.). Strata.

Park, C. S., Liu, Q., & Kaye, B. (2021). Analysis of ageism, seism, and ableism in user comments on YouTube videos about climate activist Greta Thunberg. *Social Media + Society, 7*(3) https://doi.org/10.1177%2F20563051211036059

Parker, L. (2019). *Kids suing governments about climate: It's a global trend*. National Geographic. https://www.nationalgeographic.com/environment/article/kids-suing-governments-about-climate-growing-trend

Pasbani, R. (2019, September 28). Greta Thunberg comments on death metal mashup: "From now on, I will be doing death metal only." *Metal Injection*. https://metalinjection.net/news/greta-thunberg-comments-on-death-metal-mashup-from-now-on-i-will-be-doing-death-metal-only

Patterson, T., & Barrat, S. (2019). *Playing for the planet: How video games can deliver for people and the environment*. UN Environment. https://playing4theplanet.org/

Pattinson, T. (2021, August 9). The wonders of Greta Thunberg: Read our interview with the voice of a generation. *Vogue Scandinavia*. https://www.voguescandinavia.com/articles/greta-the-great

Pauli, B. J. (2019). *Flint fights back: Environmental justice and democracy in the Flint water crisis*. MIT Press.

Pauli, B. J. (2020). The Flint water crisis. *WIREs Water, 7*(3). https://doi.org/10.1002/wat2.1420

Peng, A. Y. (2020). Alipay adds "beauty filters" to face-scan payments: A form of patriarchal control over women's bodies. *Null, 20*(4), 582–585. https://10.1080/14680777.2020.1750779

Peschau, M. (2021, June 14). *Say it loud, say it clear—youth climate action through collective action and empathy*. SciencesPo. https://www.sciencespo.fr/psia/chair-sustainable-development/2021/06/14/say-it-loud-say-it-clear-youth-climate-action-through-collective-action-and-empathy/

Pezzullo, P. C. (2011). Contextualizing boycotts and buycotts: The impure politics of consumer-based advocacy in an age of global ecological crises. *Communication and Critical Cultural Studies, 8*(2), 124–145. https://10.1080/14791420.2011.566276

Phillips, W. (2015). *This is why we can't have nice things: Mapping the relationship between online trolling and mainstream culture.* MIT Press.

Pickard, S. (2021). "You are stealing our future in front of our very eyes." The representation of climate change, emotions and the mobilisation of young environmental activists in Britain. *E-Rea, 18*(2). https://journals.openedition.org/erea/11774

Pillay, N. (2012). *The Malala effect statement.* United Nations Human Rights. https://newsarchive.ohchr.org/EN/NewsEvents/Pages/DisplayNews.aspx?NewsID=12825&LangID=E

Plant, S. (1997). *Zeroes and ones: Digital women and the new technoculture.* Doubleday.

Presley, R. (2018). Between a rock and a hard place: Rhetorical strategies for environmental protection and Tribal resistance in the Dakota access pipeline movement. In C. R. Kelly & J. E. Black (Eds.), *Decolonizing Native American rhetoric: Communicating self-determination* (pp. 285–302). Peter Lang.

Prodis, J. (1994, March 22,). Ford's new Windstar minivan designed with a woman's touch. *AP News.* https://apnews.com/0b6b02a98dd339a87cb63c0f92ba573b

Projansky, S. (2014). *Spectacular girls: Media fascination and celebrity culture.* New York University Press.

Project super bloom.(n.d.). https://www.projectsuperbloom.org.

Pulé, M., & Hultman, M. (2019). Industrial/breadwinner masculinities and climate change: Understanding the 'white male effect' of climate change denial. In H. Rydström, & C. Kinnvall (Eds.), *Climate hazards, disasters, and gender ramifications* (pp. 86–100). Routledge.

Rentschler, C. A. (2017). Bystander intervention, feminist hashtag activism, and the anti-carceral politics of care. *Feminist Media Studies, 17*(4), 565–584.

Reuters (2020, November 5). *Climate activist Thunberg hits back at Trump over anger management taunt.* Reuters. https://www.reuters.com/article/us-usa-election-thunberg/climate-activist-thunberg-hits-back-at-trump-over-anger-management-taunt-idUSKBN27M0TN

Rich, K. (2018). *Girls resist! A guide to activism, leadership, and starting a revolution.* Quirk Books.

Riggio, O. (2020). *Xiye bastida: Making room for climate activists of all backgrounds.* KCET. https://www.kcet.org/shows/tending-nature/xiye-bastida-making-room-for-climate-activists-of-all-backgrounds

Rincon, P. (2019). *Greta Thunberg: People underestimate angry kids.* BBC. https://www.bbc.com/news/science-environment-50644395

Riordan, E. (2001). Commodified agents and empowered girls: Consuming and producing feminism. *Journal of Communication Inquiry, 25*(3), 279–297.

Roche, D. (2021). *Greta Thunberg keeps on trolling world leaders with " bunny hugger" twitter bio.* Newsweek. https://www.newsweek.com/greta-thunberg-keeps-trolling-world-leaders-bunny-hugger-twitter-bio-1585907

Röderer, F. (2020). *The Greta Thunberg effect: An analysis of corporate tweets on climate change.* https://run.unl.pt/bitstream/10362/108599/1/16584_Fabienne_Roederer_1920S2_34516_Fabienne_Roederer_136101_1330703572.pdf

Rogers, N. (2016). Litigation, activism, and the paradox of lawfulness in the age of climate change. In T. Bristow, & T. H. Ford. (Eds.), *A cultural history of climate change* (pp. 211–228). Routledge.

Rosenfeld, K. (Ed.). (2020). *Gender, communication, and the digital revolution.* Cognella.

Roy, E. A. (2017). *New Zealand river granted same legal rights as human being.* The Guardian. https://www.theguardian.com/world/2017/mar/16/new-zealand-river-granted-same-legal-rights-as-human-being

Ryalls, E. D., & Mazzarella, S. R. (2021). "Famous, beloved, reviled, respected, feared, celebrated": Media construction of Greta Thunberg. *Communication, Culture and Critique, 14*(3), 438–453.

Sabherwal, A., Ballew, M. T., van Der Linden, S., Gustafson, A., Goldberg, M. H., Maibach, E. W., Kotcher, J. E., Swim, J. K., Rosenthal, S. A., & Leiserowitz, A. (2021). The Greta Thunberg effect: Familiarity with Greta Thunberg predicts intentions to engage in climate activism in the United States. *Journal of Applied Social Psychology, 51*(4), 321–333.

Sandberg, S. (2013). *Lean in: Women, work, and the will to lead.* Knopf.

Safi, M. (2017). *Ganges and Yamuna rivers granted same legal rights as human being.* The Guardian. https://www.theguardian.com/world/2017/mar/21/ganges-and-yamuna-rivers-granted-same-legal-rights-as-human-beings

Saujani, R. (2016, July 12). *How can we impact violence and hate?* Medium. https://medium.com/@reshmasaujani/how-can-we-impact-violence-hate-e47fe6d49a03

Sawchuk, S. (2019, March 12). *Meet the youth climate activists who are leading school strikes.* Education Week. https://www.edweek.org/teaching-learning/meet-the-youth-climate-activists-who-are-leading-school-strikes/2019/03

Scheinman, T. (2018). *At the GCAS in San Francisco, the youth have a voice—but only one.* PacificStandard. https://psmag.com/environment/at-the-gcas-in-san-francisco-the-youth-have-a-voice

School of Environmental Sustainability. (2021). *Indigenous youth seeking truth and justice* [Video]. YouTube. https://www.youtube.com/watch?v=oufXaMjg7Dw&t=16s

Schrum, K. (2004). *Some wore bobby socks: The emergence of teenage girls' culture, 1920–1945.* Palgrave.

Schwedel, H. (2019, Sept 12,). *"You can never see their pants for some reason."* Slate. https://slate.com/human-interest/2019/09/vsco-girls-explained-by-teens.html

Segers, I., & Arora, P. A. (2016). *Smashing patriarchy with cell phones? Critique of dominant technofeminist perspectives on mobile phone-enabled women's empowerment programmes in Bangladesh.* Unpublished manuscript.

Setzer, J., & Byrnes, R. (2020). *Global trends in climate change litigation: 2020 snapshot.* https://www.lse.ac.uk/granthaminstitute/wp-content/uploads/2020/07/Global-trends-in-climate-change-litigation_2020-snapshot.pdf

Shapiro, J. R., & Williams, A. M. (2012). The role of stereotype threats in undermining girls' and women's performance and interest in STEM fields. *Sex Roles, 66*(3–4), 175–183.

Shaw, A. (2014). The internet is full of jerks because the world is full of jerks: What feminist theory teaches us about the internet. *Communication and Critical/Cultural Studies, 11*(3), 273–277.

Shaw, J. (2021). *Why is biodiversity important.* https://www.conservation.org/blog/why-is-biodiversity-important/

Shayon, S. (2017). *State of play: Why organizations still rely on games for sustainability education.* Sustainable Brands. https://sustainablebrands.com/read/marketing-and-comms/state-of-play-why-organizations-still-rely-on-games-for-sustainability-education

Sikka, T. (2018). Technofeminism and ecofeminism: An analysis of geoengineering research. In D. A. Vakoch, & S. Mickey (Eds.), *Ecofeminism in dialogue* (pp. 107–128). Lexington Books.

Snow, D., & Bedford, R. (1988). Ideology, frame resonance, and participant mobilization. *International Social Movement Research, 1*(1), 197–217.

Srikanth, A. (2020, January 31). *After being cropped out of photo with Greta Thunberg, climate activist Vanessa Nakate speaks out.* The Hill. https://thehill.com/changing-america/sustainability/climate-change/480890-climate-activist-vanessa-nakate-is-getting

Stone, L. (2021). Youth power—youth movements: Myth, activism, and democracy. *Ethics and Education, 16*(2), 249–261.

Sturken, M. (2012). Foreword. In R. Mukherjee, & S. Banat-Weiser (Eds.), *Commodity activism: Cultural resistance in neoliberal times* (pp. ix-xi). New York University Press.

Suárez-Carballo, F., Martín-Sanromán, J-R, Martins, N. (2021). An analysis of feminist graphics published on Instagram by Spanish female professionals on the subject of International Women's Day (2019–2020). *Communication & Society, 34*(2), 351–367.

Switzer, H., Bent, E., & Endsley, C. L. (2016). Precarious politics and girl effects: Exploring the limits of the girl gone global. *Feminist Formations, 28*(1), 33–59.

Taft, J. K. (2020). Hopeful, harmless, and heroic: Figuring the girl activist as global savior. *Girlhood Studies, 13*(2), 1–17.

Te Ara Whatu. (n.d.). *India Logan-Riley.* https://tearawhatu.org/india

TED Radio Hour. (2020, May 22). *Xiye Bastida: How are young people making the choice to fight climate change?* [Video/DVD] https://www.npr.org/2020/05/22/860168455/xiye-bastida-how-are-young-people-making-the-choice-to-fight-climate-change

Telford, T. (2021, July30). These self-described trolls tackle climate crisis on social media with wit and memes. *The Washington Post.* https://www.washingtonpost.com/business/2021/07/30/greentrolling-big-oil-greenwashing/

Thomas, C. S. (2020). It's all child's play: Flint's water crisis, environmental justice, and little miss flint's ephebic rhetorics. In C. R. Schmitt, C. S. Thomas & T. R. Castor (Eds.), *Water, rhetoric, and social justice* (pp. 215–230). Lexington Books.

Thomas, T. (2020). *Tokata Iron Eyes on why the climate movement needs to listen to indigenous voices - assembly: Malala fund.* Assembly - a Malala Fund publication. https://assembly.malala.org/stories/tokata-iron-eyes-on-why-the-climate-movement-needs-to-listen-to-indigenous-voices?rq=tokata+iron+eyes

Thunberg, G. (2019). *No one is too small to make a difference.* Penguin Books.

Thunberg, G. [@GretaThunberg]. (2019, August 31). *When haters go after your looks and differences, it means they have nowhere left to go. And then you know you're winning! I have Aspergers and that means I'm sometimes a bit different from the norm. And - given the right circumstances-being different is a superpower. #aspiepower.* [Tweet]. Twitter. https://twitter.com/GretaThunberg/status/1167916177927991296

Thunberg, G. [@GretaThunberg]. (2020, January 28). *There are countless of school strikers and young climate activists around the world. Not just me. They all have names and stories waiting to be told.* [Tweet]. Twitter. https://twitter.com/GretaThunberg/status/1222135195148726272

Thunberg, G. [@GretaThunberg]. (2021, January 20). *He seems like a very happy old man looking forward to a bright and wonderful future. So nice to see!* [Tweet]. Twitter. https://twitter.com/GretaThunberg/status/1351890941087522820

Thunberg, G. (2021, July 1). The show is over. https://gretathunberg.medium.com/the-show-is-over-66e03dd38efa

Trump, D. J. [@realDonaldTrump]. (2019, December 12). *So ridiculous. Greta must work on her Anger Management problem, then go to a good old fashioned movie with a friend! Chill Greta, Chill!* [Tweet]. Twitter. https://t.co/M8ZtS8okzE

Tufecki, Z (2017). *Twitter and tear gas: The power and fragility of networked protest.* Yale University Press.

UN Climate Conference. (2019). https://unfccc.int/cop25

Unicorn Riot (2019, October 11). *Tokata Iron Eyes and Greta Thunberg discuss climate crisis* [Video]. YouTube. https://www.youtube.com/watch?v=HVW2oCe7Wwo

United Nations. (2021). *What is the United Nations framework convention on climate change?* United Nations Climate Change. https://unfccc.int/process-and-meetings/the-convention/what-is-the-united-nations-framework-convention-on-climate-change

United States Mission to the United Nations (2021, March 15). *U.S. delegation to the 65th session of the UN Commission on the Status of women.* https://usun.usmission.gov/u-s-delegation-to-the-65th-session-of-the-un-commission-on-the-status-of-women/

Van Dijck, J., & Poell, T. (2013). Understanding social media logic. *Media and Communication, 1*(1), 2–14.

van der Voo, L. (2020). *As the world burns: The new generation of activists and the landmark legal fight against climate change.* Timber Press.

Vasudevan, P., & Smith, S. (2020). The domestic geopolitics of racial capitalism. *EPC: Politics and Space, 38*(7–8), 1160–1179.

Vanner, C. (2019). Toward a definition of transnational girlhood. *Girlhood Studies, 12*(2), 115–132. doi:10.3167/ghs.2019.120209

Vickery, J., & Everbach, T. (2018). *Mediating misogyny: Gender, technology, and harassment*. Palgrave.

Vizenor, G. (2008). *Survivance: Narratives of native presence*. University of Nebraska Press.

Vu, H. T., Blomberg, M., Seo, H., Liu, Y., Shayesteh, F., & Do, H. V. (2021). Social media and environmental activism: Framing climate change on Facebook by global NGOs. *Science Communication, 43*(1), 91–115.

Wahlström, M., Wennerhag, M., & Rootes, C. (2013). Framing "the client issue": Patterns of participation and prognostic frames among client summit protestors. *Global Environmental Politics, 13*(4), 101–122. https://doi.org/10.1162/GLEP_a_00200

Wajcman, J. (2004). *Technofeminism*. Polity Press.

Wajcman, J. (2006). Technocapitalism meets technofeminism. *Labour & Industry: A Journal of the Social and Economic Relations of Work, 16*(3), 7–20.

Wieskamp, V. N. & Smith, C. (2020). "What to do when you're raped": Indigenous women critiquing and coping through a rhetoric of survivance. *Quarterly Journal of Speech, 106*(1), 2–94.

Wildemeersch D, Læssøe J, Håkansson, M. (2021). Young sustainability activists as public educators: An aesthetic approach. *European Educational Research Journal*. https://doi.org/10.1177/1474904121990953

Williams, S. (2015). Digital defense: Black feminists resist violence with hashtag activism. *Feminist Media Studies, 15*(2), 341–344.

Winner, L. (1980). Do artifacts have politics?. *Daedalus, 109*(1), 121–136.

Wonneberger, A., & Vliegenthart, R. (2021). Agenda-setting effects of climate change litigation: Interrelations across issue levels, media, and politics in the case of Urgenda against the Dutch government. *Environmental Communication,15*(5), 699–714.

Wood, M. C., & Woodward, C. W. (2013). *Nature's trust: Environmental law for a new ecological age*. Cambridge University Press.

Wu, J. (2020). Climate anxiety in young people: A call to action. *The Lancet*, https://doi.org/10.1016/S2542-5196(20)30223-0

Xue, H. (2020). *What island life taught Brianna Fruean about saving the Earth*. ASSEMBLY: a Malala Fund publication. https://assembly.malala.org/stories/what-island-life-taught-brianna-fruean-about-saving-the-earth

Yoon-Hendricks, A. (2018, July 21,). Meet the teenagers leading a climate change movement. *New York Times* https://www.nytimes.com/2018/07/21/us/politics/zero-hour-climate-march.html

Young, K. (2018). The rhetorical persona of the water protectors: Anti-Dakota pipeline resistance with mirror shields. In C. R. Kelly & J. E. Black (Eds.), *Decolonizing Native American rhetoric: Communicating self-determination* (pp. 268–284). Peter Lang.

Zoellner, D. (2021, May 21). Greta Thunberg calls out China for "fat-shaming" her in article questioning if she is really vegetarian. https://www.independent.co.uk/climate-change/greta-thunberg-china-fat-shaming-b1851860.html

Zoellner, D. (2021, May 21). *Greta Thunberg calls out China for "fat-shaming" her in article questioning if she is really vegetarian.* Independent. https://www.independent.co.uk./climate-change/greta-thunberg-china-fat-shaming-b1851860.html

Zimmerman, T. (2017). # Intersectionality: The fourth wave feminist twitter community. *Atlantis: Critical Studies in Gender, Culture & Social Justice, 38*(1), 54–70.

Zulli, D. (2020). Tweets, memes, and snaps: The way to the White House, *Spectra, 56*(1), 14–19.

Index

9/11, 75
350.org, 66
2030 temperature targets, 39

Abercrombie & Fitch, 73, 79
    Abercrombie Kids, 56
ableism, 112
abolitionism, 105
Abraham, B., 88
accountability:
    calling adults to, 4–5, 30–31, 37–40, 100, 113–14, 139
    of corporations, 116, 119
    of governments, 65–66, 72–73, 78, 124, 135, 137
    through climate litigation, 1, 122
    tracker apps for, 192
adolescence, 47, 58
adults, 2–3, 103, 140
    being called to account, 4–5, 30–31, 37–40, 100, 113–14, 139
    bullying girls, 24–32, 34, 101, 141–42
    dismissing girls, 117, 128, 138, 145–46
    fetishizing girls, 6–7, 30, 71, 102
    inaction from, 12, 30–31, 42, 56–57, 61, 115, 122
    as protectors, 135. *See also* age/generation; intergenerational coalitions
"affective injustice," 25
Africa, 8, 35, 37
African American women, 47–49, 83
age/generation, 22–23, 39, 50, 58–59, 65, 77, 139, 145
    climate girls' ages, 4, 31, 37, 44, 51, 66–72, 90, 103–5, 119, 126
    and discrimination, 2–3, 8, 10, 40, 57, 101, 117, 126, 128, 138
    Generation Z, 4, 106–7
    and heat waves, 123. *See also* adults; intergenerational coalitions; teenagers; young adults
agency, 17, 22, 34, 40, 85, 138
    anti-colonial, 70
    and climate litigation, 120–21
    developed in STEM programs, 84
    of Flint residents, 48, 57, 59–60
    and Gen Z radical strategy, 106, 109, 118, 138
    girls as agents of change, 15, 87, 89, 121, 123
    and patriarchal society, 3, 8, 64
agenda-setting, 8, 11, 20, 64, 138, 148
    and climate litigation, 128

in Flint, MI, 48
and Greta Thunberg, 29, 41–42
Ahmed, Sara, 25
Aiken, Ann, 127
air:
    pollution, 1–2, 47, 91, 119
    protections for, 119, 124, 132, 136. *See also* carbon emissions
Alimahomed, S., 100
Alipay app, 85
Ali, Rabab, 119
allyship, 3, 68, 145–146. *See also* intergenerational coalitions
Amazon, 31, 64–65, 126
American Association of University Women (AAUW), 82–84
Andersen, Inger, 87
anger, 32, 40, 59, 89, 146
    and framing of girls, 4, 20, 24–27, 31, 34, 67
    of Mari Copeny, 59
Anishinabek Nation, 72
Anshelm, J., 33
anti-Blackness, 7. *See also* Black girls; racism
anti-colonial action, 70. *See also* decolonialism
anti-consumerism, 19
antifa, 33
anti-gun movement, 101. *See also* gun violence: advocating against
anti-racist activism, 50–52. *See also* Black Lives Matter; Copeny, Amariyanna (Mari)
anti-Trump activism, 25, 31, 44, 101
anxiety, 100
    about the future, 9, 24, 27, 100, 115, 137
    from bullying, 141. *See also* eco-anxiety
Aotearoa, New Zealand, 64–65
app development, 3, 15, 21, 81, 85–87, 95, 98, 100
    for community-building, 94
    by Earth Guardians, 112

trackers, 92–93, 110, 144
Arctic Wildlife Refuge, 132
Arechiga, Samantha, 76
Arizona, 130
    Department of Environmental Quality, 132
Arora, P. A., 85, 95
Arthur, T. O., 55
Asperger's syndrome, 24, 27–28. *See also* Autism Spectrum Disorder (ASD)
#aspiepower, 28
Assembly (Malala Fund), 71
Assembly of First Nations (2016), 67
ASUS, 54
Atlantic Ocean, 23, 28
"atmospheric trust," 124
Autism Spectrum Disorder (ASD), 28, 38. *See also* Asperger's syndrome
auto industry, 47

Bachpan Andolan (Child Movement), 37
Bagley, K., 66
Bali, 15, 103, 110, 113–14
Banet-Weiser, Sarah, 13, 25, 27, 56
Bangladesh, 85, 111
Banks, Arron, 28
Bashi, G., 36
Bastida, Xiye Patrick, 66, 143
    All We Can Save, 39

Basu, Kehkashan, 102, 104, 111, 113, 115–17, 141, 144
Bay Area Youth for Climate Action, 100
Bayou Bridge Pipeline, 75
beauty filters, 85
beauty industry, 6, 53
Bedford, R., 109
Bennett, W. L., 11, 29
Bent, E., 7, 9–10, 17
Bernier, Maxime, 27–28
Beyoncé, 9
Biden-Harris Administration, 53, 77
Big Oil, 70. *See also* extraction industries; fossil fuels

Bilandzic, H., 109
biodiversity, 40, 63–64, 78–79, 147
Bioneers, 100
BIPOC activists, 37, 99, 105. *See also*
    Black feminist activism; Black girls;
    Indigenous girls; Latinx girls
Black feminist activism, 9, 20, 46–48,
    50–52, 58–60
Black feminist scholarship, 20,
    25, 45–47, 52
Black girlhood studies, 3, 7–8, 45–46
Black girls, 7, 43, 47
    resisting systemic racism, 8–9, 37,
        44–47, 55, 58–60, 138
    violence against, 9, 51–52. *See
        also* girls of color
Black, J. E., 70
Black Lives Matter, 9, 17, 58, 60,
    105, 108, 112
Blay, S., 122
Blazevik, Sara, 102, 104
blogs, 19, 98, 112
Bogost, I., 86
Bolsonaro, Jair, 31
Bolt, Andrew, 31
border-crossings, 8, 30, 64, 79, 140
Boston, MA, 130
Boulder, CO, 105
Boxed In, 94
boycotts, 18–19
boyd, d., 11
brand activism, 11, 147
    and Mari Copeny, 43–44, 53–56,
        59–60, 144
Brazil, 31, 64, 67
#BreonnaTaylor, 52
Brewer, Janice, 132
Brigham, M., 75
British Petroleum (BP), 132
Brockington, D., 18
Brough, A. R., 33
Brown communities, 66
Brown, Lyn Mikel, 98–99, 103, 146
Brown, R. N., 45
Brown v. Board of Education, 124

Bullard, Robert, 99
bullying, 79, 101
    and Autumn Peltier, 67, 141–42
    and Greta Thunberg, 24–32, 34,
        40. *See also* cyberbullying
Bush, George, 100
Butler, Jaime, 130, 132–33
buycotts, 18
Bye Bye Plastic Bags, 15, 21, 97, 106
    challenges for, 116
    international network,
        107–8, 110–11
    in mainstream media, 115
    mission, 102–104

Canada, 27, 34, 72–73, 75, 77
    Assembly of First Nations, 67–68
    and climate litigation,
        21, 119, 125
Canada News Broadcast (CNB), 67
Canadian Encyclopedia, 67
Canadian Living
    Me to the We Award, 72
capitalism, 1–2, 18, 64
    and activist funding, 55
    critiques of, 4, 15, 104,
        139–40, 147–48
    racial, 48
    resistance to, 8, 14–15, 18, 47
    and women's anger, 25
carbon emissions, 1–2, 23, 36, 41, 87
    and China, 34
    and Colombian Amazon, 126
    and Pakistan, 119
    and scientific evidence, 30, 34,
        122–23, 134
    in United States, 125–
        26, 132, 134
carbon footprint, 86, 112, 131
    tracker app, 92, 94
Carey, M. C., 48
CBC Kids News, 72
celebrity, 29, 32
    and activists, 6, 8–10, 18, 24, 31,
        38, 40, 47

Center for Young Women's
	Development (Young Women's
	Freedom Center), 102
Change the Game (Google
	Play), 21, 81–82
Chan, L. S., 85–86
Charger, Jasilyn, 68, 73–75
Chatelain:
	Woman of the Year (2019), 72
Cheyenne River Sioux Tribe, 68, 73
Children's Climate Conference
	(Sweden), 72
China, 34, 85–86
Chklovski, Tara, 82
Citizen GIS, 110
"citizen science," 48
citizenship, 11–12, 84, 105–6,
	129, 137, 139
civic engagement, 11, 45, 53, 84,
	86, 90, 95
civil rights, 131
"clapping back," 30, 34, 42, 46
Clark, L. S., 75
classism, 39, 43, 45
CLEAN4U, 93
climateclock.world, 17
climate denialism, 13, 33
Climate Fortnite Squad, 91
climate litigation, 119, 136
	challenges of, 141–42
	for Earth rights, 126
	history of Our Children's
		Trust, 123–24
	for human rights, 125–27
	and media coverage, 127–28
	and storytelling, 121–22,
		129–33, 144
	and truths, 133–35
Climate Reality Leadership Training
	Corps, 101
climate refugees, 1
#climatestrike, 40
Clinton, Hillary, 25
coal industry, 100, 119, 127, 130, 132
"code red," 1

Coleman, Haven, 41, 59
Collins, P. H., 47, 52
Colombia, 119, 126
colonialism, 64, 68, 70, 76, 78, 104,
	112–13. *See also* neocolonialism;
	settler colonial ideologies
Colon, Xavier, 75–76
commodity activism, 18, 20, 56, 147
community-building, 15, 94–95, 105.
	See also intergenerational coalitions
connective action, 11–12, 29, 109, 112
consumerism, 6, 16, 18, 21, 36
	and climate nonprofits,
		97–98, 106–7
consumption, 21, 95, 98
	of media, 84
	of plastics, 107, 110
	of water, 91–92
Copenhagen Conference of the Parties
	(COP), 125
	COP23, 65
Copeny, Amariyanna (Mari), 20,
	139–41, 143–44
	about, 43–45
	and anti-racist activism, 51–52
	and branding, 53–56
	and fame, 47
	mural of, 60
	and place-based activism,
		49–51, 89, 129
	rhetorical strategies, 56–61
	Shorty Award in Activism
		(2019), 54
#CoronaOutbreak, 50
#coronavirus, 50
Couchiching First Nation, 63
counterpublics, 38, 143
COVID-19 pandemic, 2, 49–51, 77,
	112–13, 147
crisis communication, 26–27, 40
critical consciousness, 129, 134, 138
critical discourse analysis (CDA), 18.
	See also methodology of book
critical literacy, 46, 83–84
Croatia, 102

crowdfunding, 44. *See also* fundraising
cyberbullying, 3, 12, 28, 33, 83, 102, 141. *See also* bullying
cyberfeminism, 109. *See also* feminism; techno-ecofeminism; technofeminism

Daggett, C., 140
Dakota, 84, 90
Dakota Access Pipeline (DAPL), 68–69, 108
Dave, A., 33
Davisson, A., 86
#DearFlintKids, 58
Dear Flint Kids campaign, 57–58
death threats, 13, 28, 102, 141
d'Eaubonne, Françoise, 14
decolonialism, 4, 74–75. *See also* anti-colonial action
de Finney, S., 7
deforestation, 40, 89, 126
degrowth, 4, 19
Dei Filippone, Glori, 130–33
Denver, CO, 41
depression, 24, 26. *See also* anxiety
design. *See* app development; video game design
Detroit River, 43
Diaconu, L. C., 125
Diana, Princess of Wales, 102
Dierking, L. D., 84
digital footprint, 13
disinformation campaigns, 13, 42, 88, 147
Disney, 79
dissent frameworks, 19, 35–36, 60, 119
donations, 51, 55, 97, 106–7, 118. *See also* fundraising
doxxing, 3
Driscoll, C., 6, 8
drought, 1, 41, 66, 92, 130, 132
Droughtout, 92
Dr. Phil, 58
D'Souza, Dinesh, 28
Dump That, 93

Earth Day, 31, 99, 115, 143
Earth Guardians, 97, 99, 105–8, 112
EchoHawk, Crystal, 74
ECO-18, 73
eco-anxiety, 1, 60, 105, 141, 145. *See also* anxiety
EcoDIY, 94
ecofeminism, 4, 13–15, 20, 36, 64, 76–77. *See also* feminism; techno-ecofeminism
EcoVerse, 90
Ecuadorian Amazon, 64, 65
Edmonton, Alberta, 34
education, 6, 9, 100, 137, 146
    in environmentalism, 15, 57, 65–66, 71, 88–89, 93, 97, 103, 112
    girls' rights to, 16, 123–24
    and school-to-prison pipeline, 10, 104
    in technology, 82–83
emissions. *See* carbon emissions
empathy, 21, 86, 90, 95, 147
Encino, CA, 90
Entman, R. M., 18–19
Environmental Protection Agency (EPA), 48
Equity Project (Abercrombie & Fitch), 73
erosion, 14, 65–66, 125
Estes, N., 63
European Commission on Human Rights (ECHR), 125–26
exceptionalism, 3, 9–10, 114–15
    framing Autumn Peltier, 67, 73
    framing Greta Thunberg, 28, 38, 41
    and "Malala Effect," 16–17
extraction industries, 20, 65, 68, 76–78, 86, 120, 127, 138, 147. *See also* coal industry; fossil fuels

Facebook, 9, 11, 52, 70, 100, 102, 111–12, 115
#facetheclimateemergency, 36

fashion industry, 6, 54, 79, 145
fat shaming, 34, 141
fear, 2, 6, 50, 100, 127
femicide crisis, 20, 77, 78, 140
feminine gaze, 85
femininity, 47, 83, 139
  commodification of, 6
  correlated to environmental activism, 13
  girls' nonconformity to, 25. *See also* gender
feminism, 2, 6–9, 11–12, 14, 36, 99, 103
  anti-feminist backlash, 33
  faux feminism, 146
  feminist blogosphere, 98
  and Greta Thunberg, 19–21, 25, 27, 41
  and Mari Copeny, 46–47, 50–52, 60
  and STEM programs, 82–83, 86. *See also* cyberfeminism; ecofeminism; techno-ecofeminism; technofeminism
feminist media studies, 2
feminist scholarship, 4, 47, 52, 85
Ferguson, Eleanor, 76
Fernández, C. H., 46
Fernands, Maddy, 35
Field, C. T., 8
Fiji, 64–66
films, 24, 26, 47, 129–30, 133–35, 141, 884
fires, 1, 5, 102
First Nations, 20–21, 64, 67
  First Nations Assembly, 73
  water ceremony, 72
FisH20, 90
Fixmer-Oraiz, N., 47
#Flint, 51
Flint Girl Effect, 20, 44, 59
Flint H20 Justice coalitions, 48
Flint Kids Read, 57
Flint, MI, 12, 49–50, 53–55, 58
  environmental racism in, 43–44
  historically overrun by pollution, 47–48
  inspiration from, 82, 129
  letter to Obama from, 20, 44–45, 59, 139
  longevity of water crisis in, 44, 51, 57, 59–60. *See also* Copeny, Amariyanna (Mari)
Flint River, 43
#FlintWaterCrisis, 51
floods, 1, 66, 102, 130
Florida, U.S.A.
  Parkland, 10, 30, 37
fossil fuels, 30, 39, 65, 77
  economies, 36, 64, 86, 101
  and human rights violations, 126–27, 134
  and patriarchy, 140
  and political corruption, 104, 120. *See also* coal industry; extraction industries
Foyntlin, Jayden, 130
Frazer-Carroll, M., 38
freedom of speech, 35
Freire, Paulo, 138
Fridays for Future (FFF), 5, 11, 23, 29, 40, 42, 66, 147
  India chapter, 35
#fridaysforfuture, 35, 40, 144
Fritch, J., 120–21
frontline communities, 20–21, 63–65, 70, 78, 115, 140
"Frontline to DC" pipeline protests, 77
Fruean, Brianna, 66
fundraising, 21, 44, 109, 116–17, 138
  with earth-friendly merchandise, 16, 97–98, 106–7, 147. *See also* donations
Funk, Ashley, 130–33
future, 1–3, 9–10, 16, 21, 24, 27, 53, 137
  and failed futurity, 30–31
  gaming for, 88

girls' visions of, 77–79, 100–102, 105–6, 120–22, 124–25, 129, 132–35, 139, 144–45
opened up by temporal rhetorics, 39–40
young people's claim to, 12, 23, 65, 67, 69–70, 72, 113
Galactic Restoration, 90
gamification, 112. *See also* video game design
gaming industry, 82, 87–88. *See also* video game design
Gandhi, Mahatma, 102
Ganges River, 126
GapKids 2020: Be the Future, 53–54
Garbage Goodbuyers, 92
Garcia, P., 46
Garza, Alicia, 9
Gee, J., 90
Gehm, D., 86
gender, 6, 13, 15, 74, 76–77, 79, 85, 95
and attacks online, 33–34
and climate litigation, 122
as diluting girls' radical views, 10
disparities in gaming, 87
as environmental vulnerability, 120
and grassroots organizing, 109
mortality rates of women, 123
nonbinary critique, 4. *See also* femininity; masculinity
Generation Z, 4, 105–7. *See also* age/generation
Genesee Power Station, 47–48
Ge, Tang, 34
"The Girl Effect" (Nike Foundation), 16
Girlhood Remixed Technology Camp, 83
"girl power" discourse, 6–7, 9–10, 16–17, 56
Girl Scouts of America, 83, 106
Girls Make Games, 82, 89–91

girls of color, 8, 35, 37–38. *See also* Black girls; Indigenous girls; Latinx girls
girls' studies, 3–4, 7–8, 22, 45–46, 64, 138–40
history of, 5–6. *See also* Black girlhood studies
Girls Who Code, 21, 81, 89
Girl Up (United Nations Foundation), 16
glaciers receding, 60, 109, 125
Global Climate Action Summit, 115, 137
"global future games," 88
The Global Landscapes Forum, 72
"global saviors," 9–10, 16, 20, 41
global warming, 1, 92, 99, 104
and climate litigation, 119, 123, 125, 130, 132
in video games, 90
Global Youth Activist, 53
Goal 17 Media, 112
GoFundMe, 44. *See also* fundraising
González, Emma, 10, 17, 37, 101
Goodnight, G. T., 120–21, 133
Google, 21, 81–82, 95
Grady, C., 6–7
Grassroots Climate Girl Effect, 21, 117–18
grassroots organizing, 48, 55, 68, 97–99, 138
challenges for, 115–16
and climate litigation, 122, 127
as dissent strategy, 117–18
and Gen Z radicals, 105–6
hopeful messages through, 100–103
political influence of, 109–10
and TED talks, 113–14. *See also* nonprofits
Great March for Climate Change, 131
green energy, 1, 33
Greenfield, N., 77
Green Hope Foundation, 21, 97, 106–8, 111, 117, 141, 144

limitations of, 115–16
mission of, 102, 104
greenhouse gas emissions, 1, 119, 125–27. *See also* carbon emissions
Green, L., 12
Green New Deal, 104, 106–7, 117
"green nudges," 87
Green Revolution in India, 14
green technologies, 14
greentrolling, 145
greenwashing, 31, 145, 147
"Greta Effect," 20, 24, 41–42. *See also* Thunberg, Greta
"Greta of India" (Licypriya Kangujam), 37
Grey, S. H., 70, 74–75
Griffin, A., 45–46
Gualinga, Helena, 65
Gulf of Mexico, 132
gun violence, 16, 30
  advocating against, 5, 9–10, 17, 37, 101
Gutheir, Sophie, 112

Happy Globe, 92–93
harassment, 12, 46, 83, 85, 87, 141
Haraway, Donna, 109
Harm to Table, 88
Harris, Anita, 6
Harris, Kamala, 25, 53, 60
Harvey, A., 18
hashtags, 9, 11–12, 32, 40, 49, 51–53, 55, 110. *See also individual hashtags*
Hawaii, 105
Hayes, E. R., 90
heat waves, 1, 123
hero narratives, 9, 38, 48, 71, 79
Hero Project (Marvel), 71
Hesford, W. S., 10, 16
heterosexism, 139. *See also* sexism
Hinzo, A., 75
Hip Hop Caucus, 52
Hirsi, Isra, 35, 41
Hispanic women, 83
hooks, bell, 146

hope, 49–50, 60, 102
  activism as source of, 9–10, 145–46
  in the face of bullying, 141–42
  as false, 2, 26
horizontal leadership, 10, 17
Houdek, M., 39
Houska, Tara, 63
Hultman, M., 33
human rights, 16, 119, 121–27, 136
human trafficking, 64, 123
Humphries, Mark, 32
hurricanes, 1, 5, 102, 115, 130
Hydroviv water filters, 55
hypersexualization, 47, 76, 87

I am Greta, 24, 26
Ice, R., 120–21
iconicity, 33, 36, 137
  and Autumn Peltier, 73
  and Greta Thunberg, 19–20, 23–24, 29–31, 40–42
  and Mari Copeny, 47, 54
Idaho Department of Natural Resources, 132
#IdleNoMore, 77
#IGotMySeatAtTheTable, 53, 60
IllumiNative, 74
#imjustsayin, 53
India, 35, 37
  climate litigation in, 21, 119, 126
  Green Revolution in, 14
Indigenous Climate Girl Effect, 20–21, 78–79. *See also* Indigenous girls
Indigenous Environmental Network (IEN), 63, 69–70
Indigenous girls, 2, 8, 70–72, 130
  and activist networks, 67–70, 75–77, 104, 125, 139
  and femicide, 64, 71, 76–79, 140, 144
  ignored by girls' studies, 7
  and Indigenous knowledges, 15, 63–66, 78–79, 147–48

and media representation, 38, 71, 73, 138
and survivance rhetorics, 20, 64, 70, 74–76. *See also* Native American girls
Indigenous girls' studies, 3. *See also* girls' studies
Indigenous knowledges, 1, 63–64, 65–66
    and activist organizing, 67–70, 76, 125
    defended by ecofeminists, 15, 20–21, 31, 38, 40, 78–79
    and radical empathy, 147–48
    and sacredness of water, 72–73
#IndigenousRights, 40
Indonesia, 104, 117
influencers, 6, 36–37, 53–55, 72–73
Ingraham, Laura, 28
Inland, 89
Instagram, 11, 46, 52, 111–12
    and Autumn Peltier, 73
    and Greta Thunberg, 20, 35–36, 38, 40
    and Jaime Margolin, 101
    and Mari Copeny, 20, 55–56, 60
    and Tokata Iron Eyes, 71
InterAmerican Commission for Human Rights (IACHR), 125
intergenerational coalitions, 3, 38–39, 98–99, 105, 116
    for climate litigation, 122, 124, 126, 146
    and family, 59, 67, 73, 130–31, 146
    and #MatriarchMonday campaign, 77
    and tribal elders, 69–71, 73–74
International Indigenous Youth Council (IIYC), 75–76
intersectionality, 20, 41
    as analytical framework, 7–8, 11, 19, 45, 64, 98, 139–40, 142
    and Indigenous girls, 64, 67, 70, 77–78
in organizing, 17, 36, 39–40, 43, 104–6, 108, 112, 137
Inuit, 125
Iron Eyes, Tokata, 69–72, 75, 78–79, 143

Jackson, A., 9, 46, 52
Jackson, D. Z., 48
#JadaCounterPose, 52
#JadaPose, 52
Japan, 104
Jayemanne, D., 88
Jenkins, H., 11, 31
Jewish girls, 101, 132
Johnson, A. E., 31
joy, 25, 32, 54, 58, 108, 148
Juliana, Kelsey Cascadia Rose, 21, 119, 130–31, 133, 137
Juliana v. United States, 126–30, 133, 141–42
Jung, J., 32
#JusticeforJada, 52

#KAG (Keep America Great), 32
Kaiyo, 90–91
Kalch, A., 109
Kaler-Jones, C., 45–46
Kangujam, Licypriya, 37
Kay, J. B., 25, 27
Kearney, M. C., 5–6
Keeler, B., 100
Keller, J., 12, 30, 34, 140
Kelly, C. R., 70
Kelly, L. L., 46
Kelly, S., 88
Kempf, C., 129, 135
Keystone XL pipeline protests, 68–69
Khan-Cullors, P., 9, 60
Kiazolu, Nupol, 58
Kids Against Plastic, 15, 21, 97, 106–7, 110
    mission, 102–3
Kids F.A.C.E. (Kids for a Clean Environment), 97, 99–100, 107
Kids Footlocker, 56

Kill Adlets, 93
Kimmerer, Robin Wall, 148
KlimaSeniorinnen lawsuit, 123. *See also* climate litigation
Knowles, Michael, 28
Kunda, L., 55–56
Kwauck, C., 123
Kyoto Protocol, 124–25

Lacks, Henrietta, 49
Lake Huron, 43
Lakota culture, 69–71, 76
Lakota Times, 71
#landback, 72
Latinx girls, 2, 101
lawsuits. *See* climate litigation
Lawyer Up Climate Girl Effect, 135–36. *See also* climate litigation
"leaderful movements," 17
leadership pipeline, 117
lead poisoning, 20, 43–44, 82
"leaky pipeline," 83
"lean in" discourse, 6
Lebanon–Syria border, 104, 111
legal system, 15, 21–22, 124, 133, 144
  empowering girls, 134–35
  as technology, 121. *See also* climate litigation
Legionnaires' disease, 43
letter-writing
  campaigns, 35–36, 57–58
  and Dakota Access pipeline protests, 69, 139
  to President Bush, 100, 139
  to President Obama, 20, 44–45, 56, 59, 132
LGBTQ community, 2, 74, 99, 101
Lichtenwalter, J., 48
Lindo, S., 45–46
LinkedIn, 111
litter cleanups, 93, 95, 100, 105, 107, 110–11, 117, 131–32, 144
Little Miss Flint. *See* Copeny, Amariyanna (Mari)
Little Miss Flint Clean Water Fund, 55

local knowledge production, 121, 137
Logan, G., 45
Logan-Riley, India, 65
Lottie dolls, 54
Louisiana, 74–75

Mabrey, P., 75
Mackey, J., 45
#MAGA (Make American Great Again), 32
MAI Water, 91
"Malala Effect," 16
Malala Fund, 71
Mandela, Nelson, 102
Maori, 65
  tribe of Whanganui, 126
March for Our Lives, 5, 10, 17, 23, 101
Margolin, Jamie, 13, 36, 115, 139, 145
  TED talk, 113
  and This is Zero Hour, 2, 7, 38, 59, 101–2, 104, 106–8
  Youth to Power, 107, 140
Marshall Islands, 130, 132
Martín, M., 36
Martin, Trayvon, 9
Marvel comics, 71, 79
masculinity, 74, 76
  correlated to climate denialism, 13, 33
  "petro-masculinity," 140
  in STEM fields, 82–83, 121. *See also* gender
mashups, 32
#MatriarchMonday, 77, 144
Mazzarella, S. R., 28, 37–38
McArthur, S. A., 7, 46
McCreedy, D., 84
McRae, Avery, 117, 128, 134–35, 141–42, 144, 146
meat industry, 101
media literacy programs, 46
medium.com, 112
Meek, Amy, 102–3, 107
  TED talk, 113
Meek, Ella, 102–3, 107

TED talk, 113
memes, 23–24, 29, 31–33, 112
Mendes, K., 12
mental health, 24–25, 27–28, 59, 108, 135. *See also* anxiety; self-care
Meta platforms, 146. *See also* Facebook; Instagram
methodology of book, 18–19
#MeToo, 9, 25
Mexico, 64, 94, 132
    Mexico City, 66
migrant justice, 112
Milstein, T., 18, 106
Miltner, K. M., 13
mining, 14–15, 127, 140. *See also* coal industry; extraction industries
misinformation campaigns, 3, 13, 33–34
misogyny, 9, 11, 25, 33–34, 40, 120, 140
    networked, 13, 42, 83, 143
    online, 3, 12–13
    and racism, 6, 60–61, 79, 112
MIT App Inventor, 92
#MMIW (Missing and Murdered Indigenous Women), 20, 64, 71, 76–78, 140
Mollusk, John, 32
Moore, Michael
    Roger and Me, 47
Moors, M. R., 49–50
Morgan, Piers, 27
Morrow, K. L., 122
Moses, L. B., 121
Mother Earth, 63, 67, 76, 143
Mother's Day (2011) lawsuits, 124. *See also* climate litigation
Mountain Mamas, 110
Muhammad, G. E., 7
Mukherjee, R., 56
Murphy, P. D., 31, 41
Muslim girls, 16

Nahuas Nation, 76
Nakate, Vanessa, 35, 37, 142
"name and shame" initiatives, 10, 110, 113
Namugerwa, Leah, 41
Nardi, B., 88
Nashville, TN, 100
National Child Day, Canada, 72
National Youth Parliament, 116
Native American girls, 64, 68–70, 75, 130. *See also* Indigenous girls
nativism, 147
Navajo identity, 130, 133
Nazar, Nadia, 101, 104
Nelson, A. C., 129
neocolonialism, 7–8. *See also* colonialism; settler colonial ideologies
neoliberalism, 4, 6, 16, 27, 30, 147
networked misogyny, 13, 42, 83, 143
"networked publics," 11, 53, 127, 135
New Jersey, 89
New York City, NY, 23, 66–67
Nicholson-Cole, S., 109
Nike, 56
    The Girl Effect campaign, 16
#NoDAPL, 69, 75
"no-fly movement," 41
non-governmental organizations (NGOs). *See* grassroots organizing; nonprofits
nonprofits, 19, 102, 109–10, 123, 132
    started by girls, 15, 18, 21, 76, 97–100, 105, 107. *See also* grassroots organizing
North Dakota, U.S.A., 68
Northwest Alliance for Media Literacy, 128
Nosek, G., 122, 127

Oakland, CA, 100
Obama, Barack, 20, 32, 44–45, 48, 53, 58–59, 132
O'Brien, K., 19, 36, 117, 121
Ocasio-Cortez, Alexandria, 60
oceans, 23, 28, 119
    pollution of, 89–91, 93, 111, 115

sea rise, 1, 66, 126, 130
Oglala Lakota Nation, 76
Ojibwe values, 72
"Okay, Boomer," 39
Olesen, T., 29–30, 33
Olson, Julia, 119, 124, 130
Omar, Ilhan, 41, 60
O'Neill, K., 102–3
O'Neill, S., 109
One Mind Youth Movement, 68–69
Oregon, 21, 126, 130
Osea, 93
Otomi-Toltec Peoples, 66
Our Children's Trust, 21, 119, 122, 129–35
    history of, 123–24
Our Climate Voices, 73, 129

Pacific Islander youths, 66
PacificStandard, 115
#PACKETin, 110
pageant culture, 44–45, 47, 53
Pakistan, 16, 21, 119
Palczewski, C. H., 120–21
Paris Agreement, 1, 23, 125
Park, C. S., 33–34
Parkland shooting, 10, 30, 37
participatory culture, 3, 19–20, 31, 41
patriarchy, 3, 13, 85–86, 115, 138, 140
    and colonialism, 8, 113
    girls challenging, 84, 140, 144
    and science, 14, 121
    and tribal elders, 74
Patrick, Xiye Bastida, 39, 143
    Re-Earth Initiative, 66
Pauli, B. J., 43
Pawnee Nation, 74
Pelosi, Nancy, 25, 112
Peltier, Autumn, 2, 20–21, 64, 67, 75, 79, 141
    ECO-18 Eco-Maven (2020), 73
    Me to the We Award (2016), 72
    Woman of the Year (2019), 72
Peng, A. Y., 85
Pennsylvania, 101, 130, 132

People for the Ethical Treatment of Animals (PETA), 101
People's Climate March (2017), 58
People's Climate Movement, 66
personhood, environmental, 126, 136
Peschau, M., 147
"petro-masculinity," 140
Pettus Bridge event, 68. *See also* Standing Rock protests
Pezzullo, P. C., 18
philanthropy, 20–21, 33, 54
Phillips, K. R., 39
Pillay, Navi, 16
Piotrowitcz, R., 122
pirrahla (brat), 31
place-based activism, 12, 44, 49–52, 59–60, 68, 89–90, 129
Plant for the Planet, 132
Plant, Sadie, 109
plastic bag bans, 103, 110, 113–14, 117
Plastic Clever Schools, 107
Plastic Pollution, 89, 91
plastic waste, 97, 102, 103, 107, 110–11, 113–14
Playing for the Planet Alliance, 87
podcasts, 84, 98, 112
Poell, T., 49–50
Poe, Melissa, 100
police violence, 9, 52, 56
policy reform, 5, 100, 106, 111, 123–24, 127, 132
Polluters Out campaign, 65
pollution, 2, 43, 97, 100, 102, 107, 120, 139
    of air, 1–2, 47, 89, 91, 119, 132
    of oceans, 65, 89, 93, 103, 111
    of rivers, 126
Portugal, 125–26
positionality, 4, 24, 133, 139
    of authors, 3, 47, 64
    needed for school strikes, 116
Potawatomi, 148
Power to the Youth, 53
Powwow.com, 72

Prakash, Varshini, 104
Presley, R., 74
Principle of Public Trust Doctrine, 119
prison-industrial complex, 10, 104
Projansky, S., 9
Project Super Bloom, 101
protests, 2, 11, 15, 18–19, 99–100, 105, 108, 111, 133
   anger in, 25
   for clean water in Flint, 45
   and freedom of speech, 35
   against gun violence, 5
   against oil pipelines, 20, 64–65, 68–71, 73, 77, 138, 140
   against racial injustice, 58, 147
   and school strikes, 23–24, 29–30, 40
Pulé, M., 33
Putin, Vladmir, 31

queer girls, 2, 101
Quibbit, 89

racism, 6, 11, 104, 131, 139
   and bias, 25, 48, 79, 82, 142
   Black girls' resistance to, 45–47, 50, 52–53, 60–61, 144
   environmental, 20, 43–45, 48, 59–60, 112, 132
   and violence, 9, 51–53
Raging Grannies, 39
rape imagery, 33–34, 51
Ravi, Disha, 35
Rayne, LA, 130
Reciclamex, 93
recycling, 92–94, 99–100, 102, 110
Red Warrior Camp, 69
Re-Earth Initiative, 66
refugee camps, 104, 111
remixing, 2, 11, 31–32
resilience, 36, 54, 59–60, 71, 141, 145, 147–48
"respair," 27
Rezpect Our Water, 69

rhetorical strategies, 16, 22, 29, 33, 38–39, 41
   "clapping back," 30, 34, 42, 46
   crisis communication, 26–27, 40
   in girls' video games, 89
   remixing, 31–32
   revolutionary language, 106
   seasonal cycles of communication, 53–54
   solution telling, 60
   stories in climate litigation, 129–34
   survivance rhetorics, 64, 74–75, 78
   of unity, 143
   used at Standing Rock, 70
   "We call B.S.," 10
   youth as, 2–5, 56–57. *See also* storytelling
rhetorical studies, 39, 56–57
Rich, KaeLyn:
   Girls' Resist!, 99
Ringrose, J., 12
Riordan, E., 18, 56

The Rise Up Movement in Africa, 35

Röderer, F., 41
Rodrigo, Olivia, 6
Rogers, N., 122
Rosenfeld, K., 12
Ruether, Rosemary, 76–77
Runnels-Black Fox, Maya Monroe, 77
Ryalls, E. D., 28, 37–38

Sacred Stone camp, 68
Sakshi, Shalvi, 65–66
Sami People, 40
Samoa, 64, 66
Sandberg, Sheryl, 6
   Lean In, 146
San Francisco, CA, 100, 115
Sarayaku, 65
#SayHerName, 9, 52
school shootings, 9, 10, 30, 37

#schoolstrike4climate, 40
School Strike for Climate, 2, 23–24, 40
school strikes, 2, 5, 23–24, 35, 40, 116, 139
school-to-prison pipeline, 10, 104
Schrum, K., 6
Schuck, M., 64, 68
science and technology studies (STS), 13
scientific knowledge, 121–23, 134, 137
sea levels, 1, 66, 126, 130
Sea Shepherd, 18
Seattle, WA, 39, 101
Segerberg, A., 11, 29
Segers, I., 85, 95
self-care, 140, 144. *See also* anxiety; mental health
settler colonial ideologies, 3, 63–64, 75–76, 78. *See also* colonialism; neocolonialism
sexism, 52, 74, 79, 87, 104, 120, 131. *See also* heterosexism; misogyny
sexual violence, 7, 9, 12, 51–52, 123. *See also* femicide crisis; rape imagery
Shabir, Leila, 82
Shaw, A., 12–13
ShellNo Action Coalition, 39
Sheshe, 92
Shirley, Eshe, 130, 131, 133
Shorty Awards, 54
ShowerDuck, 92
Sikka, T., 14, 121
Skol Strejk för Klimatet. *See* School Strike for Climate
Snapchat, 46
Snow, D., 109
Snyder, Rick, 44–45
Soentgen, J., 109
solar energy, 23, 106, 115
Soros, George, 33
South Dakota, 68, 70–71, 78
Spain, 92
"spectacular" girls, 7, 9, 19, 30, 61, 98, 114, 116–17, 140, 142–43

Indigenous girls as, 20, 65, 73
"Spirit Camp," 69
spirituality, 63, 66, 67, 76
Spokane Tribal People, 1
stalking, 12, 102, 141
Standing Rock protests, 20, 64, 68–71, 73
Standing Rock Sioux Tribe, 68, 74
Standing Rock Youth Council, 77
#StandWithDishaRavi, 35
STEM fields, 6, 21, 28, 145
and gender inequality, 3, 81–83, 86–87, 95, 110
STEM programs for girls, 81–84, 95, 145
stereotypes, 36–37, 122, 139, 140
and Black girls, 46, 55
and Black women, 47, 52
and Indigenous girls, 7
in STEM fields, 83
#StopFakeRenewables, 40
storytelling, 72–73, 105, 112, 114, 144
and climate litigation, 22, 129–33
and grassroots organizing, 117
hero narratives, 9, 38, 48, 71, 79
localized, 16, 49–50, 54, 65
and truth, 133–34
in video games, 89–90. *See also* rhetorical strategies
Straus, Rose, 100–101
Sturken, Marita, 18
Suajani, Rehmas, 81–82
Sunrise Movement, 21, 38, 97, 100, 112, 114, 117
fundraising, 107
mission, 102, 104–5, 108
revolutionary language of, 106
Supreme Court of Justice of Colombia, 126
"survivance," 20, 64, 70, 74–75, 78
sustainability, 1, 2, 19, 21, 33, 98, 104, 111, 137
and fashion industry, 53–54
and food traditions, 111
and packaging, 110

speaking at schools about, 116
through TEK, 79
in travel, 23, 41
video games about, 84, 88
Sweden, 23, 29, 41, 139
Syed, Ish, 82

Taft, J. K., 9, 10, 20, 28, 41
Taino Nation, 75
Tap Tap Trees, 91
Tasya, 111, 115–16
Taylor, Breonna, 52
Team GG, 89
Teaneck, NJ, 114
Te Awa Tupua river, 126
techno-ecofeminism, 4, 22, 81, 95
    as analytical framework, 14–15
    and climate litigation, 120–22, 129, 136
    and grassroots organizing, 110
    and technologies for protection, 144–45
    and Traditional Ecological Knowledge (TEK), 79
    water filters as, 55. *See also* ecofeminism; feminism; technofeminism
technofeminism, 21, 95, 122, 133
    as analytical framework, 13–14, 85–86. *See also* feminism; techno-ecofeminism
Technofeminist Climate Girl Effect, 94–95
Technovation Girls, 82, 90, 91, 92
TED talks, 113–15, 118
teenagers, 3–4, 17, 60, 70–71, 107, 140
    activists' ages, 31, 37, 44, 51, 66–68, 90
    and climate litigation, 21, 126, 130
    as depressed, 26
    framed as influential, 5–7, 28, 72, 115. *See also* age/generation; intergenerational alliances
temperature targets, 23, 39, 104, 126

Tew, Madelaine, 114
Texas, 51, 83
Thatcher, Margaret, 25
#ThisIsAmerica, 51
This is Zero Hour, 2, 7, 21, 38, 59, 97, 101, 104, 112, 114–15, 127
    and fundraising, 107
    mission, 101, 104, 108
    revolutionary aesthetic of, 106
Thomas, C. S., 56–57, 139
Thomas, Tess, 71
"thoughts and prayers," 115
Thunberg, Greta, 19–20, 25–26, 117, 143, 145
    at Battery Park 2019 global climate strike, 67
    and the "Greta Effect," 40–42
    influence on other activists, 34–38, 66, 70–71, 78
    and intergenerational conflict, 38–40
    misinformation campaigns against, 33–34
    No one is too small to make a difference, 23–24
    public bullying of, 27–28, 141
    rhetorical strategies of, 29–32, 34, 40–42
    and school strikes, 2, 5, 23–24, 35, 40, 139
TikTok, 60
toxic waste, 99, 130
Traditional Ecological Knowledge (TEK), 63, 79
TransCanada Energy, 68
transnational girlhoods, 8, 30, 64–65, 78, 138, 140
Trash up, 91
Treaty Rights of Indigenous Nations, 104
Tree Leaf, 94
tree planting, 2, 40, 87, 89, 91, 100, 102, 105–6, 111
tribal elders, 69–70, 73–74, 79

trolling, 3, 13, 33, 83. *See also* greentrolling
Trudeau, Justin, 72–73
#Trump2020, 32
Trump, Donald, 25, 27, 31–32, 101
    anti-trump rally, 44
Truth, Sojourner, 55
Tufecki, Z., 11, 19
Tumblr, 52
Twitter, 11, 20, 46, 111
    and adult bullies, 27–28, 31
    and girls' agenda-setting, 29, 31–32, 35, 37, 41, 50–52, 112, 115
    as negative space, 12–13, 50
    and self-branding, 31–32, 53, 55–56, 58, 60

Uganda, 37, 41, 124, 142
Ukraine, 124
United Arab Emirates, 91
United Nations:
    Climate Change Conference, 65, 72
    Climate Summit, 23, 25–26, 28, 31–32, 34, 37, 87, 137
    Commission on the Status of Women, 53
    Development Goals, 104
    Environmental Program, 87
    Framework Convention on Climate Change (UNFCCC), 1, 124
    General Assembly, 26, 72
    Girl Up project, 16
    Global Goals for Sustainable Development, 102
    Intergovernmental Report of Climate Change (IPCC), 1
    supporting grassroots activism, 138

United States Army Corps of Engineers, 68–69, 139
United States Mission to the UN, 53

United States Supreme Court, 124, 126–27
Urgenda Foundation, 125
Urgenda Foundation v. the Netherlands, 125, 128
Utrecht Sustainability Game Jam, 88

Valentine, Sahara, 128, 134–35, 142–43
van der Voo, L.:
    As the World Burns, 129
Van Dijck, J., 49–50
Vanner, C., 4, 8, 16, 140
vegetarianism, 34, 100–101, 131
Venice canals, 2
Vergun, Miko, 130, 132
video content, 32–33, 37, 55, 60, 69–73, 101–2, 130, 135
video game design, 3, 15, 21, 95
    aesthetics, 91
    and all-girl STEM programs, 81–87
    benefits of play, 87–88
    girls' environmental stories in, 89–90
    goals in, 90–91
    hypersexualization in, 86–87. *See also* gaming industry
Vietnam, 104
Villaseñor, Alexandria, 41
violence, 33, 78
    threats of, 13, 24, 102, 141
    against women and girls, 9, 25, 42, 52, 64, 68, 71, 75–79, 140. *See also* femicide crisis; gun violence; police violence; sexual violence
Vizenor, Gerald, 20, 74–75
Vliegenthart, R., 128
voting rights, 4, 53, 55, 120–21, 124, 138
Vu, H. T., 109

Wajcman, Judy, 13–14, 85, 135
Walker, J., 129
Walmart, 51

Washington D.C., U.S.A., 45, 71, 77, 143
water, 14, 54, 75, 94
    consumption of, 81, 91–92
    crisis in Flint, MI, 12, 20, 43–45, 47–51, 55–61
    filters for, 3, 50–51, 55, 144
    protection of, 2, 63–64, 67, 72–73
    quality of, 2, 43, 65, 68–70, 72–73, 93, 119, 143–44
    rights to, 2, 68–70, 124
    scarcity of, 50–51, 66, 130. *See also* drought; floods; oceans
"Water Protectors," 70
Waters, Maxine, 58
"We call B.S.," 10
#WednesdaysforWater, 143
Western-centrism, 8, 12, 14, 16
Western Scientific Ecological Knowledge (WSEK), 63
Weybrecht, Giselle, 84
What They Don't Sea, 90
White Earth Ojibwe, 20, 74
whiteness, 6, 7, 38–40, 66, 73
    and authors of book, 3, 47, 64
    and bullying, 20, 24, 28, 32
white supremacy, 46, 74
Wide Awake, 105
Wiikwemkoong First Nation, 2, 67, 141
Wijsen, Isabel, 102–3, 113–14
Wijsen, Melati, 97, 102–3, 113–15
Wildemeersch, D., 5, 137

wildfires, 1, 5
Wilkie, J. E., 33
Williams, Evan, 32
Williams, S., 51
Women's March, 101
Wonneberger, A., 128
Wood, J. T., 47
Wood, Mary, 124
World Economic Forum, 37, 142
#WorldWaterDay, 51

Xakriabá, Artemisa, 67, 143
xenophobia, 147
X-site Energy Services, 34

Yamuna river, 126
#YesAllWomen, 9
young adults, 3, 57, 140. *See also* age/generation; teenagers
Young, K., 70
Yousafzai, Malala, 16–17, 71
Youth Climate March, 101
Youth Climate Strike (U.S.), 35, 41, 59
Youth v. Gov (2020), 129–30, 133–34, 141
#youthvgov, 129
YouTube, 33, 69–71, 98, 102, 109, 112

Zero Hour. *See* This is Zero Hour
Zimmerman, George, 9
Zulli, D., 55

About the Authors

Carolyn M. Cunningham and Heather M. Crandall have been researching, publishing, teaching, and presenting together on topics of gender, technology, and social media activism.

They have published together on nonprofits' use of social media, hashtag activism, and social change video games. They have offered workshops on gender and technology to a variety of groups. Both are affiliate faculty in the Women's and Gender Studies program at Gonzaga University, and both are on the board of directors of the Northwest Alliance for Media Literacy.

As educators, Dr. Cunningham and Dr. Crandall designed and taught a course on Women, Communication and Leadership that turned into their edited collection, *Gender, Communication, and the Leadership Gap* (2017). Drs. Cunningham and Crandall are excited to share insights from their new book, *The Climate Girl Effect.*

Carolyn M. Cunningham, Associate Professor in the Communication and Leadership Studies Department at Gonzaga University.

Heather M. Crandall, Associate Professor in Communication Studies at Gonzaga University.

Lightning Source UK Ltd.
Milton Keynes UK
UKHW041302141022
410480UK00004B/79